MW00824798

PARANORMAL
ANIMALS
OF NORTH AMERICA

FASA CORPORATION ● 1990

TABLE OF CONTENTS

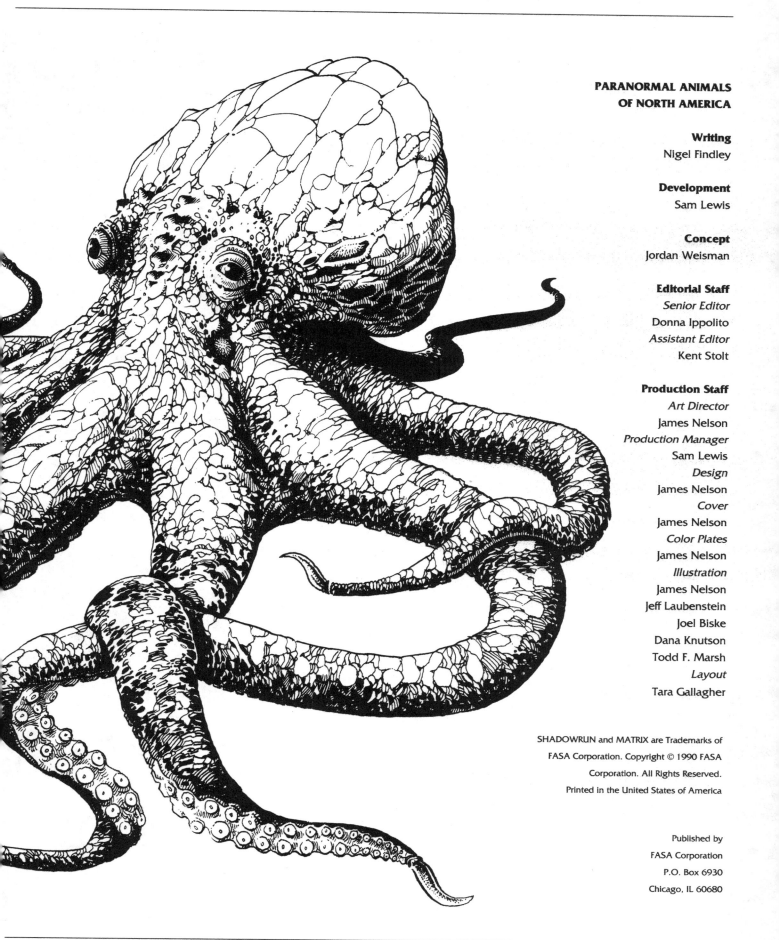

PARANORMAL ANIMALS OF NORTH AMERICA

Writing
Nigel Findley

Development
Sam Lewis

Concept
Jordan Weisman

Editorial Staff
Senior Editor
Donna Ippolito
Assistant Editor
Kent Stolt

Production Staff
Art Director
James Nelson
Production Manager
Sam Lewis
Design
James Nelson
Cover
James Nelson
Color Plates
James Nelson
Illustration
James Nelson
Jeff Laubenstein
Joel Biske
Dana Knutson
Todd F. Marsh
Layout
Tara Gallagher

SHADOWRUN and MATRIX are Trademarks of
FASA Corporation. Copyright © 1990 FASA
Corporation. All Rights Reserved.
Printed in the United States of America

Published by
FASA Corporation
P.O. Box 6930
Chicago, IL 60680

It was cold in the woods. Rain drizzled through the trees, and the gusting wind cut like a razor. As the full moon showed briefly through a gap in the clouds, Harley's cybereyes immediately adapted to the changing light levels. He saw his surroundings with a clarity that an unaugmented human couldn't know even at brightest noon. The trees stood in serried rows, cleared of their lower limbs and the underbrush that would normally surround them. That was a bad sign, but Harley had no time to worry about that now. He was more interested in the fence that his enhanced vision picked up surrounding the MTC compound a few hundred meters away. That fence was probably charged with enough juice to fry a juggernaut, but Harley wasn't going to worry about that either. Not yet.

It was the dark figures moving inside the fence that concerned him, and he gave them his total attention. At the same time, his peripheral vision assured him of the presence of his back-up, two street samurai. Calvin and Hobbes they called themselves, an obvious joke that nobody ever got. Harley hadn't hired them for their sense of humor, however, but because they were a good team, a pair of street brothers—related by decision rather than blood.

Indeed, Calvin and Hobbes synchronized their actions in uncanny fashion, as though one mind inhabited the two armored and boosted bodies. They almost never spoke to one another, their communication being limited to grunts, gestures, or glances. Harley didn't know how they did it, and he didn't really care. All that mattered was that it worked. The two street samurai were chipped so high they were almost vibrating. And that was the kind of back-up he needed tonight.

Tonight's run was a good one, the high-risk, high-pay kind that Harley liked best. There was something in the MTC depot that he wanted: data he could use personally as well as sell for a healthy profit. But he had gotten his first surprise after trying to make it a simple snatch-and-grab through the Matrix. He hadn't been able to get into the depot via the Matrix because it wasn't *on* the Matrix. The barbarism of a completely isolated, stand-alone computer system had stunned Harley.

Physical intrusion would be the only way in. But then came the second surprise.

Security surrounding the depot was mega. For starters, the depot was smack in the middle of a 500-meter zero zone. Zero incursion, zero survival. If you were outside, you didn't get in. Or if somehow you did manage to penetrate, you were buried there. Thanks to some techniques Harley'd bought from his friend Blacknight, however, he and his little team had gotten this far. But it had been tight. Then came the juiced-up fence. And now something else. Something new. Biologicals, and not just the normal guard dog.

Piasma. Bear-like and Awakened, with all the potential power and danger that implied. Harley unslung his cyberdeck and slipped the fiber-optic lead into the ceramic-lipped datajack in his temple. Calvin was beside him almost before Harley saw the man move.

"What's up?" the samurai breathed.

"Last check with Paterson's," Harley whispered as his fingers danced an intricate pattern across the keys. "Maybe somebody's got something new on those bear-things. Watch me while I'm gone." His eyes rolled upward as he slipped into the technorealm of the Matrix. (Remote linkups like this were part of Harley's edge over the other deckers competing for big corp contracts. His satellite uplink had set him back almost a million, but it had paid for itself in less than a year. And if he hit with this run, he'd be able to afford even more techno-toys.) He was out again quickly, extracting the jack and coiling the lead.

"Well?" It was Hobbes this time. For a big man, he moved quickly, with an almost preternatural silence.

"Nothing new," Harley told them. "Shadowtalk confirms these things are piasma. Straight Gain still thinks the squealers are going to do the job." He patted one of the small, grenade-like objects hanging from his bandolier.

His face split in a ragged street grin. "You guys up for it?"

The samurai didn't even have to exchange glances for that one.

"Then let's do it," Harley said.

Without a backward glance, he and his small command moved out into the night.

INTRODUCTION

>>>>>[Welcome to Shadowland, the latest in exclusive BBS (Bulletin Board Systems). Unsupported by the megacorps, unsanctioned by any government. No initiation fee, no sign-on charge. We figure that anyone who can deck his way in here deserves to be a member.

Shadowland is a non-profit venture, but only because that's the way it's turned out. So, yes, chummers, we gladly accept donations to help defray operating costs, but don't expect donations to be tax-deductible or that we'll be giving you a receipt.

Our main database is safe in Denver, with thousands of affiliated boards constantly uploading and downloading information in cities around the world. So if you want the real chiptruth about anything, Shadowland is the place to visit.

As shown on the main menu, Shadowland is broken into various topic areas. The data areas of a topic are sacrosanct and very well-protected. Don't try any writes or deletes on the main topic. We've packed it with IC, on the theory that anyone who wants to deck into that stuff is either corporate or stupid, neither of which we want prancing around our database. In the last three months, our black IC has killed two "customers." Let's not make it three.

If you are really interested in a topic, log onto its Special Interest Group (SIG). The SIGs (we call them "Shadowtalk") aren't protected. You're free to write what you want. Think of it as an FIFO (first in, first out) rolling picture of public opinion. When the Sysop (system operator) gets around to it, she housecleans Shadowtalk to get rid of stuff that's out-of-date or an obvious waste of memory.

So that's about all you have to know. Check out the main menu, see what interests you, and go to it.]<<<<<
—Control (12:29:57/07-10-50)

2. PATERSON'S GUIDE

Routing:
> **Or:** Seattle 21
> **Des:** Denver SLBBS
> **Date:** 12:34:01/11-13-50

>>>>>[Welcome to Paterson's Guide, as it is informally known. If you aren't already informed, Paterson is the premier cataloguer and classifier of paranormal creatures. His *Paranormal Creatures of North America: Awakened Animals* is the major authority consulted by zoologists, naturalists, and taxonomists the world over. To most of these specialists, Paterson is like Hoyle. If it's "by the book," it's got to be right.

You may not be too shocked to learn that that isn't really the case. When Shadowland started getting requests to put Paterson's Guide on-line, we did a little digging. It turns out that Paterson produced his guide under a UCAS government contract, with a couple of interesting riders. (The whole contract is in Reference if you want to give it a scan.) The most important rider gave government biologists (read "trained monkeys") the final say on what does or doesn't go into the guide.

Did old Paterson bridle under those conditions? No-o-o. He's supposed to be the expert, but apparently, he didn't kick at the idea of some bureaucratic types editing his work. The government nuyen must have been too enticing.

So the great Paterson's Guide is, presumably, neither accurate nor complete. Big Brother inserted disinformation that he wants disseminated while expunging stuff he doesn't want us to know.

That's why we put in a Shadowtalk section when uploading the Guide to the BBS. In a highly unauthorized manner, of course. (My heart bleeds to think of the thousands of nuyen in royalties lost to the good Dr. Paterson.) We figured you runners are the best authorities on whatever gaps and fallacies the Guide suffers. You're out there working the shadows or maybe doing research for someone who needs to know the real truth. If you haven't yet run into some of the critters described here, you probably know people who have. If you know something, chummer, upload it to the Shadowtalk section. That way, the next runner who bumps into the beastie just might live a little bit longer.

You'll notice that we haven't uploaded the whole guide, and that our selection leans heavily toward carnivores or other types that will geek you just for fun. Good Dr. Paterson spends inordinate amounts of megabytes on metacows, metahummingbirds, and even—I drek you not—metasilverfish. In many cases, the only difference between the Awakened critter and the original is a changed restriction enzyme in the digestive process or some other such drek. Not the kind of thing a runner needs to know. If a hummingbird hasn't geeked you before now, this year's model isn't likely to waste you either.

Dr. Paterson also devoted more than a 1,000 Mp on metaspecies who died out because they could not adapt to the postindustrial environment to which they had Awakened. You can't be killed by something already dead, including ghosts, so we dumped that drek out of this unauthorized edition of the Guide, too.]<<<<<
—Amanda Wilson, Sysop (12:34:01/11-13-50)

POWERS OF THE AWAKENED

POWERS OF THE AWAKENED

The sizes and weights given in the following descriptions are typical for an adult member of the species. Larger (often 10 – 20 percent, and occasionally, as much as 30 percent) and smaller (typically 60 – 75 percent in a species displaying gender size differences) individuals are possible. A description of coloration and distinctive characteristics follows.

The Habitats listed are those preferred by the creature. It is, of course, possible to encounter a creature away from that environment, especially if it serves in a guardian or watchdog capacity.

Many beings display magical powers or abilities without being active magicians. Some creatures can accomplish feats possible only through the use of magic, such as flight in defiance of aerodynamic laws or casting illusions. This magical capability is described as *innate*. Other creatures use magical energies to simply enhance such natural abilities as strength or vision. This use of magical power is described as *parabiological*.

Described below are the various powers of the Awakened creatures in this guide. Though game mechanics are included, these are intended mainly as guidelines. The gamemaster is free to make any modifications to Target Numbers, Damage Codes, or effects to suit his campaign and to keep his players on their toes. The gamemaster is also free to accept or reject any information given in the Shadowtalk sections of the creature descriptions.

In general, a creature may use only one power to attack a victim per action during combat, unless otherwise noted. All non-attack powers are considered to be permanently operable during combat.

ACCIDENT

Accident gives a being the power to cause an apparently normal accident to occur. The nature of the accident and its result will vary according to the terrain the being controls.

A character hit with Accident must roll an Unresisted Test using Quickness or Intelligence (whichever is higher) with a Target Number equal to the Essence of the being utilizing the power. If he fails the test, his action is lost as he trips, gets a face full of leaves, or even a cream pie in the face. Accident is not itself dangerous, but the environment can make it so. A fall on a narrow mountain ledge, for instance, can be most unfortunate.

ADAPTIVE COLORATION (SELECTIVE)

The most common form of Adaptive Coloration affects the visual band of the electromagnetic spectrum, including the spectrum used by dwarfs and trolls. This power gives a creature the ability to refract light around itself and become almost invisible. When the creature remains immobile, the Target Number to detect it is 10; when the creature is moving, the Target Number is 8. As this effect plays merry hell with the depth perception of anyone attacking the creature, add +2 to the Target Number for all ranged attacks. Adaptive Coloration is effective only against devices or forms of perception that use visible light, infrared or ultraviolet. Thus, it would affect thermographic sights and most forms of cybereyes, but would not affect a character using sonar sights or antipersonnel radar.

Less common forms of Adaptive Coloration refract sound waves, microwave radars, or are limited to narrower bands of the electromagnetic spectrum.

ALIENATION

Alienation gives the being the power to enshroud its victim(s) in an aura that makes the victim invisible to others. Treat this as an Invisibility Spell, with a Force equal to the being's Essence. A victim will remain under Alienation for a number of hours equal to the empowered creature's Essence.

The Alienation power is not intended as a beneficial power of invisibility. Victims of this power are invisible, intangible, and inaudible to those around them. It is as if those who are afflicted by this power do not exist at all. Drivers don't stop for them, no one talks to them, their friends shoot through them to hit targets.

The being's Essence is the Target Number the victim must achieve, using whatever attribute or skill seems appropriate, in order to avoid dangerous situations, or get someone's attention.

ANIMAL CONTROL

Some beings have heightened empathy with animals, usually limited to a particular type, such as predators or scaled animals. Animal Control gives the being the power to automatically prevent the animal from attacking, giving an alarm, and so on. With concentration, the empowered being can control an individual animal, experiencing the world through its senses and directing its behavior. This behavior would fall within what is normal for the animal's type. That is, a controlled monkey could not drive a car. The number of small animals (cats, rats, and so on) that a creature may control is equal to its (Charisma)D6. A being may control a number of larger animals (wolves, lions, and so on) equal to its Charisma.

BINDING

Binding gives the power to make its victim "stick" to a surface or to itself. The binding has a Strength Rating equal to the being's Essence.

BLINDNESS

This power can induce blindness in a single target, who can make a Willpower Resistance Test against the effect's Damage Code, which is (being's Essence)S2. If the victim manages to stage the damage down to nothing, there is no effect; otherwise, the victim is totally blind for 1D6 turns (no other physical damage is actually taken). The being can use this effect once per turn against a single target. (Cybereyes are no protection.)

COLD AURA

Cold Aura gives a being the power to sheathe itself in an area of extreme cold, inflicting damage on anyone who touches it. The aura extends out from the creature's body for a distance equal to the being's Essence in centimeters. The temperature of the cold region is approximately –100 degrees Celsius. Most liquids freeze almost instantly, and metals tend to become brittle.

Any successful melee attack against a creature possessing Cold Aura means that the attacker also takes damage from the intense cold. The attacker must make a Body Resistance Test against a damage code of (being's Essence) M2 Stun. Armor does count in resisting this damage if the gamemaster believes that the attacker has struck the creature with an armored portion of his body.

Any successful melee attack by a creature with Cold Aura increases the stage of its damage code by +2 for the victim's Resistance Test only.

COMPULSION

A being with Compulsion power can compel its victim to perform a specific action, as in posthypnotic suggestion. Often, a being may compel only one particular action. Treat as a Control Actions spell, using the being's Essence for the Force of the spell.

CONCEALMENT

Concealment power allows a being to hide within its terrain rather than becoming invisible. A being can use Concealment to hide its summoner (if it is a Nature Spirit) and its companions from danger, or alternatively, can use the power to hide something that people are seeking, including itself. Concealment adds the being's Essence Rating to the normal Target Number for any Perception Rolls the gamemaster requires. Thus, if the gamemaster decides that a search for the being would normally be a Target Number of 5, he should increase the Target Number to 5 + (being's Essence).

CONFUSION

Confusion gives a being the power to make its victims lose their sense of direction and wander confusedly through the terrain it controls. The consequences may vary widely. A Hearth Spirit causing Confusion in a house might lead to nothing worse than someone bumping into walls or mistaking a closet door for an exit. Confusion in the realm of a Mountain Spirit could easily lead someone over the nearest cliff.

Characters who attempt any form of Success Test while under this power are subject to a negative Target Modifier equal to the Essence of the being using the power. In addition, whenever the victim must make any decision, he must roll an Unresisted Willpower Test with a Target Number equal to the being's Essence. If this fails, he is unable to make up his mind. Something or someone must remind him of the need for a decision. An attack, or a verbal reminder from a companion, will allow for another test. If left alone in this state, a character will eventually wander off.

The power remains in effect as long as the victim remains within the area of terrain controlled by the being.

CORROSIVE SALIVA

With this power, the creature's saliva is highly corrosive. It will rapidly degrade armor and do considerable damage to unprotected flesh. At the end of each turn that a character is in melee combat with a creature possessing Corrosive Saliva, the player should make an Opposed Quickness Test against the creature. Make this test regardless of whether or not the creature's attack was successful. Each of the creature's net successes permanently reduces the Ballistic and Impact Rating of the character's armor by 1 (up to the creature's Essence). Once both the Impact and Ballistic Ratings of his armor are reduced, the character must make a Body Resistance Test against a damage code of (being's Essence)L(net successes).

CORROSIVE SECRETIONS

With this power, the creature's skin secretions are highly corrosive. Touching its body with bare flesh will cause damage on each turn the contact is maintained.

Any successful melee attack against a creature with Corrosive Secretion power means that the attacker might also take damage. The attacker must make a Body Resistance Test against a damage code of (being's Essence)M2.

Any successful melee attack by a creature with Corrosive Secretion increases the staging of its damage code by +2 for the victim's Resistance Test only.

Corrosive substances are particularly damaging to delicate bodyware such as smartgun link palm contacts. To avoid equipment damage, the character with the bodyware makes an Unresisted Test using his Body Rating, with a Target Number of 8.

DARKNESS

This power permits a being to cloak itself in darkness, making itself appear as a shadow. Though this tactic is useless for concealment in daylight or bright illumination, it makes it almost impossible for even thermographic vision to spot the being at night, though sonar and radar devices are not affected. The power adds +2 to all Target Numbers for Perception Tests to detect the being.

DESIRE REFLECTION

Desire Reflection gives a being the power to discover the greatest desire of a selected single target within range, and then appear as that object. Treat this as an Entertainment Spell, with the Force equal to Essence +4. Use of this power does not require a voluntary subject.

ELECTRICAL PROJECTION

Electrical Projection gives a being the power to strike a target with an electrical discharge. Depending on the being, results may range from a mild shock to a lightning bolt. A victim can neither dodge nor defend against Electrical Projection attacks. Such attacks typically do (Essence)M3 damage and disorient the target for a number of turns equal to the being's Essence.

EMPATHY

Empathy empowers a being to feel the dominant emotions and attitudes of a selected target or targets within range. The being is also able to project its own emotional state. Treat this as an Essence Success Test, with the subject's Willpower as the Target Number.

ENGULF

Engulf gives a being the power to draw its victim either into itself or the terrain or element appropriate to its nature. The victim is subject to all effects of being submerged in the substance, the least of which is usually suffocation.

The gamemaster should make an Opposed Test between the victim's Willpower and the creature's Essence. If the creature wins the test, the victim will enter the substance and begin to suffocate or suffer other appropriate damage. The victim may not escape as long as the creature maintains his power against him. An attack on another victim (using either a power or else physically) will release the first one from the Engulf power.

For each turn that a victim is suffocating, he makes a Body Resistance Test against a damage code of (being's Essence)M2 Stun. Dermal plating and armor do not count in resisting this damage.

Spirits with this power follow these rules:

The Engulf attack is a Melee Attack. The Spirit uses its Quickness to hit the target. Targets must counterattack successfully to avoid **engulfment**. If a victim is engulfed, the effects vary.

Every time it is the *victim's* action, he can try to escape. Roll an Opposed Test of the victim's Strength against the Spirit's Essence. The base Target Number is 4. If the victim wins, he breaks free.

On each of the *Spirit's* actions, engulfed victims must resist appropriate damage:

Fire Engulf: Same as if struck by the Spirit in combat; 3M4 damage, +2 Staging for Flame Aura, so resist 3M6 damage (impact armor helps against damage; not ballistic, which tends to melt).

Water Engulf: Victim must resist (Essence)M(Actions) Stun Damage. The Staging is equal to the number of actions that the Spirit has had since engulfing the victim. This is rougher than normal drowing, since the Spirit is capable of exerting great pressure on engulfed victims. Victims who pass out are still exposed to damage on the Spirit's actions, and will take lethal damage as a result. Eventually, they will drown.

Air Engulf: Victim must resist (Essence) S2 Stun effects of the Noxious Breath Power, using Willpower or Body, whichever is greater. Since the Spirit can astrally penetrate breathing gear or other protective systems, these provide no defense. The engulfed victim begins to take lethat damage after being rendered unconscious, eventually suffocatin.

Earth Engulf: Victim must resist 4S3 damage from crushing weight of the Spirit. Impact armor defends against this, not ballistic.

ENHANCED PHYSICAL ATTRIBUTES

With Enhanced Physical Attributes power, a being adds its current Essence Rating to its physical attributes. This power to enhance may be limited to specific attributes and/or in duration and number of uses.

ENHANCED MOVEMENT

With Enhanced Movement power, the creature can multiply its own movement rate by its Essence, and maintain this enhanced rate for a number of minutes equal to its (Essence)D6. This enhanced speed can only be used for uninterrupted cross-country travel; it cannot be used in tactical or combat situations.

ENHANCED REACTIONS

With Enhanced Reactions power, a being adds (Essence/2) dice to its Initiative Roll (round fractions down). This power to enhance may be limited in duration and number of uses.

ENHANCED SENSES

Enhanced Senses includes heat-sensing organs, sonar, improved hearing and smell, low-light and thermographic vision, motion detection (ability to detect electrical field disturbances), and so on.

ESSENCE DRAIN

This power allows a being to drain the Essence from another, adding the points to its own rating. The being may increase its Essence Rating up to twice the maximum for its type. (See page 176, **Shadowrun** rules for more details.)

FEAR

Fear power allows a being to fill its victims with overwhelming terror of either the terrain or of the being. The victim will race in panic for the nearest apparent point of safety.

The gamemaster should make an Opposed Test between the victim's Willpower and the creature's Essence. The creature's net number of successes is used to gauge the severity of the victim's fear.

FIRE RESISTANCE

A being with Fire Resistance power is totally unaffected by normal fire. Nonmagical fire, regardless of its temperature, does absolutely no damage to the creature. If the fire is magically based (e.g., a fireball), this power has the same effect as Immunity to Fire (i.e., the being gets automatic successes equal to its Essence Rating when resisting damage).

FLAME AURA

Flame Aura gives a being the power to make its surface ripple with flame, burning any who touch it. The aura extends out from the creature's body for a distance equal to the being's Essence in centimeters. Intense forms of this power may make wooden weapons burst into flame at a touch or even melt metal or plastic weapons.

Any successful Melee Attack against a creature with Flame Aura means that the attacker also takes damage from the intense heat. The attacker must make a Body Resistance Test against a damage code of (being's Essence) M2. Armor does count in resisting this damage if the gamemaster feels that the attacker has struck the creature with an armored portion of his body.

Any successful Melee Attack by a creature with Flame Aura increases the stage of its damage code by +2 for the victim's Resistance Test only.

FLAME PROJECTION

With this power, a being can project flames, often in the form of fiery breath. This attack has a damage code of (Essence)L1.

A being may sustain the attack, but will suffer Drain the way a magician does: Drain (Essence)S2. When the attack is sustained, the being spreads the effects over a number of square meters equal to its Essence.

Highly flammable items may be ignited by a Flame Projection attack.

GUARD

Guard gives the being the power to prevent any accident—both natural and those caused by the Accident Power, within the terrain controlled by the being.

HYPNOTIC SONG

The being's song has a hypnotic effect on any creature able to hear it. The song has the same effect as an attack of code (Essence)M1, with the damage resisted by Willpower and applied to the Mental Condition Monitor. When all spaces on the track are filled, the victim becomes immobile, fascinated, and unable to initiate any physical, mental, or magical action. The effect lasts as long as the being continues to sing. Cyberears with dampening decrease the attack code to (Essence)L1. Earplugs, depending on their effectiveness, can alter the attack code to (Essence – 1)M1, or can totally negate it.

ILLUSION

Illusion gives a being the power to project images or impressions directly into the mind of a selected target or targets within range. Treat as a Entertainment Spell, with the Force equal to the being's Essence. This does not require a voluntary subject.

IMMUNITY TO AGE

With this power, a being does not age. Thus, he will never suffer the debilitating effects of advanced years.

IMMUNITY TO COLD

The being with Immunity to Cold power is able to live comfortably in the coldest of environments. It also gets automatic successes equal to twice its Essence Rating when resisting damage from cold-based attacks.

IMMUNITY TO FIRE

The being gets automatic successes equal to double its Essence Rating when resisting damage from fire or fire-based attacks (including magical fire).

IMMUNITY TO NORMAL WEAPONS

The being gets automatic successes equal to twice its Essence Rating when resisting damage from ordinary weapons. This power has no effect against magical weapons. Against elemental damage (such as fire, lack of air, water cannon, and so on), the effect is halved.

IMMUNITY TO PATHOGENS

The being gets automatic successes equal to double its Essence Rating when resisting infections or diseases.

IMMUNITY TO POISONS

The being gets automatic successes equal to double its Essence Rating whenever resisting the effects of a toxin (poison or drug).

INFECTION

When a being that Drains Essence (such as a vampire) has reduced a victim's Essence to 0, the victim will sicken and apparently die. Shortly after this "death," the individual will return to life as a being of the type that drained his Essence (Essence still equals 0). Such "newborn" creatures are dangerous. Though they are barely conscious of their new state, instinct will drive them to satisfy their hunger in any way they can.

After their "deaths," infected characters are no longer under the control of their player, but come under the gamemaster's control.

INFLUENCE

Influence allows a being to insinuate suggestions into the mind of a victim, predisposing that person to some form of action, reaction, or emotion. Match the being's Charisma Attribute (or Essence, if it has no Charisma) in an Opposed Test against the victim's Willpower. Use the number of net successes as a guide to how strongly the suggestion is taken.

Note: The ability to Influence fear is considerably less effective than the power of Fear.

MAGICAL GUARD

Magical Guard power (which is equal to its Essence) is used as Spell Defense by the person(s) it is warding.

MAGICAL RESISTANCE

The creature with Magical Resistance power adds its Essence to its Body or Willpower Rating (whichever is appropriate) when resisting the effects of a spell.

MANIFESTATION

Spirits in Manifest form assume the attribute values listed with their entry. While in Astral form, their attributes are equal to their Essence. Spirits in Manifest form are vulnerable to physical damage.

When an attacker strikes or shoots at a manifested Spirit with a mundane weapon, his Willpower Attribute should be used instead of his usual attack skill. Against Spirit foes, unshakable strength of will is more important than weapon skill. Attacks with Weapon Focuses, other magical attacks, and attacks using a Vulnerability of the Spirit are not subject to this rule.

In addition, manifested Spirits have the power of Immunity to Normal Weapons against Fire Combat Attacks, for these do not carry the full "charge" of the attackers's will. Against firearms, Spirits have "armor" equal to twice their Force.

They do not, however, have this power against Melee Attacks, since there is nothing to reduce the effects of their opponent's courage in close combat.

Additionally, spirits in Astral form receive a +10 to their Initiative, and a +5 when Manifest.

MANA DETECTION

The creature with Mana Detection power can detect and localize the manipulation of magical energy within a range of (Essence)D6 x 10 meters.

MIMICRY

Mimicry power gives a being the ability to imitate a variety of sounds, including the hunting calls of other creatures. This mimicry is almost perfect. The Target Number to identify the sound as false is (being's Essence) +3.

MIST FORM

Mist Form gives a being the power to transform its body into a mist, apparently by controlling the molecular cohesion of its cells. The mist can pass through any crack or crevice that is not airtight, even penetrating filtration systems that are proof against gases or pollution. Systems that are proof against bacterial or viral incursions will stop it, however. While in Mist Form, the being has the additional power of Immunity to Normal Weapons, including weapons to which it has a Vulnerability. While in Mist Form, a being can be affected normally by magic. If the being is exposed to a substance to which it is allergic, it will be forced to return to its corporeal form. (The easiest such allergen to apply is Sunlight. Other substances require that fine sprays of powder or liquid be directed into the Mist.) A being requires a complete action to shift form. If forced out of Mist Form, the change is instantaneous.

MOVEMENT

Movement gives a being the power to increase or decrease its victim's movement rate within the terrain it controls, multiplying or dividing the rate by the being's Essence.

NOXIOUS BREATH

With Noxious Breath power, the nauseating effects of the being's breath incapacitate the victim. The victim makes a Willpower or Body Resistance Test (whichever rating is greater) against the spell's Damage Code, which is (being's Essence)S2 Stun. Armor and dermal plating do not help in making the Resistance Test.

PARALYZING TOUCH

Any Paralyzing Touch (including an attack that does no damage) reduces the victim's Quickness by the being's Essence Rating for 2D6 minutes. Multiple touches can cause multiple reductions. A victim whose Quickness is reduced to 0 is incapable of any movement. To continue breathing, he must make an Unopposed Willpower Test each minute against a Target Number of the being's Essence. If the victim fails one of these tests, he has stopped breathing and will die in 1D6 minutes unless the paralysis effect wears off before that time or if someone applies first aid.

PESTILENCE

If touched by a being with Pestilence power, the victim is subject to infection by a disease similar to VITAS-3, or as described in the creature's description. See page 147 of **Shadowrun** rules for details.

PETRIFICATION

Petrification gives the power to affect a victim in a manner similar to the Petrify Spell. The effect is usually permanent. The effectiveness and extent of this power can vary. Use the being's Essence as the Force of the spell.

PETRIFYING GAZE

If a victim meets the eyes of a being with Petrifying Gaze power, he must make an Unopposed Intelligence Test, with the being's Essence Rating as the Target Number. Failure means that the victim is petrified. A being can keep a number of victims petrified equal to its Essence Rating. Failure means that the only actions a victim can perform are attempts to break the spell, which require the same Resistance Test as above.

PSYCHOKINESIS

This power allows a being to generate psychokinetic energy, similar to the Magic Fingers spell, with a Strength equal to its Essence Rating.

REGENERATION

The being with Regeneration power cannot be killed by wounds, except when there is damage to the spine, brain, or other vital apparatus. Check for this damage whenever the being takes a Deadly Physical Wound or its cumulative wounds kill it. Roll 1D6. A result of 1 indicates that the being is, indeed, dead. Wounds still hurt the being, giving penalties to actions as for normal characters, but if the wounds do not kill it, they vanish at the end of the turn.

Damage from weapons that cause massive tissue damage (fire, explosion, and so on) will also kill on a result of 1 or 2 on a die roll of 1D6.

SEARCH

Search allows a being to seek any person, place, or object within its terrain. Its rating for perceiving hidden objects or persons is equal to twice its Essence. Use an Opposed Success Test against the victim's Intelligence.

SILENCE

Silence gives a being the power to surround itself with an area of total silence whose diameter is equal to the being's Essence in meters. Within that area, no sound can be heard, either by the being or anyone else. Sounds whose source is within this area are silenced at the source; nobody can hear them.

SONIC PROJECTION

Sonic Projection gives a being the power to emit a cry that is physically painful to other creatures. The cry usually enrages unintelligent creatures. Humans and metahumans who do not somehow block the sound add +2 to all Target Numbers in the turn during which the creature cries out. This penalty does not apply to characters with cyberears equipped with dampers, but increases to +3 for characters with cyberears equipped with extended high-frequency response. Some creatures will utter this cry at such a high frequency that it is inaudible to humans and metahumans who do not have aug-

mented hearing. In these cases, unaugmented characters suffer no ill effects; creatures able to hear super-high frequencies suffer the effects listed above, however.

VENOM

Venom makes a being's attack poisonous, with a Damage Code of (Essence)S2. Treat as a Toxin, with a speed of 1 turn.

WEATHER CONTROL

Weather Control allows a being to "call" certain weather conditions. These cannot be totally anomalous (i.e., a blizzard in Death Valley), and require an appropriate precursor (e.g., a low-pressure system for a thunderstorm). The weather condition builds over a period of time, reaching its peak in 1D6 hours. Once the weather condition has been called, it is no longer under the being's control. (Thus, a being who has called an electrical storm cannot command the lightning.)

WEAKNESSES

ALLERGY

Many beings react negatively to one or more substances or conditions. Normally, the effects last only as long as the being is in contact with the substance. Common allergy-causing substances include sunlight, ferrous metals, holy objects (such allergies appear to be psychosomatic), plastics, and pollutants.

Nuisance: Annoys the being but has no significant game effects.

Mild: Causes discomfort and distracts the being (+1 to all Target Numbers).

Severe: In addition to the Mild effects above, the allergen's touch is painful to the being, often forcing retreat. Weapons made of the substance add +1 to their staging when the being is resisting damage.

Extreme: In addition to the Severe effects above, the slightest touch of the allergen results in a reaction and causes physical damage to the being. Weapons made of the substance cause an additional Light wound.

DIETARY REQUIREMENT

The being's diet must contain certain substances (often trace minerals, but sometimes more esoteric compounds). Without this substance or suitable dietary supplement in its diet, the creature will sicken and die.

ESSENCE LOSS

The being has no inherent Essence Attribute. It gains Essence only by regularly consuming the Essence of others. The being loses a point of Essence every month.

A being whose Essence is reduced to 0 will die in the following month. During this period, the being is dangerous because, whatever its normal nature, it now behaves as a starved predator who will hunt fresh Essence with mindless ferocity.

REDUCED SENSES

Any or all of the being's senses may be limited in effectiveness. Typically, Reduced Senses function at half the normal rating.

VULNERABILITY

The metabolism of some beings is disrupted drastically by weapons made of particular substances. Such weapons increase their Wound Category by one step. For example, a 2L1 wooden club would be a 2M1 weapon against a being vulnerable to wood.

Beings recover (or regenerate) from wounds inflicted by the substance to which they are vulnerable with the same speed as they do from wounds due to other sources.

Simple contact with the substance is treated as a Nuisance Allergy.

AWAKENED ANIMALS

Name	B	Q	S	C	I	W	E	R	Attacks
Aardwolf	3	4 x 5	3	—	2/4	2	6	4	4M2

Powers: Concealment (Self Only)
Weaknesses: Allergy (Pollutants, Mild)

Name	B	Q	S	C	I	W	E	R	Attacks
Agropelter	2	4 x 3	3	—	3/4	2	6	4	3M2 or Humanoid

Powers: Enhanced Senses (Improved Hearing and Smell, Low-Light Vision)
Note: Multiplier for Arboreal Movement is 4.

Name	B	Q	S	C	I	W	E	R	Attacks
Bandersnatch	8	3 x 4	7	—	2/4	4	(6)	4	8S2, +1 Reach

Powers: Adaptive Coloration, Mimicry

Name	B	Q	S	C	I	W	E	R	Attacks
*Bandit	2	4 x 3	2	4	3/5	2	6	5	3L1

Powers: Enhanced Senses (Improved Hearing and Smell, Low-Light Vision)

Name	B	Q	S	C	I	W	E	R	Attacks
Behemoth	10/2	4 x 3	25	—	2/2	5	6	3	7D2

Name	B	Q	S	C	I	W	E	R	Attacks
*Birdman	2	5 x 4	1	—	1/5	3	6	5	3L1

Powers: Enhanced Senses (Improved Hearing, Sonar), Sonic Projection
Weaknesses: Allergy (Sunlight, Mild), Reduced Senses (Vision)

Name	B	Q	S	C	I	W	E	R	Attacks
Black Annis	9	4 x 5	10	—	2/3	4	(5)	4	8S2

Powers: Enhanced Physical Attributes (Strength, once per day, for (Essence)D6 turns), Enhanced Reactions, Enhanced Senses (Low-Light Vision), Influence (Depression)
Weaknesses: Allergy (Sunlight, Mild)

Name	B	Q	S	C	I	W	E	R	Attacks
*Blood Kite	1	5 x 5	1	—	1/4	2	6	5	2L1

Powers: Enhanced Senses (Improved Vision, Thermographic Vision)

Name	B	Q	S	C	I	W	E	R	Attacks
Bogie	3	5 x 4	4	—	2/4	3	(6)	4	4M2

Powers: Accident, Enhanced Movement, Enhanced Reactions, Enhanced Senses (Improved Hearing and Smell, Low-Light Vision, Motion Detection), Fear
Weaknesses: Allergy (Aconite or Horseradish, Severe)

Name	B	Q	S	C	I	W	E	R	Attacks
Bombardier	1	4 x 4	1	—	2/3	2	6	4	2L1

Name	B	Q	S	C	I	W	E	R	Attacks
Boobrie	2	3 x 5	2	—	2/3	2	6	4	4L2, +1 Reach

Powers: Pestilence
Note: Swimming multiplier is 3.

Name	B	Q	S	C	I	W	E	R	Attacks
Century Ferret	2	4 x 4	2	—	2/4	2	(6)	5	2M2

Powers: Enhanced Physical Attributes (Quickness, once per day, for (Essence)D6 turns), Enhanced Senses (Improved Hearing and Smell, Low-Light Vision, Thermographic Vision), Mana Detection
Weaknesses: Allergy (Mana, Mild)

Name	B	Q	S	C	I	W	E	R	Attacks
Chimera	5/1	3 x 3	4	—	1/3	4	(5)	2	4M2, −1 Reach

Powers: Concealment (Self Only), Immunity to Poisons, Venom
Weaknesses: Vulnerability (Iron)

Name	B	Q	S	C	I	W	E	R	Attacks
*Corpselight	5	10	—	—	2	5	2D6/A	5	3M2, −1 Reach

Powers: Essence Drain, Immunity to Normal Weapons, Manifestation, Movement (Decrease in Swamps and Marshes), Psychokinesis, Regeneration
Weaknesses: Essence Loss

Name	B	Q	S	C	I	W	E	R	Attacks
*Deathrattle	3	3 x 4	3	—	1/5	2	6	5	4L1, +1 Reach

Powers: Enhanced Senses (Thermographic Vision), Immunity to Poisons, Venom

Name	B	Q	S	C	I	W	E	R	Attacks
*Devil Jack Diamond	5/3	3 x 5	5	—	1/3	4	6	4	7S3

Name	B	Q	S	C	I	W	E	R	Attacks
*Devil Rat	2	5 x 3	1	5	2/5	3	(4)	5	4L1, −1 Reach

Powers: Animal Control (Normal Rats), Concealment (Self Only), Immunity to Pathogens, Immunity to Poisons
Weaknesses: Allergy (Sunlight, Mild)

Name	B	Q	S	C	I	W	E	R	Attacks
Devilfish	9	3 x 5	10	—	2/3	4	(6)	4	5M2

Powers: Fear, Venom

Name	B	Q	S	C	I	W	E	R	Attacks
Dour	5	4 x 3	5	3	2/4	3	5	5	4M2, +1 Reach or Humanoid

Powers: Enhanced Senses (Low-Light Vision)
Weaknesses: Allergy (Sunlight, Nuisance)

Name	B	Q	S	C	I	W	E	R	Attacks
Dzoo-Noo-Qua	9/2	5 x 2	10	1	3/3	4	(5)	4	7S2, +1 Reach

Powers: Enhanced Senses (Thermographic Vision), Essence Drain, Magical Resistance
Weaknesses: Allergy (Sunlight, Mild)

Name	B	Q	S	C	I	W	E	R	Attacks
Embracer	8	4 x 3	8	—	2/3	3	(6)	5	7S2, +1 Reach

Powers: Corrosive Secretions, Immunity to Fire, Movement (Decrease)
Weaknesses: Allergy (Cold, Mild)

Name	B	Q	S	C	I	W	E	R	Attacks
*Fideal	4	3	3	—	1/3	2	4	4	3M2, +1 Reach

Powers: Corrosive Secretions, Engulf, Enhanced Senses (Motion Detection), Invisibility (Non-Magical), Regeneration
Weaknesses: Vulnerability (Fire)
Note: Movement on land is 1.

Name	B	Q	S	C	I	W	E	R	Attacks
Firebird	2	5 x 3	2	—	2/3	3	(6)	4	5L2

Powers: Fire Resistance.

Name	B	Q	S	C	I	W	E	R	Attacks
Firedrake	4	4 x 4	4	—	2/4	3	(6)	5	3M2

Powers: Enhanced Senses (Wide-Band Hearing), Flame Projection, Immunity to Fire

Name	B	Q	S	C	I	W	E	R	Attacks
Gabriel Hound	3	4 x 4	3	—	2/3	4	(5)	4	(Str)M2

Powers: Compulsion (Immobility), Concealment (Self Only), Enhanced Movement, Enhanced Physical Attributes (Strength or Quickness, once each per day, for (Essence)D6 turns), Enhanced Reactions, Enhanced Senses (Thermographic Vision).
Weaknesses: Allergy (Sunlight, Mild)

Name	B	Q	S	C	I	W	E	R	Attacks
Gargoyle	10/3	4 x 3	8	—	2/4	4	(5)	3	(Str)S2

Powers: Concealment (Self Only), Enhanced Physical Attributes (Strength once per day for 5D6 turns), Noxious Breath
Weaknesses: Vulnerability (Iron)
Note: Flying multiplier (Males) is 4.

Name	B	Q	S	C	I	W	E	R	Attacks
Gila Demon	4/1	4 x 3	4	—	1/4	3	6	3	4L2

Powers: Enhanced Senses (Improved Smell and Vision), Venom

Name	B	Q	S	C	I	W	E	R	Attacks
Gloaming Owl	3	5 x 4	3	—	2/4	2	(6)	(4)	5L1

Powers: Blindness, Enhanced Senses (Low-Light Vision, Thermographic Vision), Fear, Silence (Non-Magical)
Weaknesses: Allergy (Sunlight, Mild)

Name	B	Q	S	C	I	W	E	R	Attacks
Greater Armadillo	4/2	3 x 3	3	—	1/3	2	6	4	2M2, −1 Reach

Powers: Enhanced Senses (Improved Smell), Immunity to Poisons
Weaknesses: Reduced Senses (Vision)

Name	B	Q	S	C	I	W	E	R	Attacks
Greater Unicorn	8	4 x 5	8	4	3/4	4	(6)	5	7M3, +1 Reach

Powers: Empathy, Enhanced Physical Attributes (Quickness), Immunity to Pathogens, Immunity to Poisons, Magical Resistance, Search

Name	B	Q	S	C	I	W	E	R	Attacks
*Greater Wolverine	7	4 x 5	4	—	2/4	2	6	5	5S2

Powers: Enhanced Physical Attributes (Quickness, once per day, for (Essence)D6 turns), Enhanced Reactions, Enhanced Senses (Improved Smell)
Weaknesses: Reduced Senses (Vision)

Name	B	Q	S	C	I	W	E	R	Attacks
Gyre	4	4 x 5	4	—	2/5	3	(6)	4	3S3

Powers: Enhanced Senses (Improved Eyesight), Immunity to Pathogens, Immunity to Poisons, Influence (Hopelessness)
Weakness: Allergy (Pollution, Severe)

Name	B	Q	S	C	I	W	E	R	Attacks
Hell Hound	4	4 x 4	5	—	3/4	3	(6)	6	6M2

Powers: Enhanced Senses (Improved Hearing and Smell, Low-Light Vision), Flame Projection, Immunity to Fire

Name	B	Q	S	C	I	W	E	R	Attacks
Hellbender	3	3 x 2	3	—	1/3	2	6	4	6L2

Powers: Enhanced Senses (Motion Detection), Immunity to Poisons, Paralyzing Touch
Weaknesses: Allergy (Unpolluted Water, Mild), Reduced Senses (Vision)
Note: Swimming multiplier is 5.

Name	B	Q	S	C	I	W	E	R	Attacks
Hoop Snake	3	3 x 4	4	—	2/3	3	6	4	6L1, −1 Reach

Powers: Venom
Note: Rolling multiplier is 5.

Name	B	Q	S	C	I	W	E	R	Attacks
Icedrake	4	4 x 4	4	—	2/3	3	(6)	5	3M2

Powers: Cold Aura, Enhanced Senses (Improved Vision), Immunity to Cold
Weaknesses: Allergy (Fire, Mild)

Name	B	Q	S	C	I	W	E	R	Attacks
*Incubus	6	2 x 2	9	3	3/5	4	(6)	4	5S2, +1 Reach

Powers: Desire Reflection, Enhanced Senses (Low-Light Vision), Illusion
Weaknesses: Allergy (Sunlight, Severe)

Name	B	Q	S	C	I	W	E	R	Attacks
Juggernaut	15/4	4 x 3	42	—	1/3	9	7	4	9D3

Powers: Enhanced Physical Attributes (Quickness, once each per day, for (Essence x 2)D6 turns), Enhanced Senses (Improved Hearing and Smell, Motion Detection), Fear, Immunity to Cold, Immunity to Fire, Immunity to Pathogens, Immunity to Poisons

Name	B	Q	S	C	I	W	E	R	Attacks
*Lambton Lizard	7/2	4 x 2	5	—	1/4	3	5	3	3S3, +1 Reach

Powers: Paralyzing Touch
Note: Swimming multiplier is 4.

Name	B	Q	S	C	I	W	E	R	Attacks
Lesser Roc	4	5 x 4	4	—	2/4	2	6	4	3M2

Powers: Enhanced Senses (Improved Vision, Low-Light Vision), Immunity to Pathogens, Immunity to Poisons

Name	B	Q	S	C	I	W	E	R	Attacks
*Lesser Thunderbird	3	6 x 2	3	—	2/5	3	(6)	6	6L2

Powers: Electrical Projection (EMP), Enhanced Senses (Low-Light Vision), Weather Control (Electrical Storms)
Note: Flying multiplier is 4.

Name	B	Q	S	C	I	W	E	R	Attacks
Leviathan	11/2	5 x 3	10	—	2/4	3	6	5	9D3

Powers: Enhanced Senses (Sonar), Mimicry

Loup-Garou	4(6)	4 x 4	7(9)	—	3/4	4	5	4(6)	3M2(6M2)

Powers: Enhanced Physical Attributes (Strength, once per day, for (Essence)D6 turns), Enhanced Senses (Thermographic Vision)
Weaknesses: Allergy (Sunlight, Severe); Allergy (Aconite or Horseradish, Severe)
Note: Statistics in parenthesis refer to the creature at peak power.

Man-of-the Woods	10	6 x 2	7	5	5	5	5A	10/15	4S2

Powers: Accident, Concealment, Confusion, Fear, Immunity to Normal Weapons, Magical Guard, Manifestation, Movement, Weather Control (Any)

Martichoras	8	6 x 4	8	—	3/4	3	6	6	7S2, +1 Reach

Powers: Enhanced Senses (Low-Light Vision), Venom
Weaknesses: Allergy (Pollution, Mild)

Megalodon	15/2	5 x 4	13	—	1/3	3	6	5	10D2

Powers: Enhanced Senses (Improved Smell), Regeneration

Mermaid	4	6 x 4	6	—	2/4	3	6	4	4S4

Powers: Enhanced Physical Attributes (Quickness, once per day, for (Essence x 2)D6 turns), Enhanced Senses (Improved Hearing)
Weaknesses: Dietary Requirement (Mercury)

Mimic Snake	4	4 x 3	8	—	2/4	2	6	4	5M1

Powers: Enhanced Senses (Low-Light Vision), Mimicry

Mist Lynx	4	5 x 4	5	–	2/4	3	(6)	4	4S2

Powers: Enhanced Senses (Low-Light Vision), Mist Form

Munchkin	3	4 x 4	6	—	4/5	5	5	5	3M2 or Humanoid

Powers: Enhanced Senses (Thermographic Vision)
Weaknesses: Dietary Requirement (Molybdenum)

New Boar	4	4 x 6	4	—	2/3	3	6	4	(Str)M2

Powers: Enhanced Physical Attributes (Strength, once per day, for Essence x 3)D6 turns), Enhanced Senses (Improved Hearing and Smell)

New Leatherback	8/3	3 x 2	5	—	2/4	3	(6)	3	3M2

Powers: Engulf, Magical Resistance, Movement
Weaknesses: Allergy (Mercury, Extreme), Vulnerability (Mercury)
Note: Swimming multiplier is 5.

*Nomad	6	3 x 3	0	6	1/6	6	9A	5	Special

Powers: Compulsion (Homicidal Mania), Essence Drain (Modified), Immunity to Normal Weapons, Manifestation

Novopossum	3	4 x 4	3	—	2/4	2	6	4	6L1

Powers: Corrosive Saliva, Enhanced Senses (Low-Light Vision)

Piasma	11/2	4 x 5	13	—	2/4	4	6	4	9D2, +1 Reach

Powers: Enhanced Physical Attributes (Strength or Quickness, once per day each, for (Essence x 2)D6 turns), Enhanced Reactions, Enhanced Senses (Thermographic Vision, Wide-Band Hearing)
Weaknesses: Allergy (Sunlight, Nuisance)

Pricuricu	1	4 x 4	0	—	1/4	1	6	4	1L1

Powers: Enhanced Senses (Low-Light Vision), Sonic Projection (High-Frequency)
Weaknesses: Allergy (Sunlight, Mild)

Rock Lizard	3	3 x 4	3	—	1/3	3	6	5	6L2

Powers: Immunity to Poisons, Venom

Rockworm	2/1	4	2	—	1/2	3	3	2	2M2

Powers: Corrosive Saliva, Immunity to Pathogens, Immunity to Poisons, Regeneration
Note: Burrowing multiplier is 0.25 for soft rock; 0.125 for hard rock.

Saber-Tooth Cat	5	5 x 4	5	—	2/4	2	6	4	5S2

Powers: Enhanced Senses (Low-Light Vision, Thermographic Vision)

Salamander	5	6 x 3	2	4	4	4	(4)A	10/51	4S2

Powers: Engulf, Flame Aura, Flame Projection, Immunity to Fire, Guard, Magical Resistance, Manifestation, Psychokinesis
Weaknesses: Vulnerability (Water)

Sea Drake	4	4 x 4	4	—	2/3	3	(6)	5	3M2, +1 Reach

Powers: Enhanced Physical Attributes (Movement, once per day, for (Essence)D6 turns), Enhanced Senses (Low-Light Vision)

Serpent, Freshwater	12/1	4 x 3	7	—	1/3	3	6	3	4S3, +1 Reach

Name	B	Q	S	C	I	W	E	R	Attacks
Serpent, Saltwater	10/2	4 x 4	18	—	1/4	4	6	4	7S3, +1 Reach

Powers: Enhanced Physical Attributes (Quickness, twice per day, for (Essence)D6 turns)

Shadowhound	4	4 x 4	5	2/4	3	6	4	5M2	

Powers: Darkness, Enhanced Senses (Low-Light Vision), Silence
Weaknesses: Allergy (Sunlight, Severe)

Siren	3	8 x 2	4	—	3/5	5	(5)	5	4M2

Powers: Enhanced Senses (Low-Light Vision), Hypnotic Song, Immunity to Pathogens, Immunity to Poisons

Snow Moose	11/1	4 x 4	9	—	2/4	3	(6)	4	6S2

Powers: Enhanced Physical Attributes (Quickness), Enhanced Senses (Improved Vision, Low-Light Vision), Immunity to Cold, Silence

Snow Snake	2	3 x 3	2	—	1/4	2	(6)	3	4L1

Powers: Enhanced Physical Attributes (Quickness), Enhanced Senses (Improved Smell, Low-Light Vision), Immunity to Cold, Venom
Weaknesses: Vulnerability (Fire)

*Stonebinder	2	4 x 4	1	—	1/4	2	(6)	4	3L1

Powers: Enhanced Senses (Sonar), Immunity to Poisons, Petrification, Venom
Weaknesses: Allergy (Sunlight, Severe)

Stormcrow	2	6 x 2	1	—	3/4	3	(6)/6	4	3L1

Powers: Enhanced Senses (Improved Hearing), Weather Control (Flock Only)
Note: A dual being only when in a flock or six or more stormcrows.

Tachypus	2	4 x 6	2	—	2/4	3	(6)	6	3M3

Powers: Enhanced Movement, Enhanced Physical Attributes (Quickness, four times per day, for (Essence)D6 turns)

Talis Cat									
As Housecat	1	4 x 4	1	—	2/4	4	(6)	5	2L2, −1 Reach
As "Cheetah"	7	9 x 4	7	—	2/4	4	(6)	5	8L2

Powers: Desire Reflection (Self, Cheetah Only), Enhanced Movement, Enhanced Physical Attributes (Quickness, Body, and Strength), Enhanced Reactions, Enhanced Senses (Low-Light Vision)

Torpedo Shark	7/2	5 x 4	6	—	1/3	3	6	5	8S3

Powers: Enhanced Physical Attributes (Quickness, three times per day, for (Essence − 2)D6 turns), Enhanced Senses (Improved Smell)

Toxic Earth Spirit	8	2 x 2	8	1	4	4	(4)A	7/12	4S3, +1 Reach,special

Powers: Alienation, Concealment, Corrosive Secretions, Fear, Manifestation, Noxious Breath

Toxic Water Spirit	6	4 x 2	4	1	4	4	(4)A	10/15	4D4 Stun

Powers: Accident, Alienation, Corrosive Secretions, Engulf, Fear, Manifestation, Movement, Search

Troglodyte	3	3 x 4	2	2	3/4	3	6	3	Humanoid

Powers: Concealment, Enhanced Senses (Thermographic Vision)
Weaknesses: Allergy (Sunlight, Mild)

Unicorn Fish	7	5 x 4	9	—	2/4	3	(6)	4	6S3, +1 Reach

Powers: Immunity to Pathogens, Magical Resistance

White Buffalo	9	4 x 4	7	5	2/4	5	6	3	5D3, +1 Reach

Powers: Animal Control (Buffalo), Enhanced Senses (Improved Hearing and Smell), Immunity to Pathogens, Search
Weaknesses: Allergy (Pollutants, Severe)

Wodewose	2	4 x 4	6	—	2/4	3	6	4	3M2, +1 Reach

Powers: Enhanced Senses (Improved Smell), Immunity to Age, Immunity to Pathogens, Immunity to Poisons, Pestilence

Wyvern	9	3 x 2	8	—	2/4	4	(6)	4	8S3, +1 Reach

Powers: Enhanced Senses (Low-Light Vision), Immunity to Poisons, Influence (Fear), Venom
Note: Flying multiple is 6.

TABLE KEY

NOTE: An asterisk before an animal's name indicates that further game mechanics are given with the being's complete description.

B: Body. The first number is the rating. The second is any "armor" for the being.

Q: Quickness. The first number is the rating. The second is the multiplier for running.

S: Strength.

C: Charisma.

I: Intelligence. The first number is the being's basic rating, used for puzzles and magic throws. The second is its perception rating, used to detect prey or enemies when its best sense is working (sonar for bats, nose for dogs, and so forth).

W: Willpower.

E: Essence. If the number appears in parentheses, the animal has a dual nature. If a capital A follows the number, the being exists primarily in astral space. A being with variable Essence has a range of numbers.

R: Reaction. The Reaction Rating for some beings is a function of their other attributes.

Attacks. This is the Attack Code for nonintelligent beings or the designation Humanoid for those that can use weapons and follow the normal combat rules for characters. This column also tells which beings have extended reach.

PARANORMAL ANIMALS
OF NORTH AMERICA
COLOR PLATES

PARANORMAL
ANIMALS
OF NORTH AMERICA
AWAKENED
ANIMALS

AARDWOLF
Proteles novalis

IDENTIFICATION

The North American aardwolf stands 0.9 meter at the shoulder and weighs about 37 kilograms. It is a modified form of *Proteles cristatus*, an African mammal resembling a hyena. Its coat is short and bristly, with longer hackles on the back of the neck that the aardwolf can raise in a threat display. Its base color is a dusty tan, with darker patches on the flanks and a dark patch running from between the ears down the spine. The Awakening has given the creature longer, sharper teeth than its conventional African predecessor.

The aardwolf is fast-moving and aggressive, particularly in packs.

As the conventional aardwolf (*p. cristatus*) is not native to North America, the *novalis* strain may derive from specimens that escaped from zoos. (A particularly large population exists in southwestern North America. One theory (unsubstantiated) posits that the aardwolf descends from a single family group originally confined in the San Diego zoo.)

MAGIC CAPABILITY

Parabiological.

HABITS

The conventional aardwolf is primarily an insectivore; the *novalis* strain is a carnivore. By preference a scavenger, it feeds from the kills of other, more aggressive, creatures. If no carrion is available, however, the *novalis* is an efficient hunter. The animals typically travel in packs of up to 30, using speed and sheer numbers to pull down their prey. Though they frequently hunt rabbits and other small desert mammals, aardwolf packs have also been known to pursue and outrun herd animals. They concentrate on the slowest-moving creature (usually the infirm or the old) in a herd, which prevents over-hunting an area or disturbing its ecology. There are tales, again unsubstantiated, of aardwolf packs attacking and killing humans.

Aardwolves are cunning and make good use of their camouflage and concealment abilities. They remain motionless, almost impossible to detect visually, until their prey is within range. They then burst from hiding in a high-speed dash. The creatures have little stamina, and can only maintain high speed for less than a minute before being forced back to a slow run.

Aardwolves balance aggressiveness with a streak of cowardice. Packs are likely to attack just about anything that moves in their initial attack, but if they encounter determined opposition that inflicts losses, the pack will turn tail and run.

COMMENTARY

The aardwolf displays a limited form of magical concealment. When they are immobile, it is nearly impossible to spot one visually, though its coloration and patterning do not change. (This ability is not effective against methods of detection not dependent on the visible spectrum.) If one sees an aardwolf while it is moving and keeps one's eye on it when it becomes immobile, there is no concealment effect. If the observer looks away for a moment, however, and then tries to reacquire his view of the aardwolf, the concealment power takes effect. Though unintelligent and definitely non-sentient, the aardwolf seems well-aware of the effectiveness (and limitations) of this ability.

The North American aardwolf has never been sighted near large human settlements, and seems to avoid vehicles.

POWERS

Concealment (Self Only).

WEAKNESSES

Allergy (Pollutants, Mild).

>>>>>(Don't be too sure about these things staying away from you just 'cause you're in a car or on a bike, chummer. A pack of these fraggers followed me and my Harley Scorpion through the whole of the Pueblo Council. (No, I don't know how they kept up. I had a handful of throttle and I didn't let up for about six hours.) When I stopped, they tried to jump me. Tried. One of their pelts looks real nice on my wall.)<<<<<
   —Casper (09:23:02/1-22-51)

>>>>>(Not to cast aspersion on our friend Cap the Knife, but I seriously doubt that it was the same pack. They're fast, but not that fast.)<<<<<
   —Archangel (11:07:53/1-24-51)

>>>>>(I'll go along with Cap. I've seen them move right bloody fast, for long stretches.)<<<<<
   —Brat (15:15:06/1-24-51)

>>>>>(Right you are, chummer.)<<<<<
   —Casper (15:20:54/1-24-51)

>>>>>(And don't be too sure about them backing down when they take casualties. A pack of them came after me and Davey, just sprang out of nowhere. They didn't back down and we had to kill every last one of them. Nasty fraggers, they are.)<<<<<
   —Brat (16:00:53/1-24-51)

GAME INFORMATION

	B	Q	S	C	I	W	E	R	Attacks
Aardwolf	3	4 x 5	3	—	2/4	2	6	4	4M2

   Powers: Concealment (Self only)
   Weaknesses: Allergy (Pollutants, Mild)

AARDWOLF
   Proteles novalis

HABITAT
   Desert and scrubland

RANGE
   Southwestern regions of North America, spreading into the Midwest

RANGE

SIZE COMPARISON

AGROPELTER
Pithecocephalus hermestes

IDENTIFICATION

The agropelter is a small hominid, up to 0.9 meter tall when standing erect, with a slender, wiry body, an ape-like face, and long, thin (but very strong) limbs. Short, thick brown or black fur covers its body, and both hands and feet have sharp claws. Though it can stand erect, it is more comfortable moving as a quadruped.

Gene typing has confirmed the agropelter as a metaspecies arising from the rhesus monkey (*Macaca mulatta*). The genetic changes have been so extensive, however, that taxonomists have decided to classify it as a totally distinct genus: *Pithecocephalus*. (Exactly how the agropelter or its predecessor species came to run loose in North America is not known.)

The agropelter is an aggressive, arboreal creature, and has been known to attack in order to drive humans away from its territory.

MAGIC CAPABILITY

Parabiological.

HABITS

The agropelter is an omnivore, but prefers meat. It lives on owls and other birds it can catch. Agropelters hunt in small, cooperative family units.

The agropelter is not intelligent, but it displays significant cunning. It is also a nasty-spirited creature, seeming to revel in destruction for its own sake. Some animals might pillage a campsite for food (or perhaps to attack the inhabitants), but the agropelter actually vandalizes such sites, wrecking what it can and despoiling the rest with excrement. Though even a family unit of agropelters is probably not capable of killing a well-defended human or metahuman, the creatures often stage "nuisance" attacks. These usually consist of dropping items such as rocks, branches, or excrement from trees. (Such ambushes are usually not fatal, though recurring "tall tales" report agropelters killing unsuspecting travelers).

COMMENTARY

Though aggressive when challenged, an agropelter is unable to overpower anything as large as a human. This does not minimize its nuisance level, however.

Agropelters can and do damage equipment, and they can make passage through their territory decidedly uncomfortable.

POWERS

Enhanced Senses (Improved Hearing and Smell, Low-Light Vision).

WEAKNESSES

None.

>>>>>("Tall tales," eh? Drek. Agropelters geeked my best bud, Tandi, up north near Vancouver. Dropped a fraggin' log on her head. Splattered her real good. So don't slot me around about "nuisance attacks.")<<<<<
    —Mr. A (03:22:09/2-4-51)

>>>>>(Ditto. Little fraggers dropped a rock on me down near Oregon City. If I hadn't been chipped so high, they would have got me, too.)<<<<<
    —Tyke (15:59:59/2-5-51)

>>>>>(I've got some gen on where those things came from. Heard it from Neddy. When things started to go strange, a research lab in Portland—Genesee, he says—had a whole population of rhesus monkeys. The lab was using all kinds of techniques to replicate Goblinization: carcinogens, irradiation, teratogens, mutagens—you name it. Neddy says they "expended" a couple hundred monkeys in the process. Then, out of the blue, the research subjects started to goblinize. It didn't matter if the little bugger had been force-fed cyclamates or was part of a control group. One day all the Genesee monkeys turned into agropelters. The same thing happened to all the primates across the country. Chimps, apes, spider monkeys, all started to undergo an Awakening, just like us.
    So what happens? A bunch of ecofreaks (you know, those guys who firebomb butcher shops and throw blood on people who wear leather shoes) broke into Genesee and let the little fraggers go. Killed some sec-guards in the raid, then torched the lab, leaving the scientists still inside. They did that with labs and zoos all across the country. Charming, ain't it?)<<<<<
    —Peachy (23:43:34/2-7-51)

>>>>>(We were justified in our actions at Genesee and other enslavement facilities around the world. Mankind must respect the rights of other living creatures.)<<<<<
    —Byron Wordsworth (01:00:01/2-8-51)

>>>>>(Like they respected the rights of Tandi? Drek.)<<<<<
    —Mr. A (10:47:34/2-8-51)

GAME INFORMATION

	B	Q	S	C	I	W	E	R	Attacks
Agropelter	2	4 x 3	3	—	3/4	2	6	4	3M2 or Humanoid

Powers: Enhanced Senses (Improved Hearing and Smell, Low-Light Vision)
Note: Multiplier for Arboreal Movement is 4.

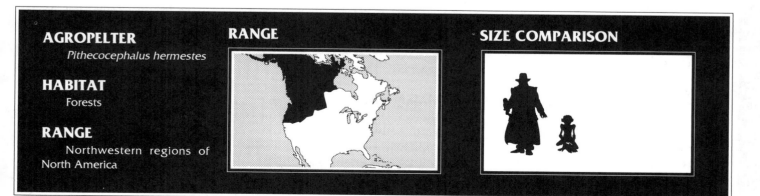

AGROPELTER
    Pithecocephalus hermestes

HABITAT
    Forests

RANGE
    Northwestern regions of North America

RANGE

SIZE COMPARISON

BANDERSNATCH
Pesvastus dissimulatus

IDENTIFICATION

The bandersnatch stands 2.9 meters tall and weighs 400 kilograms. It is a form of sasquatch that has been infected with a virus similar in effect to Human-Metahuman Vampiric Virus (HMHVV), but without the manifestation of the vampiric aspects of the HMHVV infection. The virus alters the thick sasquatch pelt, making it more tatty-looking. The bandersnatch's strong arms are also somewhat longer than its progenitor's, and its teeth are those of a carnivore.

Because of the bandersnatch's ability to refract light around its body, its true form is rarely seen. The creature has full, conscious control of this ability. When the power is in effect, the bandersnatch appears as a shifting image of the terrain around it, formed into a humanoid shape. Though not as effective as true invisibility, this power provides the creature with a startlingly effective adaptive camouflage. When the animal remains still, it is almost impossible to detect. It is difficult to focus on it even when the animal moves. As shorter and longer wavelengths are refracted as well as those of the visible spectrum, devices that depend on infrared or ultraviolet are no more effective in detecting the bandersnatch than the naked eye. Very short wavelengths such as microwaves and radar are not refracted.

The bandersnatch shares the sasquatch's mimicry abilities.

MAGIC CAPABILITY

Innate.

HABITS

The bandersnatch is active at all times. It is an omnivore, but much prefers fresh meat, preferably alive or freshly killed. It is cunning and dangerous, using its mimicry and camouflage abilities to their best advantage. The creature is able to use rudimentary tools and weapons, and has enough abstract reasoning ability to devise such simple traps as pits and deadfalls.

The bandersnatch is a solitary creature, living alone in caves or groves. It often plants traps to guard its lair.

Some sasquatch family units have been totally infected, turning the entire unit into bandersnatch. Observation of these family groups shows that the bandersnatch is extraordinarily fecund, giving birth to infant bandersnatch rather than sasquatch. The animal's tendency to let offspring fend for themselves almost from birth results in a high rate of infant mortality, keeping the bandersnatch population mercifully low.

The bandersnatch usually kills only for food or in self-defense, but it can be driven into a homicidal rage. In that state, the animal attacks anything that moves, whether it needs to hunt or not. In the absence of an animal victim, the creature will vent its rage on the surrounding terrain, uprooting or tearing limbs off trees, and so on.

COMMENTARY

Though closely related to the sasquatch, the bandersnatch is not considered a sentient being. The trauma that turned a peaceful creature into a killer apparently so damaged the bandersnatch's brain that sentience was lost. That no bandersnatch has ever shown evidence of language use bears out this assumption.

The creature's adaptive camouflage ability is unique in both nature and "paranature," but its source is unknown. Speculation is rampant, but none of the prevalent theories seems worthy of notice.

The derivation of the name "bandersnatch" is also somewhat obscure. Fictional creatures by that name appear in 19th and 20th century novels, but the actual creature bears no similarity to its fictional predecessors.

POWERS

Adaptive Coloration, Mimicry.

WEAKNESSES

None.

>>>>>(What's this "adaptive coloration" drek? What do these bleeders look like?)<<<<<
—Brat (09:18:33/3-26-51)

>>>>>(You into old movies? Pre-simsense, I'm talking. Check out an old classic, Predator, with Arnold Schwarzenneger before he went into politics. That's what this bleeder looks like, pretty close.)<<<<<
—Bladerunner (13:58:02/3-26-51)

>>>>>(This entry worries me. We say the creature is non-sentient, and so we can justify killing it, enslaving it, oppressing it. But how can we say what sentience is? We, who view everything through the filter of our own, humanocentric world-view. Isn't this another example of an age-old (1 Mp deleted by Sysop).)<<<<<
—Deborah Bailey (4-1-51/11:28:47)

>>>>>(The broad kinda rambles on, but she do got a point. Them things use weapons, set traps. I use weapons, set traps. I'm sentient.)<<<<<
—Trasher (15:33:00/4-2-51)

>>>>>(The guide states that "no bandersnatch has ever shown evidence of language use." This merely indicates that no observer has shown the patience and dedication necessary to (.5 Mp deleted by Sysop).)<<<<<
—Deborah Bailey (07:35:09/4-3-51)

>>>>>(My dear lady, non-sentient creatures like monkeys have been taught to use language.)<<<<<
—Lethe (11:23:32/4-3-51)

>>>>>(We make decisions too fast, decisions that can have a catastrophic effect on a whole race. We should take time to find them a niche as we did with the sasquatch. If the bandersnatch can function in (2.3 Mp deleted by Sysop).)<<<<<
—Deborah Bailey (19:44:53/4-3-51)

>>>>>(If a bandersnatch can be trained to take out the garbage—without eating it—does that make it sentient? Who can propose a good definition of sentience? Even a rule of thumb?)<<<<<
—Lethe (22:53:13/4-3-51)

>>>>>(How about "Can they color-coordinate their clothes?")<<<<<
—Nighthawk (00:54:13/4-4-51)

GAME INFORMATION

	B	Q	S	C	I	W	E	R	Attacks
Bandersnatch	8	3 x 4	7	—	2/4	4	(6)	4	8S2, +1 Reach

Powers: Adaptive Coloration, Mimicry

BANDERSNATCH
Pesvastus dissimulatus

HABITAT
Forested areas

RANGE
Northern regions of North America

RANGE

SIZE COMPARISON

BANDIT
Procyon latri

IDENTIFICATION

The bandit is a larger version of the raccoon (*Procyon lotor*), growing up to 1.0 meter in length, with disproportionately longer front legs. The Awakening process has given the bandit opposable thumbs and considerably better control of its manipulative digits than its progenitor enjoys. Its coloration is identical to that of the *lotor* strain.

Claims abound that the creature's eyes show some "spark of intelligence" and that it is a language-user. All such claims are specious, based purely on imagination, wishful thinking, or out-and-out fabrication.

MAGIC CAPABILITY

Parabiological.

HABITS

The bandit, as its name implies, is an accomplished thief of food and shiny objects, the latter of which it hoards in its den. In the wild, it subsists on water birds and small mammals (which it catches by lying in wait for the creatures to blunder within reach of its "hands") and on berries and roots. It has no apparent fear of mankind, and like its progenitor species, sometimes dwells in parklands within cities. The bandit is notorious for rummaging through garbage bins in search of food.

The bandit has excellent motor control of its hands and is expert at manipulating objects. There are reports, partially substantiated, that the bandit is adept at using improvised tools. This tool-use does not extend beyond such behavior as using a discarded piece of metal to pry the lid off a garbage can, however. Recurring, unsubstantiated reports assert that this creature has "an innate understanding of locking mechanisms."

Bandits usually remain in and around small bodies of water. They are excellent swimmers, and appreciate that a pond can act as a "larder" by attracting ducks and the like. Like raccoons, bandits sometimes wash their food before eating it.

Bandits prefer flight to combat. If forced into confrontation, however, or when protecting their offspring, they fight with astounding ferocity. Instances are on record of a single bandit killing a Doberman guard dog. Such ability most often occurs through guile, however, such as luring the dog into a pond or lake and then drowning it.

Bandits often travel in family bands.

COMMENTARY

Bandits display animal cunning and limited tool use, but there is no evidence that they are intelligent. Use of simple tools is common in nature and is no indication of even the glimmerings of sentience.

POWERS

Enhanced Senses (Improved Hearing and Smell, Low-Light Vision).

WEAKNESSES

None.

>>>>>(Here's another unsubstantiated rumor for you. Terrance tells me he left a "borrowed" C-N Jackrabbit parked and locked by Lake Union. When he got back, he claims the thing was unlocked and there was a slotting bandit sitting in the front seat. Says the animal was trying to work the tape deck, but that's just Terry.)<<<<<
—Iris (20:48:16/4-20-51)

>>>>>(Interesting. And why can't Terrance substantiate the story?)<<<<<
—Wing (03:52:39/4-21-51)

>>>>>(Couple of days after he told me, he got geeked by the guy who "lent" him the Jackrabbit. R.I.P., Terry.)<<<<<
—Iris (12:01:09/4-21-51)

>>>>>(Don't get me wrong, I'm no animal rights activist, but I've been thinking about opposable thumbs and intelligence. A pack of raccoons used to visit me every day, and they'd trash my garbage if I didn't feed them. Those buggers were smart. Now, I've often thought that real manipulative digits were a prerequisite for intelligence. Raccoons don't really have them, and so might be...I dunno, kind of held back. Bandits, now...they do have them.)<<<<<
—Trent (13:31:44/4-30-51)

>>>>>(If you're trying to tell me that we've got to class those ring-tailed rats as sentient just because they've got thumbs...)<<<<<
—Scuz (17:32:33/4-30-51)

>>>>>(Easy, chummer. Just a thought, O.K.?)<<<<<
—Trent (18:03:52/4-30-51)

GAME INFORMATION

	B	Q	S	C	I	W	E	R	Attacks
Bandit	2	4 x 3	2	4	3/5	2	6	5	3L1

Powers: Enhanced Senses (Improved Hearing and Smell, Low-Light Vision)

Note: Bandits do have an innate understanding of locking mechanisms. Using simple tools such as a discarded nail or bit of wire, they can often pick simple mechanical locks. Treat this ability as a skill with a 2 rating. Suggested Target Numbers for different types of lock are listed below. The gamemaster should, of course, modify Target Numbers to suit the situation.

Type of Lock	Target Number*
Hook (as on a chicken coop)	3
Window Latch	4
Simple Door Lock	6
Complex Door Lock (Deadbolt)	9
Car Door Lock	9
Combination Lock	Forget it

BANDIT
Procyon latri

HABITAT
Forests, parkland, and some urban areas

RANGE
Central to northern regions of North America

RANGE

SIZE COMPARISON

BEHEMOTH
Alligator gigas

NELSON

IDENTIFICATION

Looking distinctively like a hippopotamus, the behemoth was, for a time, believed to have sprung from escaped zoo stock. However, recent gene mapping has revealed that the behemoth is a paraspecies of the common alligator (*Alligator mississipiensis*). The behemoth stands 3 meters high at the shoulder and is 4.9 meters long. Its rough, leathery skin is thicker than that of species *mississipiensis*, and the epidermis is built up along the creature's spine to form overlapping plates.

Like the alligator, the behemoth is a carnivore, with teeth appropriate to its diet. In addition, the behemoth has developed two upward-pointing tusks, similar to those of the wild boar, long enough to protrude between the lips even when the creature's mouth is shut. The behemoth's feet are much larger than an alligator's, presumably providing additional traction when it pursues its prey.

MAGIC CAPABILITY

None.

HABITS

A territorial animal, the behemoth exhibits aggressive hunting behavior. Its preferred method is to remain motionless just below the water's surface, with only nostrils and eyes protruding, where it waits for unsuspecting creatures to pass. The behemoth will, however, sometimes actively pursue its prey, which includes water birds, amphibians, and reptiles (*A. mississipiensis* is a favorite food). Behemoths will also attack almost anything up to human-size and larger that swims by.

COMMENTARY

A population of behemoths has been confirmed in the Florida Everglades and nearby bodies of fresh water. There are also persistent claims that the Louisiana bayous are also home to behemoths.

POWERS

None.

WEAKNESSES

None.

>>>>>(No weaknesses? Don't think I like that.)<<<<<
  —Dog (13:08:41/5-13-51)

>>>>>(They got the same weakness every animal do: they don't like high-velocity, steel-jacketed lead.)<<<<<
  —Silver (17:17:18/5-13-51)

>>>>>(Guess it's some kind of allergy, huh?)<<<<<
  —Bung (00:10:52/5-14-51)

>>>>>(Funny man. By the way, the guide sucks wind. These things are definitely in the bayous. And they sure as hell will attack small boats.)<<<<<
  —Nighthawk (01:12:19/5-14-51)

>>>>>(O.K., Nighthawk. Let's hear the story.)<<<<<
  —Dog (11:22:25/5-14-51)

>>>>>(Not much of a story. It almost cost me my Aztech Nightrunner, though. I saw what looked like a log, nor did it show as anything special on the thermo. (It was a stealth night job, so I had all the gear up.) Then this sucker surges out of the water and rams me, almost staves in the hull. Then it tries to snatch me out of the cockpit. Silver's right. They don't like high-vee rounds. When he backed off, I put a grenade over the side. I figured the blast underwater would hurt him worse than an airburst, and I wouldn't have to dodge shrapnel.)<<<<<
  —Nighthawk (23:13:02/5-14-51)

>>>>>(And?)<<<<<
  —Dog (23:27:30/5-14-51)

>>>>>(Didn't kill him, but he hollered and backed way off. Of course, this little interlude brought all kinds of heat down on me. Sec-guards in a patrol boat and a couple on those jet-ski waterbike things picked up on the ruckus, so I had to light out of there real fast. The behemoth was still around and madder than all hell. My partner was watching with night goggles, and saw the behemoth pluck one of the sec-guards off his jet-ski, just as neat as you'd like. We didn't wait around to see the final outcome, though.)<<<<<
  —Nighthawk (23:33:49/5-14-51)

>>>>>(The smart money's on the sec-guards.)<<<<<
  —Dog (00:55:47/5-15-51)

>>>>>(Yeah, but I'd still like to see the scorecard. That behemoth was big and mean.)<<<<<
  —Nighthawk (00:59:08/5-15-51)

GAME INFORMATION

	B	Q	S	C	I	W	E	R	Attacks
Behemoth	10/2	4 x 3	25	—	2/2	5	6	3	7D2

BEHEMOTH
  Alligator gigas

HABITAT
  Subtropical swamps and waterways

RANGE
  Southern regions of North America

RANGE

SIZE COMPARISON

BIRDMAN
Eptesicus avehomo

IDENTIFICATION

The so-called "birdman" is related to neither bird nor man. As its taxonomic name indicates, its relation is to the common big brown bat (*Eptesicus fuscus*). Its other common name, the manbat, is more descriptive, though still not fully accurate.

The birdman is a large bat whose body is up to 0.6 meter long, with a wingspan of up to 2.0 meters. *E. avehomo* has short, soft body fur, velvety to the touch. Its head resembles that of a fox, with a pointed snout and small, pricked ears. Its color ranges from dark brown to light tan to an almost tawny red. The long claws at its wingtips are used to cling to tree branches rather than as weapons.

From a distance, the birdman vaguely resembles a winged man or harpy. Though a harmless creature, its menacing appearance often frightens the uninformed into attacking it.

MAGIC CAPABILITY

Parabiological.

HABITS

Like its progenitor, the birdman, or manbat, feeds on fruit. It is not by nature, inclination, or metabolism a carnivore.

Forming flocks for mutual protection, birdmen travel in groups of up to 20 members. If one birdman is attacked, the others will swoop down, beating at the attacker with their wings in an attempt to drive it away. Such behavior will not daunt a determined attacker, of course, and often brings the entire flock within range of a predator.

Individually, birdmen are curious. They seem particularly fascinated by the actions of both humans and metahumans, and often circle overhead to watch. (This behavior is often misinterpreted.)

If cornered or wounded, a birdman will deliver a painful bite that can cause a dangerous infection.

A birdman flock can sometimes be driven away by loud noises.

Like other bats, the creature is nocturnal or crepuscular, avoiding brightly lit areas.

COMMENTARY

Like most other bats, *E. avehomo* uses echo-location to make up for less than acute vision. Perhaps because of its size, the creature's sonar "squeals" are physically painful to many other creatures (particularly dogs, which may be driven into a frenzy). *E. avehomo*'s echo-location is almost unfailingly accurate.

As with many paraspecies, the creature's generic name is the result of some whimsy by an early paranaturialist.

POWERS

Enhanced Senses (Improved Hearing, Sonar), Sonic Projection.

WEAKNESSES

Allergy (Sunlight, Mild), Reduced Senses (Vision).

>>>>>(There's a place I gotta get into that actually uses manbats as watch animals. Seems their sonar makes them better guard creatures than dogs. Their sonar is so precise that it can pick up texture, and it's particularly attuned to movement. I've got to get past these bleeders. Anybody got ideas on how to defeat the sonar?)<<<<<
—Tanis (15:18:11/2-27-51)

>>>>>(Yeah, sure. It's obvious. White noise generator. That'll slot them up but good. They'll be blind as...well, bats. No guarantees, but it might also protect you against their cries. (If the pain effect is purely sonic and not some kind of magic drek. If it's magic, all bets are off.))<<<<<
—Straight Gain (17:21:49/2-27-51)

>>>>>(Tanis, if I'm right about where you want to go, you're welcome to it. Whatever the pay, it probably ain't enough. Watch out for those bats. The hooks on their wingtips are sharp as knives, and the buggers know how to use them. Given a chance, they'll slit you up for dessert. Noise does drive them off—loud noise—but if you're on a run, that probably ain't an option. Good luck.)<<<<<
—Falcon (10:27:04/2-28-51))

>>>>>(Sounds like you know from experience. If it's O.K. to tell me, where'd you meet up with these things? And have you got anything else I need to know?)<<<<<
—Tanis (10:30:21/2-28-51)

>>>>>(To the first question, get on what used to be I-5 and head south a ways. That's all I can tell you. Second question. They sometimes come in flocks bigger than 20, and they don't always eat fruit. I saw a manbat geek an owl and gobble it without missing a wingbeat. They're fast, and if you make 'em mad, the whole flock will make you hate life. Take lots of antidote patches.)<<<<<
—Falcon (10:42:48/2-28-51)

>>>>>(Thanks, Falcon. I'll let you know in about a week how the run went. See ya around.)<<<<<
—Tanis (10:55:56/2-28-51)

>>>>>(Tanis?)<<<<<
—Falcon (8:40:36/3-8-51)

>>>>>(Tanis?)<<<<<
—Falcon (11:51:27/3-13-51)

GAME INFORMATION

	B	Q	S	C	I	W	E	R	Attacks
Birdman	2	5 x 4	1	—	1/5	3	6	5	3L1

Powers: Enhanced Senses (Improved Hearing, Sonar), Sonic Projection

Weaknesses: Allergy (Sunlight, Mild), Reduced Senses (Vision)

Note: Manbats frequently carry a plasmodial infection similar to malaria. Each time a character is bitten by a manbat, roll 2D6. On a result of 11 or 12, the character has been infected. The disease does Damage 4L3 and a speed of 24 hours. Its symptoms are cramps, blurred vision, and profuse sweating.

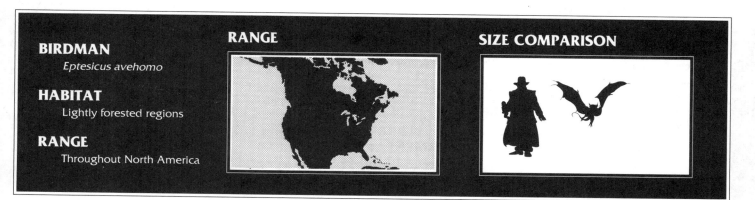

BIRDMAN
  Eptesicus avehomo

HABITAT
  Lightly forested regions

RANGE
  Throughout North America

RANGE

SIZE COMPARISON

BLACK ANNIS
Papio annisae

IDENTIFICATION

The black annis is a humanoid standing 1.7 meters, but its posture is hunched, almost twisted. Though basically bipedal, sometimes it does travel on all fours. From a distance the creature resembles an aged, yet powerful, hag. Up close, however, its human resemblance diminishes. The eyes are too large, the facial structure more akin to that of the great apes, and it has no truly opposable thumb. Hair grows from the creature's head most of the way down the spine, with thick tufts across the tops of the shoulders and hands.

The annis is broad-shouldered and has disproportionately long arms. Though showing little overt muscle development, it is exceptionally strong. Its canine teeth are hypertrophied (to efficiently kill its prey), and its digits are tipped with sharp, hard claws.

MAGIC CAPABILITY

Innate.

HABITS

The black annis is exclusively carnivorous, using its speed and strength to catch and kill its prey. It will eat any living creature it can overpower, from squirrels and owls to deer and even bear cubs. The annis is believed to be cannibalistic toward others of its species that invade its territory.

The highly territorial black annis is a solitary hunter. Its threat display consists of howling and throwing rocks, but it uses the behavior only to establish dominance over another annis, and then only rarely. Other creatures are either avoided or attacked on sight. In response to territorial infringement by another annis, the creature's response depends entirely on the apparent strength of the intruder. If it seems weak, the resident annis will attack immediately; if the intruder seems stronger, the territory-holder will avoid it. Only if the two creatures appear well-matched will the first annis attempt the threat display to drive off the intruder.

The only time more than one annis occupies the same territory is for mating. Having impregnated the female, how-ever, the male usually runs her out of the territory. An annis is an aggressive hunter from birth, and can usually subsist inde-pendently within a week or less of par-turition, when the mother abandons it.

The black annis prefers to live in rocky caves or to dig out a lair among the roots of large trees. It is nocturnal, with exceptional night vision. (The annis suffers no loss of vision in full sunlight, however.)

The black annis seems to prefer the dreariest areas of forest (or perhaps it is the presence of the creatures that blights the area).

COMMENTARY

Though no consensus exists on the origin of the black annis, most taxonomists believe it to be an Awakened form of the mandrill (*Papio sphinx*), which is why the creature was assigned to the *Papio* genus.

POWERS

Enhanced Physical Attributes (Strength, once per day, for (Essence)D6 turns), Enhanced Reactions, Enhanced Senses (Low-Light Vision), Influence (Depression).

WEAKNESSES

Allergy (Sunlight, Mild).

>>>>>(The guide goes for drek once again. These things use that "threat display" at the drop of a bleeding hat...but at what? At a fragging Banshee panzer, that's what. Started howling and chucking rocks. I was up top, and I saw it. We could have filled it so full of 30 millimeter that the damn thing would have sunk like a rock.)<<<<<
— Kaz (18:28:50/1-30-51)

>>>>>(Why didn't you?)<<<<<
— Larry (19:09:35/1-30-51)

>>>>>(Dunno. Just didn't get around to it, you know? Nobody was feeling too good...Frag it. Dunno.)<<<<<
— Kaz (19:09:35/1-30-51)

>>>>>(Yeah? Weird. I saw one of those things once around Deception Pass (guess they come pretty far north sometimes). I was on a run, tracking—it doesn't matter what I was tracking. Anyway, suddenly I just started feeling like hell. The forest looked ugly, and I felt like my whole life had turned to drek. Then I saw this thing watching me. Looked like a nasty-tempered old hag, kind of like a grandmother from hell. I felt so bleeding bad that I geeked it on the spot. Geeked it real good, capped off a whole bin of ammo. Turned the tree it was squatting in into toothpicks. And you know what? When the smoke cleared, the forest didn't look so bad after all, and I liked life again. Weird.)<<<<<
— Sal (22:44:45/2-5-51)

>>>>>(Kaz, my friend, don't underestimate this creature because it was bold or foolish enough to challenge a panzer. The black annis is easily strong enough to turn over a car. And once it has the vehicle immobilized, it can tear it open at leisure.)<<<<<
— Tinuviel (22:44:45/2-7-51)

GAME INFORMATION

	B	Q	S	C	I	W	E	R	Attacks
Black Annis	9	4 x 5	10	—	2/3	4	(5)	4	8S2

Powers: Enhanced Physical Attributes (Strength once per day, for (Essence) D6 turns), Enhanced Reactions, Enhanced Senses (Low-Light Vision), Influence (Depression)

Weaknesses: Allergy (Sunlight, Mild)

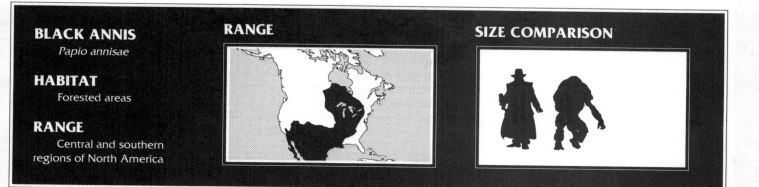

BLACK ANNIS
Papio annisae

HABITAT
Forested areas

RANGE
Central and southern regions of North America

RANGE

SIZE COMPARISON

BLOOD KITE

Buteo celeris

IDENTIFICATION

The blood kite is a small member of the *Buteo*, or hawk genus, with a wingspan of 0.75 meter and a body length of 0.2 meter. Its plumage is rich brown, with red patches on the wings. Said to resemble spilled blood, these patches give the creature its name. The blood kite has the sharp, hooked beak and powerful talons typical of its hawk relatives.

MAGIC CAPABILITY

Parabiological.

HABITS

The blood kite feeds on mice, young rabbits, and other small, ground-dwelling mammals. To hunt, it cruises at an altitude of 90 to 100 meters, waiting to spot movement on the ground, and then swoops down on its prey. Like some other hawk species, a blood kite may impale its dead prey on a large thorn or a barbed-wire fence prong while it feeds.

Blood kites often congregate in flocks of up to 30 birds. Each flock "claims" a territory of up to 20 square kilometers, defending it against other birds of prey, including blood kites from other flocks. Blood kites mate in early spring, and the females incubate the eggs until early summer. During this period, the males will attack and attempt to drive off literally anything that moves in the vicinity of the brooding females.

The males always aim for the eyes, a particularly successful tactic against even the largest animal. A male blood kite will sacrifice its own life to defend its brooding mate.

COMMENTARY

The name "blood kite" may also derive from the bird's aggressiveness and viciousness during the mating and brooding seasons.

The Awakening has had little effect on these hawks, other than to make them more aggressive in combat.

Perhaps even more than other hawks, the blood kite's vision is keyed to movement. In response to a circling blood kite, mice and other prey typically freeze in immobility. If, however, the creature panics and bolts, the blood kite will almost certainly see it and stoop on it.

POWERS

Enhanced Senses (Improved Vision, Thermographic Vision).

WEAKNESSES

None.

>>>>>(These bloody-minded little beasts will attack anything. No drek.)<<<<<
—Suki (19:38:11/2-13-51)

>>>>>(And that's their downfall. Want to know the best weapon against blood kites? A bow. Fire an arrow anywhere near a swooping blood kite, and the thing will swerve to attack the arrow, getting the shaft right down the gullet. You can usually retrieve the arrow.<<<<<
—Doc (23:33:01/2-13-51)

>>>>>(Too bad I didn't know that last spring. Me, Zinc, and the crew were in the Cascades when we walked right into a fragging nesting area. Dozens of the little bleeders, all faster than hell and hard to hit, even with a smartgun. Lucky Zinc had an autofire shotgun, which took 'em down real nice. But before we got outta there, I lost my left eye. It was new, too. Just come from Chiba, with all the toys. Fragging birds.)<<<<<
—Shiner (17:51:07/2-16-51)

>>>>>(You could try bright lights, too. Flash grenades, maybe. Look at a hawk's head: it's nearly all eyes, and the pupils open wide for low-light vision. Throwing a bright light at a kite just might overload its tiny little brain. Don't quote me, though.<<<<<
—Doc (17:51:07/2-18-51)

GAME INFORMATION

	B	Q	S	C	I	W	E	R	Attacks
Blood Kite	1	5 x 5	1	—	1/4	2	6	5	2L1

Powers: Enhanced Senses (Improved Vision, Thermographic Vision).

Note: Each time a character takes damage from a blood kite attack, roll 2D6. On a result of 12, the character has taken damage to an eye. The character can make a Body Success Test (dermal armor does not help this roll). The Target Number is 6 for an organic eye, 4 for a cybereye. If no successes are rolled, the character has lost one eye. Goggles or helmets with face shields eliminate the risk of eye loss. Neither prescription glasses nor sunglasses have any effect.

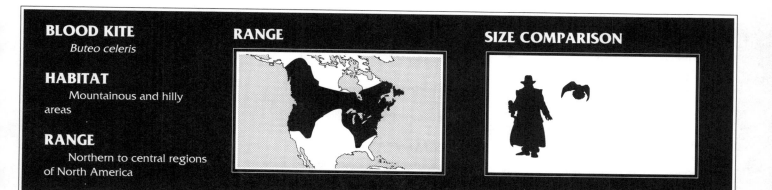

BLOOD KITE
Buteo celeris

HABITAT
Mountainous and hilly areas

RANGE
Northern to central regions of North America

RANGE

SIZE COMPARISON

BOGIE
Canis auspicii

IDENTIFICATION

The bogie is a large canine, standing up to 1.25 meters at the shoulder. It resembles an oversized rottweiler, with one significant difference: the bogie has a pair of small, horn-like protrusions growing from its brow. These "horns" are 1.0 to 2.0 centimeters long and covered with a velvety coating. Due to their extreme sensitivity, the horns do not function as weapons; the beast's powerful jaws suffice for that. One theory is that the bogie's "horns" are a form of sensory equipment. (That would certainly help explain the creature's superb sensory acuity.)

The bogie has short, bristly fur; all specimens on record are unrelieved black in color.

The bogie is faster than might be expected, considering its great size. It is an aggressive hunter.

The howl of a bogie is reputedly among the most mournful sounds in nature. One cataloger with a touch too much imagination has written that "the bogie's howl reminds us of our own mortality, producing a profound unease in the auditor."

MAGIC CAPABILITY

Innate.

HABITS

As evident from its teeth, the bogie is a carnivore. The creature hunts in packs and is ferocious. Naturalists have recorded that other creatures beside humans react negatively to the bogie's howl and that hunting bogies use this to their advantage. On record are instances of a bogie pack using howls to panic its prey, then herding them into ambush by the rest of the pack.

An individual bogie usually backs down from confrontation with any large creature (i.e., human-size or greater) that does not flee from the creature's threat displays or that responds with its own threat display. (The bogie rarely bolts, however, preferring a controlled retreat while keeping its "enemy" in view.) Packs of bogies, on the other hand, are apparently fearless.

COMMENTARY

Like the hellhound (also known as the "Baskerville hound," after a 19th-century story by Arthur Conan Doyle), the bogie's piercing howls are said to prophesy disaster and death. Though such ideas seem more suited to myth than science, some statistical evidence exists of the incidence of unforeseen and apparently acausal events, or "accidents," occurring in direct proportion to the proximity of bogies.

Bogies are closely related to dogs, who sense this kinship. Normal canines, even trained guard dogs, will not bark to announce the approach of a bogie, and the two types of creature will never fight one another.

POWERS

Accident, Enhanced Movement, Enhanced Reactions, Enhanced Senses (Improved Hearing and Smell, Low-Light Vision, Motion Detection), Fear.

WEAKNESSES

Allergy (Aconite or Horseradish, Severe).

>>>>>(Sound off. Anyone out there ever heard one of these things howl?)<<<<<
   —Casper (15:34:48/2-28-51)

>>>>>(Yeah, I have. Slotting scariest thing, too, boyo. I heard it, ran, and didn't stop until I was back in my Yellowjacket, buttoned up and out of there. I didn't feel better until the rotor noise drowned out the sound, but I fed the bleeder a couple of HE rounds, anyway. That stopped it howling, for damn sure.)<<<<<
   —Bladerunner (16:35:32/2-28-51)

>>>>>(What's this aconite stuff?)<<<<<
   —Shadowspawn (17:39:35/3-2-51)

>>>>>(Wolfsbane)<<<<<
   —Dyson (12:17:51/3-3-51)

>>>>>(Are you saying these things are fraggin' werewolves?)<<<<<
   —Casper (12:20:04/3-3-51)

>>>>>(No, no, no. Aconite, or wolfsbane, is a lethal natural toxin. It comes from a root closely related to horseradish. (Back when people grew food in their own gardens, a few folks geeked themselves every year because they couldn't tell aconite from horseradish.) These bogies show a powerful reaction to the toxin and to related alkaloids found in horseradish. Got it, chummer?)<<<<<
   —Dyson (12:21:12/3-3-51)

>>>>>(Hey, Dyson, you don't know drek. These things are is shapeshifters. I saw one geek an elf, then take her shape.)<<<<<
   —Yobo (13:33:14/3-3-51)

>>>>>(Drek! Pure slotting drek.)<<<<<
   —Casper (13:35:54/3-3-51)

>>>>>(Up yours, Cap.)<<<<<
   —Yobo (13:36:40/3-3-51)

>>>>>(Up whose...?)<<<<<
   —Casper (13:37:35/3-3-51)

>>>>>(Look, sorry, Cap, I didn't mean nothing by it, O.K.? Really. But I did see it shapeshift...)<<<<<
   —Yobo (13:38:01/3-3-51)

GAME INFORMATION

	B	Q	S	C	I	W	E	R	Attacks
Bogie	3	5 x 4	4	—	2/4	3	(6)	4	4M2

Powers: Accident, Enhanced Movement, Enhanced Reactions, Enhanced Senses (Improved Hearing and Smell, Low-Light Vision, Motion Detection), Fear

Weaknesses: Allergy (Aconite or Horseradish, Severe)

BOGIE
   Canis auspicii

HABITAT
   Light woods and plains

RANGE
   Northeast and central regions of North America

RANGE

SIZE COMPARISON

BOMBARDIER
Glaucomys teli

IDENTIFICATION

The bombardier is a paraspecies derived from the flying squirrel (*Glaucomys volans*). Like its progenitor, the bombardier is able to take long, gliding leaps because of the wing-like folds of skin connecting the fore and hind legs. The bombardier is larger than *G. volans*, growing to a length of 0.6 meter. Its color is light tan, shading to white on the belly, with a darker brown, almost black, stripe along the spine.

MAGIC CAPABILITY

None.

HABITS

The bombardier resembles other squirrels in subsisting on a diet of nuts and berries. During the fall months, it gathers and hoards nuts for the winter. Bombardiers hibernate during the coldest months. Its hibernation state is apparently intermittent, for bombardiers are sometimes sighted even at the height of winter. These creatures are, presumably, spotted during short periods of activity that interrupt their hibernation).

Bombardiers usually nest in the hollow trunks of dead trees, or they may construct nests from twigs in the higher branches of living trees. At the time of hibernation, most dig burrows among the roots of "their" tree, where they remain in a dormant state.

Bombardiers are not highly territorial, except during the birthing season and for a month or so thereafter. At these times, a male bombardier tries to protect its tree home by emitting chattering cries as it swoops down on any unwelcome visitors. Another common behavior is to carry nuts or other small objects in their mouths, which they drop at the bottom of their swoop. These "dive-bombing" attacks are usually very accurate, earning the bombardier its name.

Bombardiers prefer flight to combat, but a cornered individual can deliver a nasty bite. Bombardier bites are usually clean, with no reported cases of diseases transmitted by the creature.

COMMENTARY

Though they may appear to fly, bombardiers can only glide, launching themselves from trees and other high elevation points. Bombardiers cannot glide as well as smaller flying squirrels, however, due to their greater mass. In fact, the horizontal range of a glide is limited to twice its vertical drop. (Thus, a bombardier traveling from a 50-meter tree can glide a total of 100 meters.) During this glide, the creature is highly maneuverable. Apart from short and very limited "pull-ups," however, bombardiers cannot gain altitude during a glide.

POWERS

None.

WEAKNESSES

None.

>>>>>(I've seen these little beasties, and their glide ratio is much more than two-to-one.)<<<<<
— Wingz (10:53:49/1-30-51)

>>>>>(And they drop more than nuts, too.)<<<<<
— Slag (13:56:07/2-2-51)

>>>>>(Like what?)<<<<<
— Peachy (18:39:46/2-3-51)

>>>>>(Let's just say they generate their own projectiles. And cleaning up after a direct hit is messy.)<<<<<
— Slag (18:39:46/2-3-51)

>>>>>(Does one of these things like to hang around with a moose, by any chance? Ha ha ha.)<<<<<
— Bladerunner (10:58:00/2-14-51)

>>>>>(I don't get it.)<<<<<
— Slag (23:59:52/2-15-51)

GAME INFORMATION

	B	Q	S	C	I	W	E	R	Attacks
Bombardier	1	4 x 4	1	—	2/3	2	6	4	2L1

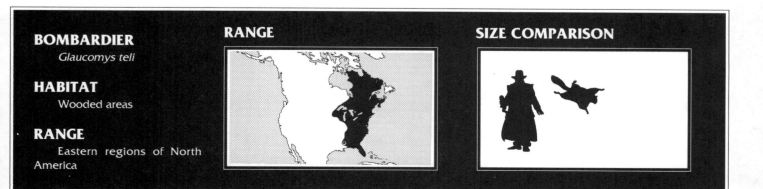

BOMBARDIER
Glaucomys teli

HABITAT
Wooded areas

RANGE
Eastern regions of North America

RANGE

SIZE COMPARISON

BOOBRIE
Grus carnivori

IDENTIFICATION

The boobrie is a large wading bird that resembles a crane and grows to a height of 1.85 meters, with a wingspan of up to 2.8 meters. Its plumage is usually black (though its hackle feathers may lighten to a dark gray), and its legs and beak are a bright red. The boobrie has a slightly hooked beak, and its webbed feet are clawed. Its distinctive cry is even more raucous than a peacock's.

MAGIC CAPABILITY

Parabiological.

HABITS

The boobrie is a fish-eater. It usually stands in the shallows, remaining completely motionless until a small fish swims near. Then, in an almost blindingly fast reaction, it seizes the fish with its beak. It uses one clawed foot to hold the fish while tearing into it with its beak. Though fish make up the major part of the boobrie's diet, the birds will also eat small mammals or birds foolish enough to wander within reach of its long neck. Some naturalists have recorded instances of boobries also eating carrion.

Boobries nest in flocks of up to 100 individuals. To feed, however, they usually spread out widely. Flocking behavior is a mutual-defense tactic. A boobrie under attack issues a cry that brings the rest of the flock to its defense. A bird the size of a boobrie is a dangerous opponent even for a creature the size of a small bear. Their wings are strong enough to snap a man's arm, and their beaks and claws are sharp.

COMMENTARY

Epidemiologists report that boobries are carriers of a viral infection similar to VITAS-3. This virus is dormant in the body of the boobrie, but rapidly expresses when it enters another host. Infection can be through open wounds (e.g., injuries inflicted by the boobrie) or through ingestion of boobrie meat.

The derivation of the name "boobrie" remains a mystery.

POWERS

Pestilence.

WEAKNESSES

None.

>>>>>(I know the derivation of "boobrie". It's the name of a bird of ill-omen from Scottish legend. Some kind of sending from the devil, I think.)<<<<<
—Bard (11:46:21/1-23-51)

>>>>>(Some experts I know think the VITAS-3 is a modified version of a retrovirus (which means its genetic material is RNA, not DNA, like in most viruses). There's no known mechanism for preventing the expression of this kind of retrovirus. How come the boobries don't get the disease? What is it in their metabolism that keeps the retrovirus dormant? It's something I think we should be trying to find out.)<<<<<
—Doc (12:54:08/1-30-51)

>>>>>(Why's it important?)<<<<<
—Lyle (13:15:02/1-30-51)

>>>>>(The VITAS-3 type of retrovirus is very susceptible to mutation. I figure it's only a matter of time before it evolves into something else. Maybe we'll end up with another VITAS-style epidemic that doesn't respond to our current treatments. If there's something in the boobrie that turns the virus dormant, I'd like to know about it. Just in case.)<<<<<
—Doc (13:27:21/1-30-51)

>>>>>(VITAS-4? Oh, just fragging peachy.)<<<<<
—Lyle (13:35:57/1-30-51)

>>>>>(Whatever it is the boobries have, I don't think it's predictable. I heard from Sylvie that whole populations of boobries suddenly just up and die. Sounds like the disease sometimes flares up and kills them all off. Great Ghu help you if you're around when that happens.)<<<<<
—Dav (20:01:46/1-30-51)

GAME INFORMATION

	B	Q	S	C	I	W	E	R	Attacks
Boobrie	2	3 x 5	2	—	2/3	2	6	4	4L2, +1 Reach

Powers: Pestilence

Note: Swimming multiplier is 3.

BOOBRIE
Grus carnivori

HABITAT
Shoreline, estuarine, and lakeshore habitats

RANGE
Western coastal regions; Gulf Coast; Florida peninsula

RANGE

SIZE COMPARISON

CENTURY FERRET
Mustela millenniae

IDENTIFICATION

The century ferret grows to a length of from 0.9 to 2 meters, with tail. It resembles a yellow-brown mink with dark brown feet, tail, and mask. Its eyes are red, like those of the domesticated ferret, but it is not albinistic. It has the speed and flexibility of all members of genus *Mustelidae*.

MAGIC CAPABILITY

Innate.

HABITS

The century ferret is carnivorous, living on rodents and other small mammals. It rarely digs its own burrow, preferring to take over the burrow of its prey. As with all ferrets, it is agile, fast, and aggressive. When challenged or attacked, it seems utterly fearless, fighting with a ferocity that belies its relatively small size.

The century ferret does not hibernate, apparently being active year-round. During the winter, it feeds by detecting the burrows of hibernating creatures and capturing and killing them as they sleep.

Century ferrets are solitary hunters. They are by preference diurnal, though they may be active at night as well.

COMMENTARY

The century ferret received its name because the first recorded specimen was captured on January 1, 2000. At the time, it was believed that the animal represented a new species of ferret. Naturalists all over the globe spent years trying to explain how such a large mammal had escaped discovery for so long. Now it is known that the century ferret is undoubtedly an Awakened creature, though the date of its appearance predates the widespread Awakening of other species.

POWERS

Enhanced Physical Attributes (Quickness, once per day, for (Essence)D6 turns), Enhanced Senses (Improved Hearing and Smell, Low-Light Vision, Thermographic Vision), Mana Detection.

WEAKNESSES

Allergy (Mana, Mild).

>>>>>(Spike baby.)<<<<<
—Doc (13:19:52/2-4-51)

>>>>>(What?)<<<<<
—Ellis (14:43:12/2-4-51)

>>>>>(Premature Awakening. UGE in humans was a statistical phenomenon, I think. Like a jagged bell curve, with the peak centered around 2011. The century ferret's Awakening curve peaked earlier. Possibly its genetic complex is more mana-sensitive. Probably extremely sensitive to magical energy, too.)<<<<<
—Doc (15:01:26/2-4-51)

>>>>>(It's fearless and ferocious. How ferocious?)<<<<<
—Leslie (1:24:00/2-10-51)

>>>>>(Fearless enough to attack me, and ferocious enough to rip me up a bit before I could kill it.)<<<<<
—Delsenora (11:26:06/2-10-51)

>>>>>(Just one?)<<<<<
—Leslie (11:27:30/2-10-51)

>>>>>(Just one. I guess I came too near its lair or something. It was bloody fast. I didn't even see it coming until its teeth were in my leg.)<<<<<
—Delsenora (11:27:30/2-10-51)

>>>>>(Isn't there anything out there that likes people?)<<<<<
—Leslie (11:28:55/2-10-51)

GAME INFORMATION

	B	Q	S	C	I	W	E	R	Attacks
Century Ferret	2	4 x 4	2	—	2/4	2	(6)	5	2M2

Powers: Enhanced Physical Attributes (Quickness, once per day, for (Essence)D6 turns), Enhanced Senses (Improved Hearing and Smell, Low-Light Vision, Thermographic Vision), Mana Detection

Weaknesses: Allergy (Mana, Mild)

CENTURY FERRET
Mustela millenniae

HABITAT
Deciduous forests and parkland

RANGE
Northern regions of North America

RANGE

SIZE COMPARISON

CHIMERA
Draco chimaera

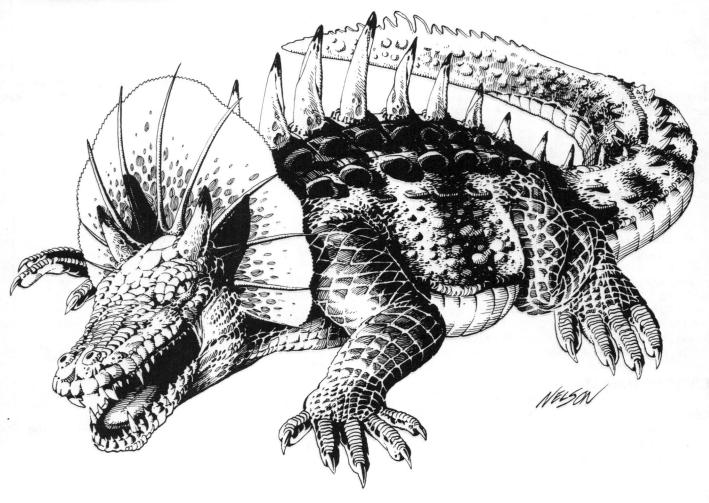

NELSON

IDENTIFICATION

Growing up to 3.7 meters long, the chimera is a powerful lizard, its appearance reminiscent of a wingless western dragon. It has a fine ruff of skin around its neck, a short, broad snout, and two short but sharp horns on its brow. It is lithe, fast, and strong. Its color varies widely, from dark gray, to brown, to a light yellow-brown or tan. The belly is usually white. Some reports indicate that the creature can change to the color of its background, like a chameleon.

The chimera has large, regular teeth and sharply curved claws.

MAGIC CAPABILITY

Innate.

HABITS

Chimera are carnivorous, eating anything they can catch. Their regular diet includes kangaroo rats and other desert-dwelling small mammals and snakes. (The venom of even the most lethal snake seems not to effect chimera.)

The chimera is a solitary hunter and highly territorial. During mating season (late spring), males fight one another for access to available females. Having impregnated the females, however, the males drive them off.

Females lay their eggs, cover them with dirt or sometimes with cairns of small stones, and then ignore them. The eggs have a distinctive odor, making it easy for predators to locate the nests.

The chimera's elaborate threat display consists of raising the neck ruff, hissing, and making mock charges. This display is used against creatures larger than 1.5 meters long. If the other creature flees from the threat display, the chimera usually pursues and attempts to kill it. If the other creature stands firm, however, the chimera most often tries to avoid it.

Even compared to other reptiles, the chimera's intelligence is limited.

The bite of the chimera is venomous.

COMMENTARY

The mythical chimera was a composite creature, with the heads of a lion and a goat and the hindquarters of a dragon. It may be assumed that the horned head of *D. chimaera* reminded an earlier cataloger of a goat, while the neck ruff resembled the mane of a lion, hence the name.

The kinship between chimera and dragons is obvious from the creature's appearance, though the Great Dragon Dunkelzahn categorically denies this kinship.

POWERS

Concealment (Self Only), Immunity to Poisons, Venom.

WEAKNESSES

Vulnerability (Iron).

>>>>>(These babies are neither dragons nor dracoforms. I proved that to the satisfaction of myself and many well-regarded parataxonomists in 2046, but Paterson continues to cling to his outmoded ideas. Gene typing and various bio-assays prove that the chimera is an Awakened iguana. Its progenitor species is Iguana iguana, and so I propose the classification of Iguana sagani.)<<<<<
    —Sagan (13:56:21/2-27-51)

>>>>>(I don't know, Sagan. They look like dragons, and they get big like dragons. I saw one that must have been almost five meters long.)<<<<<
    —Halliday (23:01:53/2-28-51)

>>>>>(They breathe fire, too.)<<<<<
    —Yobo (14:03:28/3-1-51)

>>>>>(Drek!)<<<<<
    —Casper (17:10:10/3-1-51)

>>>>>(Just who is this breeder Yobo anyway?)<<<<<
    —Jodi(17:25:08/3-1-51)

>>>>>(Let's keep the personality conflicts offline. I wish to know more about this threat behavior, if anyone can tell me.)<<<<<
    —Lethe (18:14:36/3-1-51)

>>>>>(Yeah, sure. I've seen it. I was taking my bike through the Pueblo Council land on my way to Denver when I saw a chimera on the road ahead (that's the five-meter bugger I mentioned earlier). Didn't look one bit friendly. Hissing like a leaky boiler, and the mane around its neck standing straight up, making it look even bigger. It charged...Well, I thought it was charging, but it stopped a few meters off, just kinda watching and waiting. It was like a staring contests for awhile, but I guess it blinked first, 'cause finally it just sort of slouched away.)<<<<<
    —Halliday (09:06:46/3-2-51)

>>>>>(Why didn't you just geek it?)<<<<<
    —Trasher (12:12:04/3-2-51)

>>>>>(With a fragging Streetline Special? Yeah, right. And really make it mad. Besides, the PC goon patrols don't take kindly to Anglos shooting off weapons while on their lands.)<<<<<
    —Halliday (13:10:33/3-2-51)

>>>>>(Bet you had to clean your saddle afterward. Har-har-har.)<<<<<
    —Trasher (14:51:10/ 3-2-51)

GAME INFORMATION

	B	Q	S	C	I	W	E	R	Attacks
Chimera	5/1	3 x 3	4	—	1/3	4	(5)	2	4M2, −1 Reach

Powers: Concealment (Self Only), Immunity to Poisons, Venom
Weaknesses: Vulnerability (Iron)

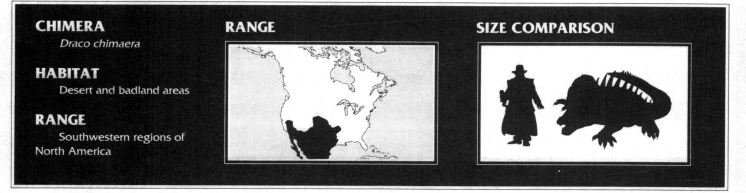

CHIMERA
    Draco chimaera

HABITAT
    Desert and badland areas

RANGE
    Southwestern regions of
North America

RANGE

SIZE COMPARISON

CORPSELIGHT
No accepted taxonomy.

IDENTIFICATION

There is no widespread consensus about whether this creature actually exists. Some so-called experts claim that reported sightings are instances of spontaneously igniting marsh or of some kind of magical activity. More reputable cataloguers acknowledge that the corpselight definitely exists. Even this latter group has reached no consensus on the creature's taxonomy, however.

The corpselight appears as a floating ball of light approximately 0.3 meter in diameter. The light is usually cold-white in color, sometimes tinged with blue, with an intensity on the order of 10 candles (i.e., 10 lumens of flux at 0.3 meter). It usually drifts slowly, though some reports indicate faster movement. It rarely achieves an altitude of more than 2.0 meters.

The corpselight seems to have no physical form. That is, no corpselight "corpse" has yet been brought in for study.

MAGIC CAPABILITY

Innate.

HABITS

With no physical form, the corpselight needs no food to maintain its metabolism. There are reports, however, of the creatures attacking travelers in desolate, marshy regions. The motive of these attacks is unknown. Other, unsubstantiated reports indicate that corpselights have killed travelers, but the manner of death is unknown.

Corpselights may be solitary, though clusters of up to six individuals have been reported in several instances.

They seem to appear only at night, and then only in desolate, deserted areas.

COMMENTARY

Of the many theories concerning the nature of the corpselight, the most cogent seems to be that it is predominantly an astral being that manifests as a ball of light in the physical world.

POWERS

Essence Drain, Immunity to Normal Weapons, Manifestation, Movement (Decrease in Swamps and Marshes), Psychokinesis, Regeneration.

WEAKNESSES

Essence Loss.

>>>>>(These things scare the fragging wits out of me. I met up with one in a mangrove swamp one night. I tried to run, but couldn't seem to move fast enough. Then this glowing puffball just drifted down and touched me on the back of the neck. What happened next was ecstasy, the best rush I've ever had (and that includes chipped and anatomical). The other runners chased it off and dragged me away, and I hated them for it. I was weak as a fragging kitten for days afterward, but I couldn't stop thinking about that ecstasy, and wanting more. I'm scared. I think if I saw one of those things again, I'd walk up to it and just let it do what it would with me.)<<<<<
    —Luka (14:50:24/1-14-51)

>>>>>(You should be scared of corpselights. They're among the most lethal creatures in existence. Yeah, they'll kill you, all the while you love every minute of it, and they're tough to kill themselves. I hear they're psychokinetic, too. Probably the best way to kill them is in astral space.)<<<<<
    —Celene (15:05:38/1-14-51)

>>>>>(They're tough bleeders there, too. But in astral their appearance isn't so innocuous: just looking at one puts you on guard. It looks like a big glowing octopus with 20 tentacles and a single eye the size of a dinner plate.)<<<<<
    —Darkcloud (03:10:00/1-15-51)

>>>>>(Some of them cast spells, too.)<<<<<
    —Trent (13:15:08/1-16-51)

>>>>>(Are you serious? Where do they come from? What are they?)<<<<<
    —Lukas (14:28:36/1-16-51)

>>>>>(Nobody knows. Least of all Paterson.)<<<<<
    —Celene (20:42:28/1-16-51)

>>>>>(What's all this drek about "10 lumens of flux at 0.3 meters"? How bright are the bleeders?)<<<<<
    —Spider (11:21:26/1-17-51)

>>>>>(No brighter than a burning torch.)<<<<<
    —Straight Gain (23:22:46/1-17-51)

GAME INFORMATION

	B	Q	S	C	I	W	E	R	Attacks
Corpselight	5	10	—	—	2	5	2D6/A	5	3M2, −1 Reach

Powers: Essence Drain, Immunity to Normal Weapons, Manifestation, Movement (Decrease in Swamps and Marshes), Psychokinesis, Regeneration

Weaknesses: Essence Loss

Note: When a corpselight is encountered, it has an initial Essence Rating of 2D6. Thus, its normal maximum Essence Rating is 12. (Note, however, that its Essence Drain Power can, theoretically, increase its Essence Rating to 24.)

CORPSELIGHT
   No accepted taxonomy.

HABITAT
   Swamps and marshy areas

RANGE
   Throughout the world

RANGE

SIZE COMPARISON

DEATHRATTLE
Crotalus nex

IDENTIFICATION

Growing up to 1.9 meters in length, this creature's appearance is indistinguishable from that of the normal (Awakened) diamondback rattlesnake *(Crotalus adamanteus)*. Its body is muscular and powerful, and its movement on land surprisingly rapid. It can also swim fairly swiftly, though it prefers land. The snake's two large fangs are hinged to fold out of the way when its mouth closes.

MAGIC CAPABILITY

None.

HABITS

The deathrattle feeds on small mammals and birds, who seem terrified into immobility at its approach. Its strike is almost too fast for the unaided eye to follow. It swallows its prey whole, unhinging its jaws in order to engulf creatures up to the size of a small rabbit.

The deathrattle's venom is more toxic than a normal rattlesnake's, with an onset time of only a few seconds. In addition to its bite, it can spit venom with great accuracy at ranges of up to 2.0 meters. The toxin is absorbed through the skin, and is as lethal as when injected by the fangs. An adult deathrattle has enough venom in its sacks for as many as five bites or spits.

Deathrattles hunt mainly at night, as their natural prey tends to be nocturnal. Sensory pits below the snake's eyes give it exceptional thermographic vision, making it an unerring hunter in complete darkness.

During the day, deathrattles often spend their time basking on rocks. Their apparent torpor is deceptive: the snake's reactions are as fast at these times as at any other.

The deathrattle's threat display consists of sounding the overlapping horny-plated rattle on its tail. Because the creature's coloration allows it to blend in well with its environment, the rattle-sound is often the first indication of its presence.

COMMENTARY

Deathrattle toxin is as lethal as Fugu-5 toxin, with the added side effect of agonizing pain.

Deathrattles are, of course, immune to their own toxin, but this immunity seems to extend to most other toxins as well.

POWERS

Enhanced Senses (Thermographic Vision), Immunity to Poisons, Venom.

WEAKNESSES

None.

>>>>>(These things extend north. No kidding. I almost got nailed by one near Vernon, in what used to be freaking British Columbia. It was just lying on a rock, and I didn't see it until it started rattling. I got it before it got me, though. Good shot. Blew it clean in half. But both halves kept thrashing around, and I'm pretty sure the head end was still trying to bite me.)<<<<<
—Tandi (16:39:5/1-1-51)

>>>>>(Here's something for any trivia buffs out there. You know the word "nex" in its scientific classification? It's Latin, and it means "violent death". Nice, huh?)<<<<<
—Clifton (09:42:33/4-18-51)

>>>>>(That answers a little question I've had for a while. I met up with this elf hit-man, called himself Nex, a real charmer. I didn't know where he got the name. Plus, this guy's favorite technique was a special poison that nobody else seemed to know about. Now I think I know where he got it from.)<<<<<
—Mr. A (13:44:50/4-21-51)

>>>>>(Correct. It seems unfortunate that my secret is now out. Perhaps I should be angry about that.)<<<<<
—Nex (01:34:48/4-23-51)

>>>>>(Well? Mr. A? You still out there?)<<<<<
—Clifton (17:48:51/5-10-51)

>>>>>(Guess not.)<<<<<
—Clifton (19:34:19/6-01-51)

GAME INFORMATION

	B	Q	S	C	I	W	E	R	Attacks
Deathrattle	3	3 x 4	3	—	1/5	2	6	5	4L1, +1 Reach

Powers: Enhanced Senses (Thermographic Vision), Immunity to Poisons, Venom

Note: The pain inflicted by the toxin is enough to add +2 to all the victim's Target Numbers, in addition to any normal wound damage. The pain lasts for 10 hours, minus 1 hour for each point of Willpower the victim has.

DEATHRATTLE
Crotalus nex

HABITAT
Desert and badland areas

RANGE
Southwestern and southern regions of North America, with some subspecies extending north

RANGE

SIZE COMPARISON

DEVIL JACK DIAMOND

Litholepis adamanticus

IDENTIFICATION

The devil jack diamond typically grows to a length of 3.0 meters and a mass of 150 kilograms, though specimens reaching 4.0 meters have been reported. It is a freshwater fish with the vicious jaws of a pike (*Esox lucuis*) or a muskie (*E. masquinongy*).

Its back is broad and flat, covered with heavy scales. Evidence exists that the devil jack diamond is an Awakened form of the pike, though its Awakening has changed it significantly enough to warrant a new classification.

MAGIC CAPABILITY

None.

HABITS

The devil jack diamond feeds predominantly on other fish. In the Mississippi River, large Mississippi catfish (*Ictalurus punctatus*) seem to constitute its main food. It will, however, attack anything else that enters the water.

Unless actively feeding, the devil jack diamond floats at the surface, with just its back awash. In this position, it can be mistaken for a floating log or deadhead.

The devil jack diamond is aggressive and ferocious, extremely fast and agile for its considerable size. There are reports of several devil jacks cooperating to overturn small boats and then feeding on the occupants, but the creature is usually a solitary hunter. If more than one is present, it is common for them to fight among themselves to establish dominance, even in the presence of prey.

The creature seems to be enraged by noises or commotion in the water. Thus, boats attract the creatures, and the sound of thrashing in the water (as when someone has fallen overboard) will almost guarantee an attack.

COMMENTARY

The scales along the back of the devil jack diamond are thick and resilient, providing it with natural armor plating.

The derivation of its name is unknown.

POWERS

None.

WEAKNESSES

None.

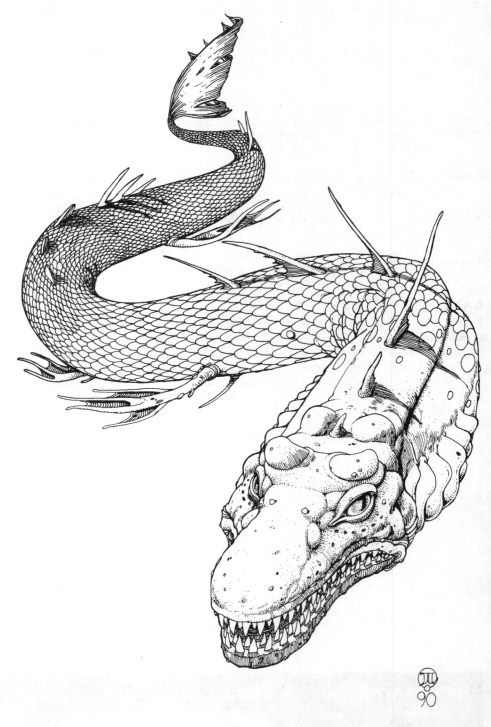

>>>>>(Hey, Clifton, you're the trivia-loving drekhead around here. Where's the name come from?)<<<<<
—Spider (17:10:44/2-23-51)

>>>>>(I'll ignore the aspersions on my character, Spider, but only because I know that the source is clinically brain-dead. One day, the DocWagon will come by to use you as a donor for a brain transplant, and if you have any friends, they won't notice the difference. In answer to your question, the name comes from Oregonian lumberjack tales about a fish that used to pretend it was a log, then eat lumberjacks who tried to roll it. Where they got the name, I neither know nor care.)<<<<<
—Clifton (21:19:33/2-26-51)

>>>>>(A buddy of mine swears these things are good eating. He had a good way of catching them, too. Attach a grenade to a noisemaker, pull the pin, and chuck it over the side. The suckers will go for it every time and blow their guts out. When they float to the surface, filet them. He's got a good recipe, too, that will feed thirty-five.)<<<<<
—Straight Gain (17:16:57/3-24-51)

GAME INFORMATION

	B	Q	S	C	I	W	E	R	Attacks
Devil Jack Diamond	5/3	3 x 5	5	—	1/3	4	6	4	7S3

Note: Natural armor gives the creature an additional Armor Rating of 2 against attacks directed at its back.

DEVIL JACK DIAMOND

Litholepis adamanticus

HABITAT

Rivers and lakes

RANGE

Southern regions of North America (predominantly the Mississippi River and tributaries)

RANGE

SIZE COMPARISON

DEVIL RAT
Rattûs diabolis

IDENTIFICATION

The devil rat is a paraspecies derived from the common rat (*Rattus rattus*). It is somewhat larger than its progenitor, up to 1.0 meter in length (including tail) and weighing as much as 4.0 kilograms.

The devil rat is hairless, except for long, sensitive whiskers, and its skin is grayish-pink and deeply wrinkled.

Devil rats are fast and aggressive.

MAGIC CAPABILITIES

Innate.

HABITS

Normal rats are omnivores and scavengers, fighting only when cornered. Devil rats, however, are vicious urban predators. They hunt in packs of up to 30 individuals, preying on less ferocious animals, children, or others incapable of defending themselves. There are unsubstantiated reports of devil rats attacking healthy adults while asleep. When a pack of rats has made a kill, the creatures frequently "celebrate" by sitting back on their haunches and setting up a high-pitched howl.

Devil rats are nocturnal. In sewer systems and other dark places, however, they are active around the clock. They hunt by stealth, showing great cunning. They adapt quickly to a new environment, immediately recognizing and distrusting anything out of place in that environment. This is why it is difficult to trap devil rats: they recognize the traps as "foreign" to the environment and avoid them.

Devil rats are prolific, and live anywhere that humans or metahumans do. Because of their instincts and their innate immunity to most poisons, exterminating the creatures is impossible.

COMMENTARY

Like their progenitors, devil rats can carry diseases. Most of these are merely irritating (rashes, soreness in the joints, enlarged lymph nodes, and so on), but some reports exist of devil rats carrying the VITAS-3 virus.

Many cities have launched campaigns to eradicate their rat populations, but these campaigns have invariably failed. Devil rats are even more tenacious and hard to kill than their progenitor species. When and if mankind ever travels to the stars, it is likely that devil rats will go along for the ride as unwelcome stowaways.

POWERS

Animal Control (Normal Rats), Concealment (Self Only), Immunity to Pathogens, Immunity to Poisons.

WEAKNESSES

Allergy (Sunlight, Mild)

>>>>>(Mild allergy to sunlight? Drek! It burns the little fraggers. Blisters, tissue death, you name it.)<<<<<
—Casper (08:45:53/1-30-51)

>>>>>(Chummer, you brain-fried or what? I seen a passel o' them peckers killin' a dog middle of Maynard at high noon on a sunny day. Didn't look blistered or tissue-dead to me.)<<<<<
—Snake (03:00:49/2-3-51)

>>>>>(You get these things in packs of more than thirty, man. Tex and me, we were doing the tunnels under Pioneer Square. A good escape route—or it used to be. We took a wrong turn into some kinda room, and found the place was just crawling with those puckered rats. They didn't hesitate, just came at us, waves of them. Great choice, huh? Security guards behind us, devil rats in front of us. You know what? We chose the fraggin' sec-guards!)<<<<<
—Yoshi (04:11:18/4-14-51)

>>>>>(Those things ain't just vicious, they're evil. I watched a handful of 'em geek a drunk in an alley. And you know what? They woke the poor bleeder up, made sure he saw them and knew what was coming. Then they geeked him.)<<<<<
—Herman (09:35:19/4-17-51)

>>>>>(Drek!)<<<<<
—Casper (23:07:04/4-17-51)

GAME INFORMATION

	B	Q	S	C	I	W	E	R	Attacks
Devil Rat	2	5 x 3	1	5	2/5	3	(4)	5	4L1, −1 Reach

Powers: Animal Control (Normal Rats), Concealment (Self Only), Immunity to Pathogens, Immunity to Poisons

Weaknesses: Allergy (Sunlight, Mild)

Note: There is a 1 in 12 chance that any given devil rat is infected with the VITAS-3 virus (a result of 11 or 12 on 2D6). Anytime a character is bitten by an infected rat, roll 2D6. On a result of 9 or more, the character has contracted the disease. (Note that infected rats are generally immune to the virus, merely acting as carriers.)

DEVIL RAT
Rattus diabolis

HABITAT
Urban areas

RANGE
Throughout the world

RANGE

SIZE COMPARISON

DEVILFISH

Manta phobi

NELSON

IDENTIFICATION

The devilfish is an Awakened version of the manta ray. Achieving a "wingspan" of 8.0 meters, it is larger than its progenitor, but shares the same shape and coloration. The devilfish's dorsal surface is black, with white markings on the ventral; these markings differ between specimens and can be used to identify individuals. The creature has a slightly elongated tail, tipped with a venomous spine.

The devilfish can swim rapidly by flexing the lateral lobes of its body in a manner reminiscent of wings. It can also leap from the water and glide for a considerable distance. Glides of 100 meters have been reported, though the longest verified was less than 70 meters).

MAGIC CAPABILITY

Innate.

HABITS

The devilfish feeds on smaller fish. If it detects a school of prey fish nearby, it often leaps from the water and then lands heavily on top of the school. The impact stuns the fish, allowing the devilfish to feed with little exertion. Under good conditions, the "slap" made by this hunting technique can be heard several kilometers away.

The devilfish is predominantly nocturnal. During daylight hours, the creature usually lies on a flat ocean bottom, partially covered with sand that it flips over itself using its "wings". At other times, it hangs motionless just below the surface.

The female devilfish's eggs are enclosed in a membranous pouch after being laid. The female will sometimes expel this pouch while airborne.

The devilfish is not aggressive toward larger creatures. As with normal manta rays, divers can sometimes "hitch a ride" with a devilfish by hanging onto the front margin of its body as it cruises slowly along. If attacked or aroused, however, its venomous spine is a formidable weapon. The mass and the strength of its muscular body allow it to inflict significant damage against targets up to the size of a small boat.

COMMENTARY

The devilfish has an innate ability to instill fear in other creatures (an ability that seems magical in nature). This "fear aura" is under the creature's conscious control, but is only used if the devilfish feels threatened.

POWERS

Fear, Venom.

WEAKNESSES

None.

>>>>>(These things are wiz. I've seen them down in the Gulf. Go out in a small boat at night, turn off the lights and the engine, and then just wait. Sometimes they'll glide right over you. Cool.)<<<<<
    —Naf (17:52:36/2-11-51)

>>>>>(Yeah, just as long as they don't land on you. A few hundred kilos of fish trying to be a bird would ruin your whole day.)<<<<<
    —Yoshi (03:31:49/2-13-51)

>>>>>(What do you have to do to make one of these babies mad? Seems they don't mind hitchhikers.)<<<<<
    —Gort (17:57:47/2-16-51)

>>>>>(Insult its mother?)<<<<<
    —Slag (18:42:20/2-16-51)

>>>>>(Unsubstantiated speculation about its sexual hygiene and proclivities?)<<<<<
    —Yoshi (18:57:15/2-16-51)

>>>>>(Drop an anchor on it.)<<<<<
    —Naf (20:34:40/2-16-51)

>>>>>(Send it out on a blind date with a chick with a "great personality"?)<<<<<
    —Slag (20:41:05/2-16-51)

>>>>>(Send it out on a blind date with Slag.)<<<<<
    —Juli (20:43:48/2-16-51)

GAME INFORMATION

	B	Q	S	C	I	W	E	R	Attacks
Devilfish	9	3 x 5	10	—	2/3	4	(6)	4	5M2

Powers: Fear, Venom

DEVILFISH
    Manta phobi

HABITAT
    Tropical oceans

RANGE
    Gulf of Mexico, southeastern coast of Florida, southern coast of California Free State

RANGE

SIZE COMPARISON

DOUR
Pan malifici

IDENTIFICATION

The dour has been described as short and stocky, humanoid, heavily muscled, and dark-skinned. In fact, the dour is not related to *Homo sapiens* at all, but is rather an Awakened form of the chimpanzee (*Pan troglodytes*).

Unlike the chimpanzee, the dour's hair growth is limited to the skull, the shoulders and chest, and the backs of the hands and feet. It maintains its progenitor's long arms and somewhat human-like facial structure, however. The dour has larger eyes than the chimpanzee, and seems well-adapted to a nocturnal or subterranean lifestyle. It stands 1.25 meters, and weighs about 70 kilograms (most of it muscle).

MAGIC CAPABILITY

Parabiological.

HABITS

The dour is omnivorous, though it prefers meat. Most of its diet seems to consist of rats and other rodents.

The dour prefers to live in caves, caverns, or abandoned mines, shying away from daylight and using its acute low-light vision to hunt in the caverns. Some individuals, however, seem to prefer an arboreal existence similar to the chimpanzee's. These arboreal dour are nocturnal, spending the day in lairs they dig under the roots of large trees. Though dour dislike bright light, it seems to cause them neither serious inconvenience nor damage.

Most dour live and hunt in small family groups of up to five individuals. These families are very territorial, and use threat displays or out-and-out attack to drive intruding dour (and other primates) from their "turf". The cave lair of a family group is usually concealed, with some reports that the creatures occasionally set rudimentary traps (simple pits or deadfalls) to protect their homes.

If recurring rumors are true, some dour have adapted to life in the abandoned zones of cities. The behavior of these individuals is significantly modified. The family group is no longer significant, and dour will often hunt alone. On the other hand, when circumstances warrant, the city dour combine into motley bands of perhaps a dozen individuals. (Rumors of city dour are, as yet, unsubstantiated. It is

only the sheer volume of these reports that suggests some truth to them.)

Other rumors that dour sometimes use weapons and tools, wear clothing, and make use of magic are certainly fanciful.

Dour are aggressive in protecting their territory, behaving as though the best defense is a good offense. They frequently set up cunning ambushes if they detect intruders. (These behaviors are examples of animal cunning rather than evidence of the creature's intelligence or sentience.)

COMMENTARY

Dour are reported to be nasty-tempered creatures. Rumor has it that the city dour, in particular, seem to enjoy destruction and vandalism for its own sake.

Dour practice little in the way of hygiene, with no compunction about fouling their own nests. Thus, dour lairs can sometimes be detected by their smell.

POWERS

Enhanced Senses (Low-Light Vision).

WEAKNESSES

Allergy (Sunlight, Nuisance).

>>>>>(I met up with some of these buggers in the tunnels under Pioneer Square. They were armed with makeshift weapons, like clubs and spears made from sharpened re-bar, and they acted like they had some basic ideas about tactics. I'm almost positive I saw one or two wearing clothes. Just scraps and tattered remnants, but still clothes.)<<<<<
 —Nova (10:40:45/1-31-51)

>>>>>(What were they doing?)<<<<<
 —Macro (10:45:33/1-31-51)

>>>>>(Trying to scrag us. I guess we walked into their turf. Timmy got nailed by a trap, some kind of trip-wired crossbow that put a spike clean through his leg. Then these little things started climbing out from behind pipes, coming up through access covers in the floor, dropping from the ceiling... Bladerunner loved it. Said it was like a scene from one of his old movies. He didn't love it so much when one of the little bleeders tried to shove two meters of re-bar through his chest. While all this was going on, there was one dour hanging back. It was chanting, and something was starting to take shape around it.)<<<<<
 —Nova (10:47:50/1-31-51)

>>>>>(What?)<<<<<
 —Macro (10:55:32/1-31-51)

>>>>>(Don't know. I figured I didn't want to know, so I fed it a grenade. I had to ignore the others doing it, too, and three of them almost geeked me.<<<<<
 —Nova (10:56:47)/1-31-51)

>>>>>(You know what you're saying, don't you?)<<<<<
 —Macro (10:59:11/1-31-51)

>>>>>(Yeah...But the color of its tie didn't match its socks, so I guess I'm O.K. with Lone Star.)<<<<<
 —Nova (11:00:35/1-31-51)

>>>>>(Tool and weapon use, enough abstract reasoning to set mechanical traps, clothing, magical activity. It's obvious: these things are sentient and must be treated as such. The behavior of humanity, and particularly the attitudes displayed on this BBS, worry me. We must (.5 Mb deleted by Sysop).)<<<<<
 —Deborah Bailey (14:53:09/2-1-51)

GAME INFORMATION

	B	Q	S	C	I	W	E	R	Attacks
Dour	5	4 x 3	5	—	2/4	3	5	5	4M2, +1 Reach or Humanoid

 Powers: Enhanced Senses (Low-Light Vision)
 Weaknesses: Allergy (Sunlight, Nuisance)

DOUR
 Pan malifici

HABITAT
 Forests, mountains, caves, and caverns

RANGE
 Temperate and subtropical regions of North America

RANGE

SIZE COMPARISON

DZOO-NOO-QUA

Homo saevitias

IDENTIFICATION

The dzoo-noo-qua has recently been confirmed as a troll (*Homo sapiens ingentis*) infected with the HMHVV virus. The virus has increased the incidence of dermal bone deposition, making the dzoo-noo-qua look more deformed and asymmetrical than *ingentis*. Horns, spines, and plates of "dermal armor" are common, with such modifications differing widely from individual to individual.

This creature typically measures 2.8 meters and weighs 120 kilograms or more. Skin color varies from pinkish-white to mahogany brown. Fingers and toes are equipped with spade-like nails. The eyes are slightly larger than in *ingentis*, and are heavily vascularized, giving a blood-shot appearance.

MAGIC CAPABILITY

Innate, though there are rumors of magically active dzoo-noo-qua.

HABITS

The dzoo-noo-qua is omnivorous, but prefers meat. There are also recurring tales of ritual cannibalism among groups.

The creature is, by preference, nocturnal. Individuals inhabiting wilderness areas dwell in caverns and converted structures such as bridges. In urban areas, they prefer deserted or normally uninhabited areas such as sewers or derelict buildings.

Populations sometimes congregate in small groups for hunting and mutual protection. These groups are territorial. Isolated individuals, however, seem to show no territorial imperative, and are considerably less aggressive unless hunting or threatened.

In addition to the physical changes, HMHVV infection also adversely effects intelligence. Though the progenitor species is undoubtedly sentient, sub-species *saevitias* possesses no more than an animal level of intelligence.

The dzoo-noo-qua is not sentient.

COMMENTARY

The superficial similarity between the dzoo-noo-qua and trolls is the source of several unfortunate misconceptions. Some people erroneously assume that trolls share the dzoo-noo-qua's cannibalistic and aggressive behavior, while others mistake the wild creature for the socialized troll.

Governmental policies with regard to dzoo-noo-qua are confused. In some jurisdictions, such as the UCAS, statutes make it illegal to kill the creature without "evidence of imminent malice or injurious intent." Other jurisdictions offer high bounties for dzoo-noo-qua pelts. Within the protected jurisdiction, some factions continue to lobby for bounties on the dzoo-noo-qua; in the bounty jurisdictions, on the other hand, others lobby for stringent penalties against killing or injuring the creature. The former group holds that the dzoo-noo-qua are unintelligent and pose a significant threat to human and metahuman life; the latter believes the creatures to be sentient and that to kill one is murder.

The name dzoo-noo-qua comes from a Northwest Indian legend of a huge, man-like beast that steals and eats infants. There is no evidence that the dzoo-noo-qua exhibits this behavior.

POWERS

Enhanced Senses (Thermographic Vision), Essence Drain, Magical Resistance.

WEAKNESSES

Allergy (Sunlight, Mild).

>>>>>(Latest news flash: It looks like the "bounty hunter" faction in Seattle has lost a whole lot of credibility. Some reporter from Nightpulse dug up links between the lobby group and the Humanis Policlub. How's that grab you?)<<<<<
— Clifton (15:01:52/3-23-51)

>>>>>(The Humanis policlub, being a socially aware organization, funds many important groups and institutions such as orphanages, hospital IC units, and more than one library. Does the source of funding decrease *their* credibility? I think not.)<<<<<
— Urnst (16:23:28/3-24-51)

>>>>>(Get off that drek, will you, Urnst? The orphanage and intensive care units get lots of business when you and your bullet-head friends go on a rampage. And we all know what kind of books your library stocks.)<<<<<
— Himem (16:35:25/3-25/51)

>>>>>(Its not that simplistic. I'm a troll, so I sure as drek don't support Urnst and his Humanis goons. But I do support the bounty. Those big armored bleeders give us trolls a bad name.) <<<<<
— Baker (10:34:03/3-26-51)

>>>>>(I don't know about this thing. I got jumped by a couple of those things while I was hiding in a drainage culvert. I tried to reason with them, but they wouldn't listen. so I tried to reason with a power bolt, and they wouldn't listen to that either. they did listen to my partner's grenade launcher, but it was a close thing. The bitch of it is that they could be intelligent. Maybe cutting them down was a bad as cutting down Baker.)<<<<<
— Suki (21:01:54/3-26-51)

GAME INFORMATION

	B	Q	S	C	I	W	E	R	Attacks
Dzoo-Noo-Qua	9/2	5 x 2	10	1	3/3	4	(5)	4	7S2, +1 Reach

Powers: Enhanced Senses (Thermographic Vision), Essence Drain, Magical Resistance
Weaknesses: Allergy (Sunlight, Mild)

DZOO-NOO-QUA
Homo saevitias

HABITAT
Any, including cities

RANGE
Potentially worldwide

RANGE

SIZE COMPARISON

EMBRACER
Gorilla rubicundi

IDENTIFICATION

The embracer is the same size (up to 1.9 meters standing height) and has much the same proportions as the (now extinct) mountain gorilla *(Gorilla berengei)*. The resemblance between the two creatures ends there, however. The embracer is completely hairless, with smooth red skin that has an almost metallic sheen. Its head is large, with a wide mouth full of sharp teeth. Above its tiny, pig-like eyes are two small, curved horns.

Like a gorilla, it usually moves on all fours, but it can rear up on its hind legs when necessary.

The creature's sweat is highly acidic and has a characteristic, sharp odor.

MAGIC CAPABILITY

Innate.

HABITS

The embracer enjoys heat and prefers to lair in caves near volcanoes or hot springs. Many live in or around the Mount St. Helens crater or near the steam vents on Mount Baker. They can tolerate much higher temperatures than can other primates, and seem to have no difficulty shedding excess heat.

Embracers are constantly hungry and always hunting. Though strictly omnivores, meat makes up more than 90 percent of their diet. They hunt birds and smaller animals. The embracer is able to catch prey much swifter than itself, almost as though it were able to prevent the prey from using its full speed. Thus, an embracer can pull down even swift species like deer and mountain sheep.

Embracers are solitary hunters who congregate only to mate. If confronted by an animal of comparable size (a human or a sasquatch, for example), they will exhibit a gorilla-like threat display (tearing up the undergrowth, pounding on the ground or chest, short mock charges, and so on). If the other creature shows subservience by crouching down and averting its eyes, the embracer may decide not to attack. If the other creature does not back down, or tries to flee, the embracer will almost certainly attack.

Though embracers have sharp teeth and can deliver a damaging bite, their most dangerous mode of attack is to grab their prey in a bear hug that literally squeezes the life out. The embracer's

perspiration is also enough to cause damage to the exposed flesh of other animals, which make its hug doubly dangerous.

Embracers are diurnal.

COMMENTARY

The embracer is not intelligent. Its progenitor species is the mountain gorilla. The original "stock" of creatures is presumed to have escaped (or been released) from zoos or medical research laboratories.

POWERS

Corrosive Secretions, Immunity to Fire, Movement (Decrease).

WEAKNESSES

Allergy (Cold, Mild).

>>>>>(Anybody ever seen one of these?)<<<<<
    —Casper (16:18:34/2-8-51))

>>>>>(Yeah, me. It was on Mount St. Helens, by the Cauldron. You know, the cave with that lake of lava. Spooky place. Spooky! Like something out of Dante's Inferno, with bubbling lava throwing red light on the walls, and that heavy smell of sulphur. The guy I was chasing, he ducked down one of those little passages. Just when I was trying to decide whether to follow him or just use a grenade to bring down the tunnel roof, I heard him scream, like the devil himself had got him. I kinda froze. Then this thing bounds out of the tunnel. Red all over, big grinning mouth full of teeth, and horns, for god's sake. I thought it was the Reaper himself out to get me.)<<<<<
    —Rory (16:34:03/2-8-51)

>>>>>(So you ran?)<<<<<
    —Scuz (16:55:01/2-8-51)

>>>>>(Slotting right, I ran.)<<<<<
    —Rory (17:00:19/2-8-51)

>>>>>(Rory, did you smell it before you saw it? I hear you can smell those things a klick away.)<<<<<
    —Tess (14:25:48/2-9-51)

>>>>>(Not over the sulphur. Sorry, Tess. Why? Planning to head out St. Helens way?)<<<<<
    —Rory (14:37:02/2-9-51)

>>>>>(No comment.)<<<<<
    —Tess (15:10:28/2-9-51)

GAME INFORMATION

	B	Q	S	C	I	W	E	R	Attacks
Embracer	8	4 x 3	8	—	2/3	3	(6)	5	7S2, +1 Reach

    Powers: Corrosive Secretions, Immunity to Fire, Movement (Decrease)
    Weaknesses: Allergy (Cold, Mild)

EMBRACER
    Gorilla rubicundi

HABITAT
    Mountainous and hilly
(preferably volcanic) areas

RANGE
    Throughout North America

RANGE

SIZE COMPARISON

FIDEAL
Scyphozoa fidealis

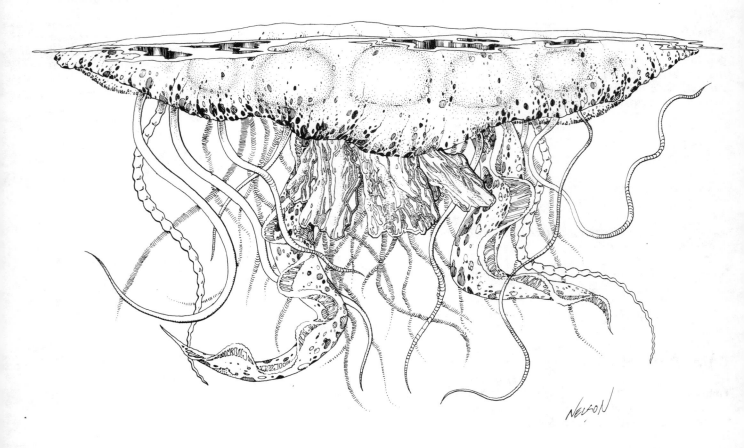

NELSON

IDENTIFICATION

The fideal is a soft-bodied invertebrate apparently related to coelenterates such as jellyfish *(Plagyodus scopelide)*. The organism appears as a large, amoeboid, jellyfish-like mass; its size varies, but can reach well over 0.5 meter in diameter. (This diameter refers to the fideal when it is in a roughly spherical shape. Because the creature has no internal structure, it can take on any shape. It can compress itself into a disk less than 1.0 centimeter thick. Such a disk would have a diameter of more than 3.0 meters.)

The fideal has multiple tentacles of up to 0.75 meter in length. (The longer these tentacles are, the thinner they are.) The jelly-like material composing the fideal is colorless and has almost exactly the same refractive index as water. Thus, when submerged, the fideal is almost undetectable, either via the visual spectrum or by thermographic vision.

MAGIC CAPABILITY

Parabiological.

HABITS

The fideal subsists on small creatures that it can engulf. These creatures remain as visible inclusions within the fideal's mass until digestive enzymes have dissolved them. These enzymes are unable to dissolve gold, stainless steel, and some other rare metals and alloys, or certain ceramics. Such objects can remain within the fideal for long periods of time before the creature expels them.

The fideal's preferred method of hunting is to lie immobile, barely submerged in shallow water, preferably among water grasses near a marshy shore. Here it waits for some creature to swim by or, in the case of larger animals, to step on the fideal. When this happens, the fideal lashes out with blindingly quick tentacles to seize the prey. If the prey is too large to absorb easily, the fideal drags it below the surface until the prey drowns. Throughout this process, the fideal secretes its highly corrosive enzymes, already beginning the job of digesting the prey.

Fideals reproduce asexually by binary fission. One fideal splits into two smaller fideals.

The fideal is not intelligent.

COMMENTARY

The fideal is believed to have sprung from freshwater jellyfish, though gene mapping is unable to give a positive match with any single species.

The creature can exist on land for limited periods of time, but is rarely encountered there. It can move slowly on land, with an oozing motion, and it can squeeze its way through the minutest openings.

The fideal has no optic sensors, apparently depending totally on motion detection.

POWERS

Corrosive Secretions, Engulf, Enhanced Senses (Motion Detection), Invisibility (Non-Magical), Regeneration.

WEAKNESSES

Vulnerability (Fire).

>>>>>(Watch out for these things. They're real nasty.)<<<<<
  —Toni (17:29:28/2-25-51)

>>>>>(No drek. I trod in one and it tried to eat my leg. Had to get new boots and everything.)<<<<<
  —Karl (18:01:39/2-25-51)

>>>>>(They ain't common, are they?)<<<<<
  —Manta (09:28:08/3-4-51)

>>>>>(Not so rare that you can just forget about them.)<<<<<
  —Toni (12:16:30/3-4-51)

>>>>>(That's right. If you're planning to go wading in the shallows in some muddy lake, best to probe the bottom ahead of you with a stick or something. If something tries to eat the stick, burn it.)<<<<<
  —Karl (02:11:14/3-5-51)

>>>>>(Yeah, burn it. Fire's the way to go. They're a bitch to kill any other way.)<<<<<
  —Toni (11:54:30/3-5-51)

>>>>>(I heard through a contact at MTC that these things didn't spring up by themselves. They were made. MTC's Bioweapons lab built them, then let them go.)<<<<<
  —Go-Boy (17:37:27/3-24-51)

>>>>>(I heard the same thing, but it wasn't about the boys at MTC. It was bioweapons people at Aztechnology.)<<<<<
  —Raver (23:59:45/3-25-51)

>>>>>(No, no, no. It was a freelance lab in Bellevue.)<<<<<
  —Warren (04:41:40/3-26-51)

>>>>>(Hold on a minute here while I get this straight. Everyone's saying these things are synthetic? Or if not synthetic, then engineered. Right?)<<<<<
  —Toni (05:10:49/3-26-51)

>>>>>(Right-o.)<<<<<
  —Warren (08:51:10/3-26-51)

>>>>>(I don't think I like the sound of this.)<<<<<
  —Toni (11:55:39/3-26-51)

GAME INFORMATION

	B	Q	S	C	I	W	E	R	Attacks
Fideal	4	3	3	—	1/3	2	4	4	3M2, +1 Reach

Powers: Corrosive Secretions, Engulf, Enhanced Senses (Motion Detection), Invisibility (Non-Magical)*, Regeneration
Weaknesses: Vulnerability (Fire)
Note: Movement on land is 1.
  *Though there is no magic involved, the fideal is under a permanent Invisibility Spell while under water, giving it a Concealability Rating of 10. This is true whether it is viewed from below or from above the surface.
  Because the fideal has no brain, it is totally immune to Illusion and Manipulation Spells.

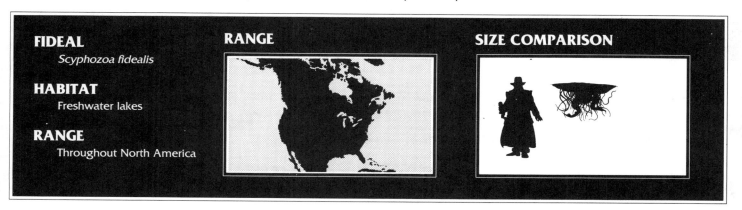

FIDEAL
  Scyphozoa fidealis

HABITAT
  Freshwater lakes

RANGE
  Throughout North America

RANGE

SIZE COMPARISON

FIREBIRD
Paradisia igni

IDENTIFICATION

The firebird is similar in conformation to a nighthawk. It has abundant orange plumage, with trailing tail feathers of bright yellow. The firebird's beak is sharply pointed, and its talons resemble an eagle's. The creature can achieve a wingspan of 1.8 meters, and a length (including tail feathers) of 1.0 meter.

MAGIC CAPABILITY

Innate.

HABITS

The firebird is an insectivore, using its powerful talons to tear open rotting logs and other habitations of grubs and insects. It can also cling to the trunk of a tree like a woodpecker, picking insects out of the bark.

Firebirds congregate in small, family-based groups of up to six individuals. These groups claim only the smallest territories, usually a radius of 10 meters from their nesting tree, but defend this area with paranoid vigor. Any creature large enough to pose a threat to the firebirds is subject to energetic mock attacks should it intrude. During such a mock attack, the birds swoop down on the outsider, screaming raucously, but they always pull out of their dive well above their apparent target. Only if the intruder continues to approach to within a "critical radius" (about 3 meters from the nesting tree), will the firebirds attack in earnest.

The firebird is so named because it is totally resistant to fire and seems to enjoy playing in it. The larger the fire, the more firebirds will arrive to swoop and soar through the flames, enjoying the chaotic updrafts and thermals. Large forest fires attract the entire firebird population for dozens of kilometers around.

COMMENTARY

This bird's affinity for fire leads many laymen to equate it with the phoenix, but no biological relationship exists. Even the relation to fire differs. The phoenix is able to project an aura of flame about itself; the firebird plays with fire but is unable to cause one.

POWERS

Fire Resistance.

WEAKNESSES

None.

>>>>>(Have you noticed that the two creatures sometimes hang out together? One phoenix might have a couple of firebird groups nearby. Coincidence? I don't think so. And doesn't that imply that the firebirds have some smarts?)<<<<<
    —Spectre (15:35:02/1-10-51)

>>>>>(Let's say some firebirds are attacking you. Can you turn them away from you by setting fire to something?)<<<<<
    —Griffon (09:02:57/1-11-51)

>>>>>(Interesting thought. Which is dominant, territoriality or love of fire?)<<<<<
    —Spectre (20:21:02/1-11-51)

>>>>>(My money's on territoriality.)<<<<<
    —Icarus (22:17:05/1-11-51)

>>>>>(Who cares? What's wiz is watching these birds in action. My buddies and I, we took out a light panzer, and brewed it up real nice. At least ten of those firebird things came to play in the flames. What a show!)<<<<<
    —Ace (11:09:39/1-12-51)

GAME INFORMATION

	B	Q	S	C	I	W	E	R	Attacks
Firebird	2	5 x 3	2	—	2/3	3	(6)	4	5L2

Powers: Fire Resistance

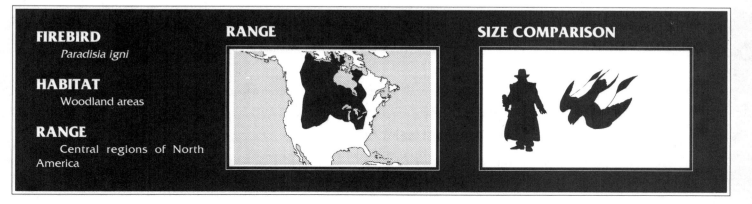

FIREBIRD
    Paradisia igni

HABITAT
    Woodland areas

RANGE
    Central regions of North America

RANGE

SIZE COMPARISON

FIREDRAKE

Draco minimalis americanus

IDENTIFICATION

The firedrake is a lizard that grows up to 1.25 meters in length. It resembles a western dragon, but has no wings. It typically moves on all fours, but can also rear up onto its hind legs, balancing with its tail. Its skin is scaled but supple, ranging in color from red-brown on the back to light tan on the belly. Its small eyes are red and malevolent-looking.

The firedrake can breathe flame.

MAGIC CAPABILITY

Innate.

HABITS

The firedrake is a fast and aggressive carnivore, attacking anything that comes within its hunting area. Rats and groundhogs are a favorite prey. When the firedrake locates the burrow of one of these creatures, it sends a jet of flame down the opening. Because such burrows usually have multiple openings, some of the adult prey have a good chance of escaping. The young are usually killed, however, and the firedrake can then dig up the cooked bodies at its leisure.

Like the wolverine, the firedrake will kill even when not hungry. Even when totally sated just after a hunt, it will almost inevitably attack an intruder into its hunting area.

Firedrakes congregate in small family groups of up to eight individuals. The family is led by the dominant female. Younger females will eventually challenge the matriarch to combat, but such contests are rarely to the death. If the younger female loses, she is driven from the group to start her own. If the matriarch loses, however, the rest of the family group immediately kills her, and the challenger becomes the new matriarch.

Firedrake groups lair in caves, preferably those heated by volcanic activity.

COMMENTARY

No consensus exists on the derivation and taxonomy of the firedrake. Most authorities believe that the firedrake is an Awakened form of a mundane reptile, perhaps a varaniad lizard or similar species. One small, but very vocal, group, however, points to the firedrake's fiery breath as evidence of kinship with dragons. It is this group of dissidents that has managed to force through the taxonomic classification of the firedrake as *Draco minimalis americanus*. Given that these creatures do not exhibit the common draco abilities of flight, thermographic vision, and sapience, we cannot accept the draco classification. It is anticipated that, as the more enlightened members of the scientific community align their efforts, this mistake will soon be remedied.

POWERS

Enhanced Senses (Wide-Band Hearing), Flame Projection, Immunity to Fire.

WEAKNESSES

None.

>>>>>(Paterson is hiding the real story here.)<<<<<
—Doc (11:33:35/2-3-51)

>>>>>(What do you mean?)<<<<<
—N.F.A. (12:01:36/2-3-51)

>>>>>(If you savvy gene typing, lend an ear. The genetic blueprint of a creature tells you everything there is to know about it, and how it relates to other creatures. For example, if you look at the genetic map of the house cat and of the cheetah, they're identical—except for one small section of DNA in one chromosome that's been inverted. Now, I'm really simplifying all this, but the point is that this proves that house cats and cheetahs are closely related.

Well, we've done gene typing on the firedrake, and it's not like anything else. Oh, sure, it's got sections of DNA that are similar to some of the large lizards (like Paterson's varaniad lizard), and it's got sections that match tissue samples from the real dragons. But the way these sections fit together is plain weird. These birds are either old, that is, they evolved some 30 million years ago, maybe from the precursor reptile that gave rise to both modern lizards and the dragons. Or else they're brand spanking new; they were engineered through chimeric gene-splicing, and it was done recently. But that still leaves big questions. If they're old, why weren't they spotted until 2012, or whenever the first one was recorded? And if they're new, who in the hell built them?)<<<<<
—Doc (12:02:55/2-3-51)

GAME INFORMATION

	B	Q	S	C	I	W	E	R	Attacks
Firedrake	4	4 x 4	4	—	2/4	3	(6)	5	3M2

Powers: Enhanced Senses (Wide-Band Hearing), Flame Projection, Immunity to Fire

FIREDRAKE
Draco minimalis americanus

HABITAT
Mountainous areas (particularly volcanic areas)

RANGE
Western regions of North America

RANGE

SIZE COMPARISON

GABRIEL HOUND

Canis mutabilis

IDENTIFICATION

The gabriel hound is a large dog, standing approximately 1.0 meter at the shoulder. The animal is lean, fast, and vicious, with a short, bristly coat that shows the same range of color as normal canines. Its face has a vaguely human appearance.

MAGIC CAPABILITY

Innate.

HABITS

The gabriel hound is an efficient urban predator. It dwells in vacant lots, junk yards, and other uninhabited urban areas, or in wild regions that sometimes border cities. It feeds mostly on other urban-adapted animals such as devil rats, but will also attack and kill humans and metahumans. (The animal rarely attacks healthy adults, preferring to snatch children or to kill sick or wounded squatters.)

Nocturnal by nature, the gabriel hound is a stealthy animal, with highly acute thermographic vision.

Gabriel hounds are usually solitary hunters. Occasionally, however, they congregate in packs of a dozen or more individuals. These packs are dangerous, often forsaking their stealthy ways in favor of outright attack on anything that moves. Gabriel hounds are exceptionally fast, fiercely aggressive, and almost preternaturally strong.

The gabriel hound has shapeshifting ability, but it is limited. It can take on a more human form, increasing the human appearance of its face and changing its body to resemble a person moving on all-fours. (The animal is unable to take on true bipedal form.) This shapeshifting ability seems to require continued concentration, for the creature always resumes its true form when attacking or when wounded.

D.K.

COMMENTARY

The "un-shifted" gabriel hound's human-like face puzzled scientists at first, particularly before its shapeshifting ability was reported or confirmed. This humanoid appearance might have been partially explained as a form of "protective coloration" to protect the animal from human hunters, but the creature's existence was first reported in 2013 and evolution cannot work that fast. This may be a unique example of metamorphosis in a paraspecies.

The name "gabriel hound" has a mythological origin. According to English legend, the gabriel hound was a mysterious flying creature whose howls and yelps signaled an ill omen.

POWERS

Compulsion (Immobility), Conceal-Iment (Self Only), Enhanced Movement, Enhanced Physical Attributes (Strength or Quickness, once each per day, for (Essence)D6 turns), Enhanced Reactions, Enhanced Senses (Thermographic Vision).

WEAKNESSES

Allergy (Sunlight, Mild).

>>>>>(Word to the wise: Do not mess with these things.)<<<<<
—Wolverine (12:26:43/3-25-51)

>>>>>(Why the frag not? They're just dogs, ain't they?)<<<<<
—Scuz (13:25:14/3-25-51)

>>>>>(Yeah, just dogs. Well, some doggies like to chase cars, but when these fraggers do it, they catch them. And when they catch them, they eat them.)<<<<<
—Wolverine (13:34:50/3-25-51)

>>>>>(Oh, bloody fraggin' drek.)<<<<<
—Scuz (14:17:09/3-25-51)

>>>>>(No, Scuz, you moron, it isn't drek. I was leaving a meet in the old industrial district, and a pack of these things chased my "borrowed" Nightsky. They tore off the bloody rear fender before I could lose them.)<<<<<
—Wolverine (14:30:14/3-25-51)

>>>>>(I don't know which is worse, one gabriel hound or a whole pack of them. With the pack, at least you know they're after you and you can do something about it. When there's just one, it sneaks up on you. And even if you see it, it becomes hard to move away from it. There's something kind of hypnotic about these things.)<<<<<
—Moffat (11:36:56/4-3-51)

GAME INFORMATION

	B	Q	S	C	I	W	E	R	Attacks
Gabriel Hound	3	4 x 4	3	—	2/3	4	(5)	4	(Str)M2

Powers: Compulsion (Immobility), Concealment (Self Only), Enhanced Movement, Enhanced Physical Attributes (Strength or Quickness, once each per day, for (Essence)D6 turns), Enhanced Reactions, Enhanced Senses (Thermographic Vision)

Weaknesses: Allergy (Sunlight, Mild)

GABRIEL HOUND
   Canis mutabilis

HABITAT
   Urban areas

RANGE
   Throughout North America

RANGE

SIZE COMPARISON

GARGOYLE

Gargoyle saxi

IDENTIFICATION

The gargoyle is a humanoid creature standing up to 2.0 meters and often weighing more than 150 kilograms. The creature is dull gray in color, and the texture and appearance of its rough skin give it a resemblance to stone. It has a single, short horn in the center of its brow, pronounced canine teeth, and wicked claws on its large hands and feet. The gargoyle is stocky and enormously powerful.

There are unsubstantiated reports of significant differences between the male and the female of the species. According to these claims, the female is as described above, with long, powerful arms. The male, however, has wings sprouting from its shoulders instead of arms. If such reports are accurate, these variations represent the greatest recorded morphological difference between sexes.

To further muddy the waters, a six-limbed subspecies has recently been identified. This subspecies, *G. saxi sexus*, has the same coloration as *G. saxi*, but is equipped with wings, legs, and fully functional arms.

MAGIC CAPABILITY

Innate.

HABITS

Gargoyles are definitely carnivores. Waiting for prey to pass by, they lie in some elevated area, hidden by their natural camouflage. They prefer swooping attacks, similar to those of hawks, but can bring down prey while remaining on the ground.

No female has ever been observed hunting, nor has their existence been conclusively proven. Either the unwinged females depend on the males for food, or they simply do not exist.

Neither has any observer ever recorded sighting an immature gargoyle, nor is anything known of the creature's reproductive habits or cycles.

The gargoyle is not believed to be intelligent.

COMMENTARY

The gargoyle's origin is unknown. All attempts at genetic mapping have produced contradictory data, with no matches even between individual members of the species. The gargoyle is exceptionally well-adapted to its

NELSON

environment, usually an indication of a long evolutionary history. Yet, in the case of this being, no evidence exists, on any level, of such a history.

A subspecies, *G. saxi sexus*, has been positively identified in deserted urban areas. Like the griffin and the western dragon, *G. saxi sexus* violates long-standing theories of vertebrate evolution.

One theory posits that *G. saxi sexus* is actually the female of the species. This has yet to be confirmed. No live *G. saxi*

sexus has been captured, and because this subspecies' flesh immediately calcifies upon death, an autopsy is difficult and the results unreliable.

POWERS

Concealment (Self Only), Enhanced Physical Attributes (Strength, once per day, for 5D6 turns), Noxious Breath.

WEAKNESSES

Vulnerability (Iron).

>>>>>(What does anybody know about these females?)<<<<<
—Tandi (09:19:57/1-2-51)

>>>>>(I've seen them. They exist, and they do hunt. Not as aggressively as the males, but they can pick off something like a small mountain sheep. The one I saw had arms and definitely did not have wings.)<<<<<
—Casper (11:25:21/1-2-51)

>>>>>(Can anyone tell me about this "noxious breath" and their vulnerability to iron?)<<<<<
—Trask (23:10:32/1-11-51)

>>>>>(Just what the guide says. Their breath is toxic, causing muscle cramps and some neurological dysfunction. I think the effect is enzymatic, but don't quote me.)<<<<<
—Doc (07:36:25/1-12-51)

>>>>>(The six-limbed ones are definitely made of stone. My chummer and I were in an alley when one swooped down out of nowhere and sunk its claws into Gabby's shoulders. I unloaded a whole clip from my Uzi, but that didn't bother the damn thing a bit.)<<<<<
—Scuz (10:24:35/1-12-51)

>>>>>(They call 'em gargoyles because they look like those stone statues they used to put on the corners of cathedrals and all that drek, right? Well, it just makes me wonder. Where did those medieval architects get the idea for their gargoyles? Maybe they'd seen them somewhere...)<<<<<
—Gray (13:01:56/1-13-51)

>>>>>(So you're proposing that we call these beings gargoyles because they look like statues that were modeled after gargoyles? Or are you proposing that the cathedral gargoyles are dead G. saxi sexus?)<<<<<
—Doc (13:23:34/1-13-51)

>>>>>(Not so much proposing as just wondering.)<<<<<
—Gray (13:26:40/1-13-51)

>>>>>(Hey, check this out! Nothing from that animal rights activist. Maybe those flakes only care about cute, little furry animals, not big armored things that'll tear your arm off. Nothing to say, Deborah whatever-your-name-is?)<<<<<
—Junior (18:22:01/1-23-51)

GAME INFORMATION

	B	Q	S	C	I	W	E	R	Attacks
Gargoyle	10/3	4 x 3	8	—	2/4	4	(5)	3	(Str)S2

Powers: Concealment (Self only), Enhanced Physical Attributes (Strength, once per day for 5D6 turns), Noxious Breath
Weaknesses: Vulnerability (Iron)
Note: Flying multiplier (Males) is 4.

GARGOYLE
Gargoyle saxi

HABITAT
Mountains and caves; increased sightings in urban areas

RANGE
Northern regions of North America

RANGE

SIZE COMPARISON

GILA DEMON
Heloderma diabolis

IDENTIFICATION

Growing up to 1.7 meters in length, the gila demon is a larger and more aggressive version of the gila monster lizard (*Heloderma suspectum*). Like *H. suspectum*, the gila demon's skin is studded with bead-like, yellow or orange and black tubercles. The animal is omnivorous and venomous.

MAGIC CAPABILITY

Parabiological.

HABITS

The gila demon eats almost anything, from roots and berries to insects and small mammals. It is fast for its size and able to dig rapidly. It is adept at detecting and excavating the burrows of kangaroo rats and other small, desert-dwelling mammals.

Gila demons seem to be active around the clock, though they spend most daylight hours basking in the sun to raise their body temperature. This state of apparent torpor is deceptive, however. Should prey come near, the gila demon reacts with exceptional speed.

A gila demon will not usually attack a creature its own size. If, on the other hand, it feels threatened, it might attack rather than back down.

Gila demons do not form family or other groups. Individuals approach one another only for the purpose of mating.

COMMENTARY

The gila demon's senses seem to be particularly acute.

There is no known antidote to its venom.

POWERS

Enhanced Senses (Improved Vision and Smell), Venom.

WEAKNESSES

None.

>>>>>(The guide should print that in big glowing letters: NO KNOWN ANTIDOTE TO THE GILA DEMON'S VENOM! Got that?)<<<<<
    —Jericho (14:40:18/1-25-51)

>>>>>(But it matter unless you get the thing riled. Just don't.)<<<<<
    —Clive (17:55:41/1-25-51))

>>>>>(You can get the bleeder riled merely by looking at it.)<<<<<
    —Jericho (18:04:27/1-25-51)

>>>>>(Jericho's right. If it was human, I'd say this being was a paranoid psychotic. It sees threats where they don't exist and then overreacts to them. Plus, I heard from Joey that some gilas can spit their venom. Just watch out for them.)<<<<<
    —Stella (20:19:21/1-25-51)

>>>>>(True, true. But on the bright side, they're damned fine eating.)<<<<<
    —Joey (03:37:37/1-26-51)

GAME INFORMATION

	B	Q	S	C	I	W	E	R	Attacks
Gila Demon	4/1	4 x 3	4	—	1/4	3	6	3	4L2

Powers: Enhanced Senses (Improved Vision and Smell), Venom

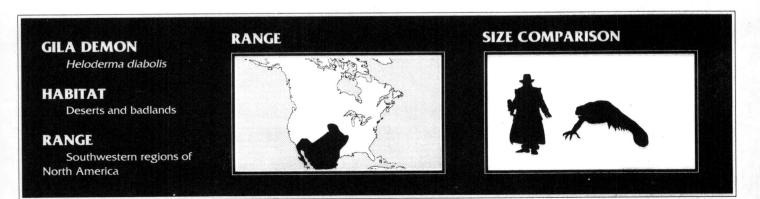

GILA DEMON
    Heloderma diabolis

HABITAT
    Deserts and badlands

RANGE
    Southwestern regions of North America

RANGE

SIZE COMPARISON

GLOAMING OWL
Bubo crepusculi

IDENTIFICATION

The gloaming owl is similar in shape and proportion to the great horned owl (*Bubo virginianus*), its progenitor species, but its plumage is all black. The gloaming owl reaches a length of 0.8 meter and a wingspan of 2.0 meters. Its beak and talons are sharp and prominently curved.

MAGIC CAPABILITY

Innate.

HABITS

Like other owls, the gloaming owl is a nocturnal hunter that feeds on mice, lizards, snakes, and other small animals. Gloaming owls also hunt small bats, which they catch on the wing. The night vision of the gloaming owl is phenomenal, and some anatomical evidence indicates that the creature has true thermographic vision.

The gloaming owl rarely hunts creatures more than about 0.3 meter in length, and there are no reports of unprovoked attacks against humans or metahumans. If the creature is attacked or directly threatened, however, it is ready and able to defend itself.

Observers have noted the feeling of menace produced by the sight of a gloaming owl gliding overhead. The creature's very presence seems to inspire irrational fear. Whether this is due to a magical effect or to some other cause is unknown.

COMMENTARY

Thanks to the complex, aerodynamic arrangement of the gloaming owl's wing feathers, it is absolutely silent in flight. In fact, reports indicate that the creature emanates a field of silence around itself (presumably to prevent the death-cry of its prey from alerting others). Other, more fanciful, reports claim that the creature can induce blindness in others.

POWERS

Blindness, Enhanced Senses (Low-Light Vision, Thermographic Vision), Fear, Silence

WEAKNESSES

Allergy (Sunlight, Mild)

>>>>>("Fanciful reports" or not, the gloaming owl can cause blindness. It's possible to fight off the effects, but it's a scary feeling.)<<<<<
   —Fox (15:38:00/2-21-51)

>>>>>(What did you do to irk an owl?)<<<<<
   —Preston (15:43:30/2-21-51)

>>>>>(Nothing. Or so I thought. I was camping out, lying low for a bit. I'd left in a bit of a hurry and had neglected to bring along food, so I set out some snares. Second night out, I was checking my snare line, and one had got something. A rabbit. I was just bending down to take it out when the world went gray, and it felt like a pressure in my brain, on both sides, near my temples. I managed to fight back the grayness, but the pressure was still there. I looked around, and this bloody black owl was sitting in a tree watching me. A gloaming owl. And it was trying to strike me blind.)<<<<<
   —Fox (15:52:59/2-21-51)

>>>>>(I guess it wanted the rabbit.)<<<<<
   —Samantha (15:56:22/2-21-51)

>>>>>(Were you scared?)<<<<<
   —Preston (16:01:36/2-21-51)

>>>>>(No, I was too scared of being blind to be scared of a fragging owl. But...now that you mention it...I was really scared about being blind.)<<<<<
   —Fox (16:03:55/2-21-51)

GAME INFORMATION

	B	Q	S	C	I	W	E	R	Attacks
Gloaming Owl	3	5 x 4	3	—	2/4	2	(6)	4	5L1

   Powers: Blindness, Enhanced Senses (Low-Light Vision, Thermographic Vision), Fear, Silence
   Weaknesses: Allergy (Sunlight, Mild)

GLOAMING OWL
   Bubo crepusculi

HABITAT
   Woods, hills, and grasslands

RANGE
   Northern regions of North America

RANGE

SIZE COMPARISON

GREATER ARMADILLO
Dasypus major

IDENTIFICATION

The Texas armadillo (*Dasypus novemcinctus*) is unusual in that two Awakened species have arisen from it: the greater armadillo (*D. major*) and the juggernaut (*D. praegrandis*), discussed later.

The greater armadillo closely resembles its smaller cousin, but grows to a length of 1.2 meters. It has the same covering of jointed, bony plates and the same abysmal eyesight. The greater armadillo's feet are equipped with long, sharp claws designed for digging, but these also make nasty weapons if the creature is aroused.

MAGIC CAPABILITY

Parabiological.

HABITS

The greater armadillo is an insectivore. It uses its powerful legs and sharp claws to burrow into the ground in search of food or shelter. So strong is the creature that it can tear into the cement-hard termite colonies ("termite towers") that have come to dot west Texas.

The creature is nocturnal, and spends the daylight hours in shallow burrows. Because its eyesight is poor, it depends on its acute senses of smell and taste.

If startled, the greater armadillo's instinctive reaction is to jump straight up in the air, sometimes up to half a meter high. (This is a carry-over from the time when the armadillo's main threat was snakes. Though the creature is now immune to most toxins, the reaction remains.) After this initial startled reaction, the creature has two optional responses to any threat. The most common is to roll up into a tight ball to protect its soft underbelly as it waits for the attacker—presumably a predator—to become frustrated with the armadillo's hard armor and wander off. The second is all-out attack, using its powerful legs and sharp, ripping claws.

The creature should, theoretically, be able to select the response best suited to the opponent, but the greater armadillo is apparently not intelligent enough to do so. Indeed, its defensive reactions are so arbitrary that it might roll itself up to defend against a curious puppy or ferociously attack a groundcar.

COMMENTARY

The phenomenal stupidity of the greater armadillo is what can make it a dangerous creature. It is best approached with caution.

The greater armadillo is edentate.

POWERS

Enhanced Senses (Improved Smell), Immunity to Poisons.

WEAKNESSES

Reduced Senses (Vision).

>>>>>(Phenomenal stupidity might be the understatement of the year. I seen one of these things walk right into the wheel of a parked car. Boink! So it backs up and does it again. Then it backs up once more—third time's the charm, right?—and walks into the wheel again. Stupid ain't the word.)<<<<<
   —Sami (16:30:23/3-10-51)

>>>>>(What happened then?)<<<<<
   —Rogue (18:01:55/3-10-51)

>>>>>(It got mad and shredded the wheel. It was my fragging car, so I blew its head off. Hollowed the little pecker out and dried the hide. Makes a great salad bowl.)<<<<<
   —Sami (18:03:01/3-10-51)

>>>>>(Remind me never to accept a dinner invitation from you, girl.)<<<<<
   — Slag (18:10:43/3-10-51)

>>>>>(You wish.)<<<<<
   —Sami (20:37:28/3-10-51)

>>>>>(Hey, you guys, get a room, why don'cha?)<<<<<
   —Bob (20:39:29/3-10-51)

>>>>>(Up yours.)<<<<<
   — Slag (20:47:15/3-10-51)

>>>>>(Up yours.)<<<<<
   —Sami (20:47:16/3-10-51)

GAME INFORMATION

	B	Q	S	C	I	W	E	R	Attacks
Greater Armadillo	4/2	3 x 3	3	—	1/3	2	6	4	2M2, −1 Reach

     Powers: Enhanced Senses (Improved Smell), Immunity to Poisons
     Weaknesses: Reduced Senses (Vision)

GREATER ARMADILLO
   Dasypus major

HABITAT
   Desert areas

RANGE
   Southern regions of North America

RANGE

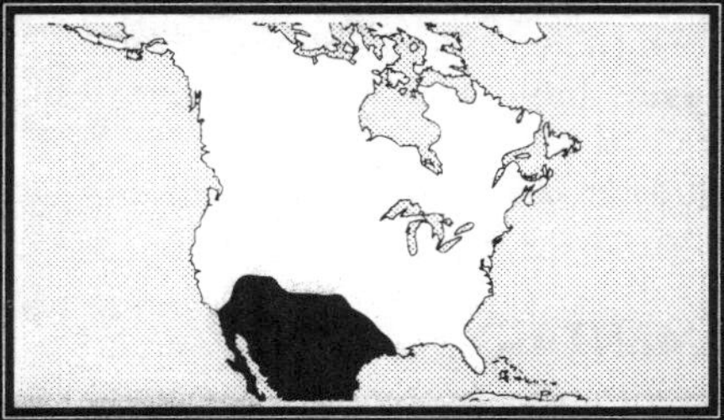

SIZE COMPARISON

GREATER UNICORN
Unicornus magnus

IDENTIFICATION

The greater unicorn is a larger, less delicate-looking unicorn, with a thick, flowing mane of coarse hair. Its typical color is honey-brown, and its hooves are tinged pink. Its eyes are larger than the unicorn's, and have a golden cast. Its single spiral horn is shorter and stronger-looking. The greater unicorn can achieve a height of 1.7 meters or more at the shoulder.

MAGIC CAPABILITY

Innate.

HABITS

The greater unicorn is a diurnal herbivore. Unlike the unicorn, it congregates only with its own kind. The animal favors a small, tightly knit family group, though such groups occasionally combine to form herds of up to 30 individuals.

The greater unicorn's response to intruders in its territory is unpredictable. Various reports indicate that it is as likely to attack without provocation, to flee, or to approach with curiosity. In combat, the greater unicorn is a formidable opponent, attacking with its hooves as well as its horn.

Many shamans consider this creature's horn ideal as a fetish or spell focus for dealing with poisons, pathogens, and/or detection/avoidance of same. This is, presumably, the reason that unscrupulous individuals have hunted down greater unicorns, cutting off the horns and leaving the bodies to rot.

COMMENTARY

Like the unicorn, the greater unicorn seems to be an Awakened creature derived from the common horse. Unsubstantiated theories link the greater unicorn's origin to the wild Przewalski horse (*Equus przewalski*), though the evidence strongly shows that both *U. magnus* and *U. validus* arose form the domestic horse, *E. caballus*.

Claims that greater unicorns can communicate telepathically with one another have yet to be proven.

The greater unicorn does not share the unicorn's sensitivity to pollutants.

POWERS

Empathy, Enhanced Physical Attributes (Quickness), Immunity to Pathogens, Immunity to Poisons, Magical Resistance, Search.

WEAKNESSES

None.

>>>>>(There used to be a large herd of greater unicorns on Blackcombe Mountain, north of Vancouver. They lived in the meadows that were the beginner ski runs before the place went Chapter eleven. I camped up there for a couple of months, just to get away from the world for a while. It was a few years ago, so who knows if they're still there.)<<<<<
—Hans (21:42:40/3-9-51)

>>>>>(I know. They're gone. The whole herd, every one of them was killed by talis-poachers. The land is poorer for their passing.)<<<<<
—Takae (13:59:44/3-14-51)

>>>>>(The guide says something about empathy. Anyone out there got more on that?)<<<<<
—Mac (04:47:18/3-21-51)

>>>>>(Sometimes, when I was near the unicorns, I felt something it's hard to describe. A kind of innocent peace. They trusted me. I knew that. I could feel it, and something more…Once some security people came up the mountain. I didn't see them, but then suddenly I felt threatened. I hid until I knew they were gone, knew it the same way I knew they had come. I'm not saying for sure that the greater unicorns warned me. You be the judge.)<<<<<
—Hans (09:15:35/3-21-51)

GAME INFORMATION

	B	Q	S	C	I	W	E	R	Attacks
Greater Unicorn	8	4 x 5	8	4	3/4	4	(6)	5	7M3, +1 Reach

Powers: Empathy, Enhanced Physical Attributes (Quickness), Immunity to Pathogens, Immunity to Poisons, Magical Resistance, Search

GREATER UNICORN
Unicornus magnus

HABITAT
Mountains and alpine meadows

RANGE
Throughout the world

RANGE

SIZE COMPARISON

GREATER WOLVERINE
Gulo impii

IDENTIFICATION

The greater wolverine is an Awakened version of the common wolverine (*Gulo luscus*). It grows to a height of 0.9 meter at the shoulder and can achieve a total length of 2.2 meters, while maintaining roughly the proportions of its progenitor species. Its fur is shaggy, light brown to almost yellow on its back, turning to a dark brown on its belly. Its claws are wickedly curved, and its teeth are like razors.

MAGIC CAPABILITY

Parabiological.

HABITS

The greater wolverine, like its progenitor, is an aggressive carnivore. It uses its surprising speed and ferocity to chase down and kill prey ranging from rabbits to small bears. Whether hungry or not, the greater wolverine will attack any creature that enters its hunting area. When finished feeding, or if it has made a kill it has no desire to eat, it despoils the remains by urinating on them.

There are exceptionally strong rivalries between individuals, whether male or female. Even when the female is in estrus, a male and female encountering one another are as likely to fight as they are to mate. (From an ecological point of view, this has the advantage of controlling the population of what might otherwise be a destabilizing influence on the local ecosystem.)

COMMENTARY

The greater wolverine has an acute sense of smell, though its eyesight is weak.

There are some reports that the greater wolverine carries a dangerous viral infection, though it is not known whether this is endemic to the population or occurs in only isolated instances.

POWERS

Enhanced Physical Attributes (Quickness, once per day, for (Essence)D6 turns), Enhanced Reactions, Enhanced Senses (Improved Smell).

WEAKNESSES

Reduced Senses (Vision).

>>>>>(These things are the size of fragging lions.)<<<<<
    —Ross (17:10:38/1-17-51)

>>>>>(You got it.)<<<<<
    —Iceman (02:27:16/1-18-51)

>>>>>(Any way of getting them to stay away?)<<<<<
    —Ross (22:12:54/1-18-51)

>>>>>(Yeah. It's gross, but it works. Find a wolverine kill, one that's been despoiled. Then rub the stuff all over you and your gear. It smells real drekky, but it definitely repels a wolverine. If you're real tough, go catch yourself a wolverine and ring out its bladder.)<<<<<
    —Chiller (09:53:41/1-19-51)

>>>>>(Chiller, wish I'd had your advice several years ago. I'm now the proud owner of a cyberarm and two cyberlegs. All thanks to a fragging greater wolverine.)<<<<<
    —Iceman (17:31:26/1-19-51)

GAME INFORMATION

	B	Q	S	C	I	W	E	R	Attacks
Greater Wolverine	7	4 x 5	4	—	2/4	2	6	5	5S2

Powers: Enhanced Physical Attributes (Quickness, once per day for (Essence) D6 turns), Enhanced Reactions, Enhanced Senses (Improved Smell)

Weaknesses: Reduced Senses (Vision)

Note: There is a chance that any given greater wolverine is infected with a virus that has a speed of 24 hours and damage of 3S3. Roll 2D6; a result of 12 means the creature is infected. Anytime a character is bitten by an infected wolverine, roll 2D6. On a result of 9, the character will contract the disease. (Note that infected wolverines are generally immune to the virus, merely acting as carriers.) After the incubation period, the victim suffers fever and breaks out in bright red blotches until the damage is reduced to Light.

GREATER WOLVERINE
Gulo impii

HABITAT
Woods, preferably at an altitude exceeding 1,000 meters

RANGE
Northern North America; also reported in mountainous regions of eastern UCAS

RANGE

SIZE COMPARISON

GYRE
Cathartes repartus

IDENTIFICATION

The gyre is an Awakened species derived from the turkey buzzard (*Cathartes aura*). Somewhat larger than its progenitor species, the gyre reaches a length of 1.4 meters and a wingspan of 4.0 meters. It is a dark brown color dorsally, shading to lighter brown on the pinions, turning off-white beneath. Its head and feet are pale pink. Its large eyes are red.

MAGIC CAPABILITY

Innate.

HABITS

Usually seen circling in the updrafts over the northern hills of California Free State and in the Rocky Mountain region, the gyre rarely touches ground except to feed. Its normal diet is carrion, though it will also attack weak or injured animals. Upon locating a suitable feed, the gyre emits loud cries to call others of its kind to the feast.

Gyres operate in loosely knit flocks of four to eight individuals. When scouting for food, a single flock may spread out over ten or more square kilometers. When food is located, however, the flock gathers together to share it. No rivalries or challenges between flocks have ever been reported. This may indicate an instinctive prohibition against one gyre flock entering the territory of another.

A gyre is capable of climbing to great altitudes (altitudes up to 4,600 meters have been reported). With its exceptionally acute eyesight, a gyre is able to spot prey at great distances.

COMMENTARY

Like vultures and other condors, the gyre usually attacks prey that is already near death. It seems to sense when a prey creature is weakening, and moves ever closer with the approach of death. Perhaps this is why the gyre can instill a feeling of hopelessness at the sight of its approach.

The creature is very sensitive to pollutants. This sensitivity, along with the fact that the first colonies of the species appeared in California Free State, led some early paranaturalists to assume that the gyre's progenitor species was the California condor (*Gymnogyps californianus*). This theory could only have been based on wishful thinking rather than solid scientific evidence, for the last California condor died in captivity in 2009.

POWERS

Enhanced Senses (Improved Eyesight), Immunity to Pathogens, Immunity to Poisons, Influence (Hopelessness).

WEAKNESSES

Allergy (Pollution, Severe).

>>>>>(I hate these buggers. They know you're wounded and out of water. They know you're going to weaken, and when you do, you're theirs.)<<<<<
    —Frostfire(11:39:07/3-26-51)

>>>>>(That's sensationalistic drek.)<<<<<
    —Delbert (11:42:30/3-26-51)

>>>>>(No, it's not. Try wandering around in the badlands with no water and a couple of Uzi rounds in your leg, and see those things watching you with their red eyes. Then tell me its drek.)<<<<<
    —Frostfire(11:43:52/3-26-51)

>>>>>(They don't attack you until you're almost dead, though, do they? I mean, if you keep moving, they'll leave you alone.)<<<<<
    —Suki (17:26:20/3-26-51)

>>>>>(They don't attack you until they think you're almost dead. There might be some difference of opinion on that point.)<<<<<
    —Frostfire (17:31:00/3-26-51)

>>>>>(Frostfire, did they attack you?)<<<<<
    —Gaston (16:43:50/3-27-51)

>>>>>(No, they didn't. I wanted so bad to just give up and lay down, but something kept me pushing on. Finally, my buddies found me. But just before the copter arrived, one of those things was so close I could have reached out and touched it. Another few minutes and they'd have started to feed, whether I was dead or not.)<<<<<
    —Frostfire (16:59:16/3-27-51)

>>>>>(Gruesome.)<<<<<
    —Suki (17:25:28/3-27-51)

GAME INFORMATION

	B	Q	S	C	I	W	E	R	Attacks
Gyre	4	4 x 5	4	—	2/5	3	(6)	4	3S3

Powers: Enhanced Senses (Improved Eyesight), Immunity to Pathogens, Immunity to Poisons, Influence (Hopelessness)
Weaknesses: Allergy (Pollution, Severe)

GYRE
Cathartes repartus

HABITAT
Deserts, arid hill country, and mountains

RANGE
Southwestern regions of North America (predominantly California Free State)

RANGE

SIZE COMPARISON

HELL HOUND
Canis tartari

IDENTIFICATION

The hell hound is a coal-black dog with red-rimmed, glaring eyes. It stands up to 0.9 meter high at the shoulder, and can weigh more than 80 kilograms. It is fast and powerful, with an impressive set of enlarged teeth.

MAGIC CAPABILITY

Innate.

HABITS

The hell hound is an efficient predator, preferring to hunt in packs of up to a dozen individuals. Though it is a rare sight, more than one pack occasionally cooperates in a hunt. Hell hound packs will chase and pull down deer and wild sheep, with reports of large or multiple packs attacking animals as large as bear.

Individual hell hounds will also feed on rabbits or squirrels that they can catch.

Pack behavior is well-coordinated. During a hunt, one portion of the pack often operates to flush the prey toward where the rest of the pack waits in ambush. The animals' barking and howling seems to strike fear into their prey, and they use this to good effect.

Though the hell hound is a good hunter, it is not above scavenging. A pack of hell hounds sometimes chases a larger predator away from its kill.

Hell hounds recognize the folly of taking on creatures that are too tough for them. Hell hound attacks against humans and metahumans are rare.

COMMENTARY

Hell hounds have excellent low-light

vision. This vision is not fully thermographic, however; the animal requires at least the equivalent of starlight to be able to see in the dark.

There are recurring reports that hell hounds show some innate resistance to fire and that they are able to breathe fire. No captive hell hounds have exhibited these abilities, but photographic records do exist of wild hell hounds burning down thickets where their prey had run to hide.

POWERS

Enhanced Senses (Improved Hearing and Smell, Low-Light Vision). Flame Projection, Immunity to Fire.

WEAKNESSES

None.

>>>>>(I've never heard of a confirmed case of a hell hound attack on humans. I think these things are like wolves: they've just got a bad rep.)<<<<<
— Phantom (9:18:51/1-27-51)

>>>>>(I'll buy that. I've even heard stories about them protecting people from other nasties in the woods.)<<<<<
— Sabre (18:00:11/1-28-51)

>>>>>(Don't count on it, bucko. Remember that you get wild rumors on both sides of things. You've got to treat them all with suspicion until there's proof.)<<<<<
— Ogre (18:19:00/1-28-51)

>>>>>(I've heard that some corps are using hell hounds as guard dogs. Anyone check me on that?)<<<<<
— Mandala (09:06:08/2-1-51)

>>>>>(Check. I've seen 'em. You know that MTC depot north of the plex where they mothballed those old panzers? It's guarded by hell hounds.)<<<<<
— Scarecrow (19:14:03/2-1-51)

>>>>>(So you can train them.)<<<<<
— Tracy (10:08:46/2-2-51)

>>>>>(Trained hell hounds are the ideal guard animal. They're dual, so you can get them to hit the spell worms coming in astrally, and they can fry the samurai coming in over the fence. Several mercenary outfits I've worked with use them to patrol supply dumps. One merc Captain I knew had two as personal pets and bodyguards. They were exceptionally well-trained and totally loyal to him. He sometimes used them as trackers.)<<<<<
— Mars (16:10:57/2-2-51)

GAME INFORMATION

	B	Q	S	C	I	W	E	R	Attacks
Hell Hound	4	4 x 4	5	—	3/4	3	(6)	6	6M2

Powers: Enhanced Senses (Improved Hearing and Smell, Low-Light Vision), Flame Projection, Immunity to Fire

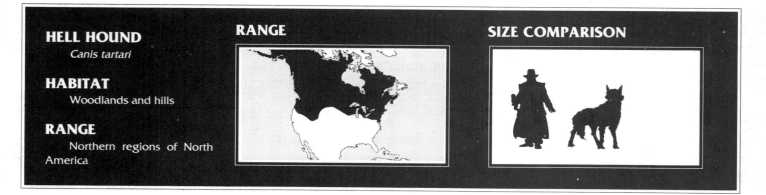

HELL HOUND
  Canis tartari

HABITAT
  Woodlands and hills

RANGE
  Northern regions of North America

RANGE

SIZE COMPARISON

HELLBENDER
Cryptobranchus pollutus

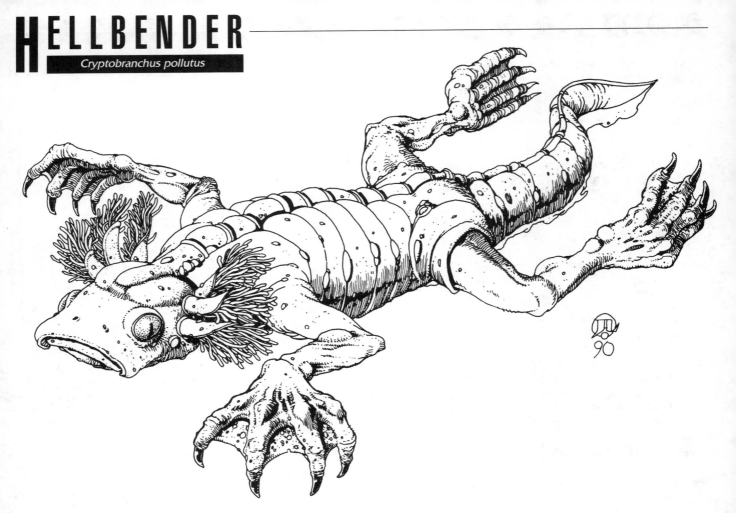

IDENTIFICATION

The hellbender is a large aquatic salamander growing to a length of 1.2 meters. It has a thick body and tail, and a rounded head with feathery external gills. Its legs are small, almost vestigial. It is predominantly light gray. The hellbender is very slow on land, but surprisingly fast in the water, where it uses its broad tail to assist with propulsion.

MAGIC CAPABILITY

Parabiological.

HABITS

The hellbender feeds on fish and small water birds. It secretes a neurotoxin that has a numbing and paralyzing effect. The hellbender's bite, or even contact with its skin, can result in temporary paralysis.

The hellbender is efficient at using this neurotoxin. It will remain motionless, either on the river bottom or floating just below the surface, until its chosen prey approaches. Then, with darting speed, it lunges for its prey with its snout, or lashes out with its tail. The intent is not to catch the prey in its mouth, but merely to make

contact. The hellbender simply waits for the paralyzing toxin to take effect (a matter of seconds for smaller creatures) and then feeds at its leisure.

The female hellbender lays her eggs in a sticky mass that adheres to water grass or weeds near the shore. One egg mass can produce several hundred immature hellbenders. On hatching, the young are about a centimeter long. They secrete the paralysis toxin immediately, but in such small concentrations that many dozens of bites or contacts would be necessary to affect a human-size creature. The newly hatched hellbenders are ravenously hungry, and will attack anything in sight, including each other. This post-hatch feeding frenzy is so intense that infant mortality among hellbenders exceeds 90 percent.

COMMENTARY

Hellbenders depend on a sensitivity to pressure changes in the water to detect the approach of their prey. So poor is their eyesight that the creature can be considered, for all intents and purposes, blind.

Prior to the Awakening, the hellbender (*Cryptobranchus alleghaniensis*)

was a species of salamander found in the Mississippi and Ohio River systems. The creature was small, no more than 0.1 to 0.2 meter long, and considered repulsive in appearance. Pollution in its river habitations brought the hellbender close to extinction. In 2012, however, the entire species appears to have undergone an Awakening, a metamorphosis that permitted the hellbender to thrive in its polluted habitat. The change was so radical that most scientists were in agreement that a new species had arisen. Thus does the current hellbender have the name *C. pollutus*.

The hellbender is immune to most toxins, and is totally unaffected by the high pollution levels in many rivers. Indeed, it seems to prefer rivers with high levels of dioxins and PCBs, and actively shuns unpolluted fresh water.

POWERS

Enhanced Senses (Motion Detection), Immunity to Poisons, Paralyzing Touch.

WEAKNESSES

Allergy (Unpolluted Water, Mild), Reduced Senses (Vision).

>>>>>(I don't think hellbenders care what they attack. Fish, bird, you, me, boat, hovercraft...it doesn't matter. If it gets paralyzed, they try to eat it, if it doesn't, oh well...Dumb as a bag of hammers.)<<<<<
     —Travis (10:40:16/2-9-51)

>>>>>(Maybe, but don't underestimate them. I lost a buddy to a hellbender. My pal was swimming, the thing got him, and he drowned before I could help.)<<<<<
     —Rusty (07:28:36/2-13-51)

>>>>>(Same thing almost happened to me, chummer. I got dragged out before I could drown, but drek, it's scary when you can't move. It was a real effort of will even to breathe, and I thought for sure I was about to cash it in. That's something I'll never forget. Sure, there's always the chance you might get geeked on a run, but I'd never been in a situation where I couldn't react, no matter how desperate that play might have been. But lying there, not being able to feel my body, and trying my hardest just to keep breathing, I realized that the shadows on the wall might be the last things I'd ever see...and suddenly it wasn't a game anymore.)<<<<<
     —Price (17:48:40/2-13-51)

>>>>>(Feet of clay, Pricey, hmmm?)<<<<<
     —Rat (20:54:19/2-14-51)

>>>>>(I hope you have a debilitating brain aneurysm, you freak.)<<<<<
     —Price (21:07:49/2-14-51)

>>>>>(The point is, don't underestimate these things, even the little ones. You fall into one of their hatching frenzies and you'll get your ticket punched just as quick as by a full-grown hellbender. Maybe quicker.)<<<<<
     —Candice (08:40:01/2-15-51)

GAME INFORMATION

	B	Q	S	C	I	W	E	R	Attacks
Hellbender	3	3 x 2	3	—	1/3	2	6	4	6L2

Powers: Enhanced Senses (Motion Detection), Immunity to Poisons, Paralyzing Touch
Weaknesses: Allergy (Unpolluted Water, Mild), Reduced Senses (Vision)
Note: Swimming multiplier is 5.

HELLBENDER
Cryptobranchus pollutus

HABITAT
Freshwater rivers

RANGE
Midwestern regions of North America, primarily the Mississippi and Ohio River Valleys

RANGE

SIZE COMPARISON

HOOP SNAKE
Natrix circumflexis

IDENTIFICATION

Also called the *amphisbaena*, the hoop snake is a short (1.6 meters) but powerful serpent with a unique manner of locomotion. It catches its tail in its mouth, forming a hoop, and rolls rapidly downhill. (Though this is normally an escape mechanism, it can also serve as a form of attack. Hoop snakes are heavy enough to put a nasty dent in a car or break bones with their impact). The hoop snake ranges in color from blue-green to brown. Its jaws are powerful, and its bite is venomous.

MAGIC CAPABILITY

Parabiological.

HABITS

The hoop snake feeds on mice, squirrels, and other small mammals. It swallows its prey whole, its jaws unhinging to allow the snake to engulf victims up to the size of a small rabbit. Unlike many other snakes, the hoop snake is a ground-dweller that never takes to the trees.

The hoop snake's rolling behavior is usually reserved as an escape mechanism. If threatened by a larger creature, the snake will attempt to roll away. Should the threatening creature be downhill of the hoop snake, however, the serpent sometimes directs its roll so as to strike the other creature. Hoop snakes can weigh up to 23 kilograms, and can pick up considerable speed on a steep slope. The impact from a rolling hoop snake can be formidable.

The hoop snake's physiology has adapted to support this behavior. The snake has a round, bullet-shaped head, and is considerably thicker and more muscular than most other serpents. It has protruding ridges of bone over its eyes, and its scales are less flexible and rougher than other species. When the snake moves normally, the rougher scales scrape against one another with a sound similar to that of two hands rubbing together. In quiet conditions, this sound is audible up to 10 meters away.

COMMENTARY

Genetic typing indicates that the hoop snake's progenitor species is the common grass snake (*Natrix natrix*); this has not been confirmed, however.

Greek myths tell of the *amphisbaena*, a two-headed snake that would clasp its two mouths together to form a ring. The second head is typical of the kind of exaggeration found in myths. It is interesting to consider whether the ancient Greeks were reporting actual sightings of a creature similar to the hoop snake, however.

POWERS

Venom.

WEAKNESSES

None.

>>>>>(So ancient Greece had hoop snakes, huh? I'm not sure I buy that.)<<<<<
—Candice (11:20:17/2-16-51)

>>>>>(Even stranger is that early American folklore is full of tall tales about these rascals.)<<<<<
—Jazzman (11:27:23/2-16-51)

>>>>>(Don't worry your head about it. The only thing that matters is that we've got hoop snakes.)<<<<<
—Brad (11:35:10/2-24-51)

>>>>>(Don't believe it that hoop snakes roll just to escape or attack. I think they do it for fun. And they understand about roads.)<<<<<
—Derek (21:24:18/2-24-51)

>>>>>(What do you mean, Derek?)<<<<<
—Candice (10:25:38/2-25-51)

>>>>>(I was in Cal Free State, driving up to Kitts Peak, the old observatory. I turn a corner, and there's four hoop snakes just booting it down the road right at me. I cut hard, almost went into a ditch, but I missed them by a hair. One of them took off my wing mirror, though. At the speed they were going, if I'd hit one head-on, it would have done some real damage.
  When I got to the observatory, the guy I was to meet told me it's common for hoop snakes to do that. Takes them a couple of days to climb the hill, then they boot it down the road again. Don't tell me that's an escape mechanism. These things are playing. Snake games.)<<<<<
—Derek (12:17:27/2-25-51)

GAME INFORMATION

	B	Q	S	C	I	W	E	R	Attacks
Hoop Snake	3	3 x 4	4	—	2/3	3	6	4	6L1, −1 Reach

Powers: Venom

Note: Rolling multiplier is 5.

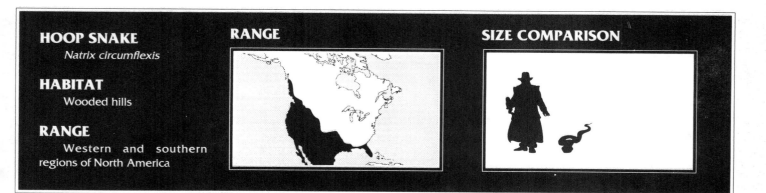

HOOP SNAKE
Natrix circumflexis

HABITAT
Wooded hills

RANGE
Western and southern regions of North America

RANGE

SIZE COMPARISON

ICEDRAKE
Draco algoris articus

IDENTIFICATION

The icedrake is a lizard that reaches a length of up to 1.5 meters. It resembles a western dragon, but has no wings. It usually moves on all fours, but can also rear up onto its hind legs, balancing with its tail. Its white skin is thick but supple. Its small eyes are red and malevolent-looking.

Despite its dragon-like appearance and probable relationship to the firedrake, the icedrake cannot breathe flame.

MAGIC CAPABILITY

Innate.

HABITS

The icedrake is a carnivore, and an even more aggressive hunter than the firedrake. It feeds on mountain sheep and goats, as well as small creatures that it can dig out of their burrows. Icedrakes hunt in family-based packs of up to six individuals. There is little organized cooperation, however, and the creatures often fight over prey. Icedrake packs are led by a dominant male; challenges from younger males are usually to the death.

With their thick skin as protection, icedrakes are fearless enough to attack much larger creatures. Another of the icedrake's defense mechanisms is its ability to emanate an aura of extreme cold around itself. This cold is intense enough to inflict damage on creatures foolish enough to get close to the icedrake.

Icedrakes have acute vision, but their other senses are weak. They move with exceptional speed.

COMMENTARY

As with the firedrake, there is much controversy over the icedrake's derivation. The same dissident faction that decided on the taxonomy for the firedrake assigned the icedrake to genus *Draco*, despite evidence to the contrary. It seems obvious to this cataloguer that the icedrake, like the firedrake, is an Awakened version of a mundane reptile, probably exactly the same species. The fact that no progenitor species has yet been identified merely shows that inadequate effort and resources have been applied to the project.

Also, gene typing has identified a close relationship between the firedrake and the icedrake. Both creatures apparently arose from the same progenitor species or from a species closely related to them.

POWERS

Cold Aura, Enhanced Senses (Improved Vision), Immunity to Cold.

WEAKNESSES

Allergy (Fire, Mild).

>>>>>(Doc, are you still out there? The points you were just making about the firedrake, are they the same for this critter?)<<<<<
    —N.F.A. (13:08:25/2-3-51)

>>>>>(Yeah, same kind of thing. Paterson's right, there's a kinship between the two drakes. That's obvious from enzyme assays. You don't even need to go as far as a gene map. The two species are closely linked in some way. That's rare for Awakened creatures, you realize. Look at the greater armadillo and the juggernaut. Both Awakened from the common armadillo (from the same species, that's the point), but the two resulting species are noticeably different on the enzymatic and genetic level. Much more different than the two drakes.)<<<<<
    —Doc (13:10:48/2-3-51)

>>>>>(Who cares?)<<<<<
    —Scragger (13:17:02/2-3-51)

>>>>>(You should. The Awakening is what made our world what it is today. Don't we need to know as much as possible about both?)<<<<<
    —Doc (13:18:20/2-3-51)

GAME INFORMATION

	B	Q	S	C	I	W	E	R	Attacks
Icedrake	4	4 × 4	4	—	2/3	3	(6)	5	3M2

Powers: Cold Aura, Enhanced Senses (Improved Vision), Immunity to Cold
Weaknesses: Allergy (Fire, Mild)

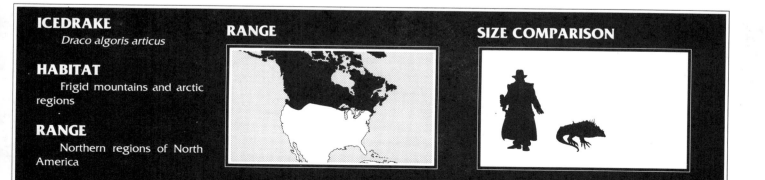

ICEDRAKE
    Draco algoris articus

HABITAT
    Frigid mountains and arctic regions

RANGE
    Northern regions of North America

RANGE

SIZE COMPARISON

INCUBUS

Incubus praetexti

IDENTIFICATION

The incubus resembles a large, land-dwelling octopus. Its soft body grows up to 1.0 meter long, and the span of its tentacles (tip to tip, diametrically) can exceed 3.2 meters. Its skin is usually dark purple, shading to a light, purplish-white on the underside. When being cautious, the creature changes to light gray speckled with black; when enraged or hunting, it becomes bright red.

The incubus's tentacles have suckers. Near the tip of each tentacle is a sharp, horny process that can cause severe tearing wounds.

The incubus's eyes are larger (proportionately) than the octopus's, and look disturbingly human. On the creature's ventral side, set among the tentacle roots, is a large, powerful beak (again, similar to the octopus's).

MAGIC CAPABILITY

Innate.

HABITS

The incubus is a skilled urban predator that hunts any city-dwelling creature, including humans and metahumans. Because it can only move slowly, the incubus uses a minor form of telepathy and illusion to attract prey within the range of its powerful tentacles.

Once a victim has wandered into range, the incubus reads its mind to discover details of the prey's innermost desires. It then projects an illusion that perfectly matches those desires directly into the victim's mind. Because the incubus remains in continuous contact with its victim's mind, it can tailor the illusion's "reactions" to match the victim's expectations. Thus, a human might "see" and be able to converse with his or her "dream-lover." The incubus can "target" only one victim at a time, though anyone else within range will be aware of the illusion.

If a creature other than the victim is within range, this second creature will also see the illusion, but the details will be flawed and inconsistent. The victim, however, sees only the most perfectly tailored image until the incubus decides to drop the illusion.

The incubus is nocturnal and has excellent low-light vision. Sunlight seems to harm the creature.

In sewers or other sunless environments, the incubus is active around the clock. Its preferred manner of hunting is to "stake out" a generally deserted area and wait for prospective prey to wander by. The incubus then uses its telepathic projection power to lure its prey close enough to the hiding place so it can attack and kill the prey. The incubus's body has no rigid members and is capable of great compression. Thus can it squeeze through a hole as small as 50 centimeters in diameter.

COMMENTARY

The name "incubus" derives from myths about devils that take male form to entice female victims; the female version is the succubus. No evidence supports the postulate that these myths are proof that an incubus-type existed in an earlier Time.

POWERS

Desire Reflection, Enhanced Senses (Low-Light Vision), Illusion.

WEAKNESSES

Allergy (Sunlight, Severe).

>>>>>(I geeked me an incubus last night down by the docks.)<<<<<
　　—Billy (15:11:28/1-8-51)

>>>>>(Like drek you did, Billy-Boy. Here's the scoop, chummer. Billy-boy had point while I followed along one of those service roads near the loading cranes. He spots something and signals, so I do the quick fade, thinking I'll either hear Bill's signal or the sounds of him taking something on. I wait a few seconds, then poke my head out. And there's Billy-boy swaggering up to a blonde wearing only a negligee and a dog collar. And Billy's carrying on a conversation, but I can only hear his voice. The girl isn't saying word one, but Billy's talking like she's answering him back.)<<<<<
　　—Blackadder (15:11:59/1-8-51)

>>>>>(Well, I thought she was a streetwalker.)<<<<<
　　—Billy (15:15:17/1-8-51)

>>>>>(On a deserted stretch of docks at three in the morning? Well, anyway, I've got an idea what's going down, so I put a couple of rounds into Billy's lady-love, and that kind of distracts the thing from its illusion. Now Billy's real mad, screaming a blue streak until he sees, kind of out the corner of his eye, just what he's been chatting with. So he yells even louder, pulls out his heat and empties the clip into the thing almost without realizing what he's doing. So, maybe you did geek it, Billy, but I wouldn't be too proud of it.)<<<<<
　　—Blackadder (15:16:02/1-8-51)

>>>>>(What happens if you've got cybereyes or you're wearing smart goggles? Can you see through the illusion?)<<<<<
　　—Oscar (20:27:05/1-8-51)

>>>>>(No. Seeing is a function of the brain, not the eyes, and that's where the incubus gets to you. Your cybereye might be feeding you an image of an octopus, but your brain sees the blonde in a negligee. Now about that dog collar, Billy...)<<<<<
　　—Doc (03:55:27/1-9-51)

>>>>>(The Doc's right, but there's another twist. If you're viewing the incubus by remote, like on-screen, maybe, and you're out of its range, you'll see it right. Or if you vid it, then watch the tape.)<<<<<
　　—Straight Gain (10:30:09/1-9-51)

GAME INFORMATION

	B	Q	S	C	I	W	E	R	Attacks
Incubus	6	2 x 2	9	3	3/5	4	(6)	4	5S2, +1 Reach

　　Powers: Desire Reflection, Enhanced Senses (Low-Light Vision), Illusion
　　Weaknesses: Allergy (Sunlight, Severe)
　　Note: The Incubus's Desire Reflection power always works in conjunction with the Illusion power. The victim is under the effect of the Desire Reflection, and any companions are subject to the Illusion. Note that the Incubus has 10 dice for its Success Test against the victim, but only 6 dice for convincing the victim's companions that the illusion is real.

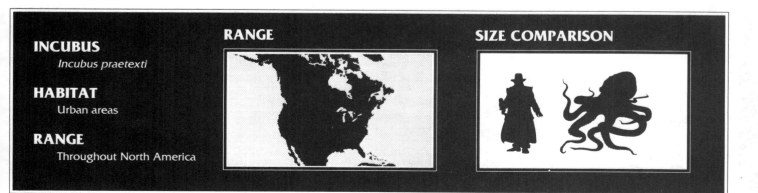

INCUBUS
　　Incubus praetexti

HABITAT
　　Urban areas

RANGE
　　Throughout North America

RANGE

SIZE COMPARISON

JUGGERNAUT
Dasypus praegrandis

IDENTIFICATION

Another Awakened creature that arose from the common armadillo (*D. novemcinctus*), the juggernaut has the same jointed armor of bony plates and the same poor eyesight. The juggernaut, however, reaches lengths of 14 meters or more.

Like the armadillo, the juggernaut has no teeth; unlike the armadillo, the juggernaut has sharp serrated ridges of bone in both upper and lower jaw. The creature's feet are clawed.

MAGIC CAPABILITY

Parabiological.

HABITS

The juggernaut is an omnivore in the truest sense of the word. Its chemical economy can absorb and extract nutrients from everything, be it plant, animal, rocks, or even scrap metal. It does seem to prefer live prey, however. This variable chemical economy allows the juggernaut to respire anaerobically for hours. When its metabolism has switched over to anaerobic, it needs no air. (Though it cannot swim, a juggernaut can hunt fish in a lake by walking around on the lake bed.) When operating aerobically, however, the creature is considerably faster (reflecting the greater chemical efficiency of aerobic respiration).

To compensate for its weak eyesight, the juggernaut has enhanced hearing and smell, and motion detection (apparently based on detection of electrical fields). Juggernauts do not have thermographic vision. On the other side, they show a very small IR signature, and thus are difficult to detect using thermos. (This is an apparent consequence of the insulating nature of the juggernaut's hide plates, though how the excess heat is dissipated remains a mystery).

Juggernauts are aggressive hunters. They are also solitary creatures. Unless one is male and the other a female in estrus, an encounter between two juggernauts almost inevitably leads to a fight to the death of one or both.

COMMENTARY

A juggernaut will cut a swath through a region, eating and destroying everything in its path. They are the ultimate killing machine, and conversely, exceedingly

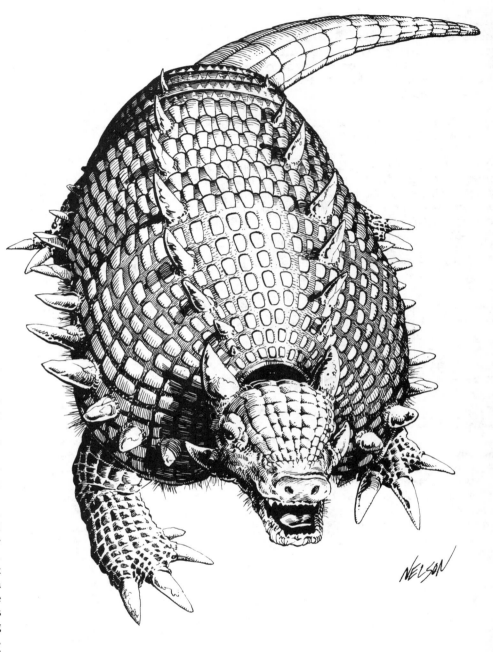

NELSON

hard to kill. Most governments offer a significant bounty for the destruction of a juggernaut. (It is perhaps instructive that very few juggernaut bounties have ever been paid out.)

POWERS

Enhanced Physical Attributes (Quickness, once per day, for (Essence x 2)D6 turns), Enhanced Senses (Improved Hearing and Smell, Motion Detection), Fear, Immunity to Cold, Immunity to Fire, Immunity to Pathogens, Immunity to Poisons.

WEAKNESSES

None.

>>>>>(How the slotting hell do you kill one of these things?)<<<<<
—Greyhawk (16:01:18/2-23-51)

>>>>>(Panzer with an assault cannon. Say it with sabots.)<<<<<
—Mad Merc (16:43:27/2-23-51)

>>>>>(I'm not kidding. There's no easy way to take these guys down?)<<<<<
—Greyhawk (16:47:34/2-23-51)

>>>>>(If you're thinking of going for one of those bounties, I'd advise against it. The bounty's a good purse, but you'll spend most of it getting yourself put back together again—if you make it back at all.)<<<<<
—Casper (18:04:57/2-23-51)

>>>>>(No, Greyhawk, there's no easy way. You just got to pound on it till it croaks. If you can face up to it without running.)<<<<<
—Eagle (04:05:59/2-24-51)

>>>>>(I've thought about that. Does this bleeder really cause fear, or is that just the only logical reaction?)<<<<<
—Neddy (08:07:32/2-24-51)

>>>>>(Hey, Greyhawk. If you're serious about going after a jugger, I can kluge together something that might save your butt. For a price, of course. The guide says they do their motion detection trick by detecting electrical fields. I can whip you up a random field generator, an electrical analog of white noise, and it should throw the big bleeder for a serious loop. Of course, it might only make it mad.)<<<<<
—Straight Gain (18:27:08/2-24-51)

>>>>>(I agree with Cap the Knife, Greyhawk. I've seen one of these things from the air. It must have been a baby, no more than eight or nine meters. The thing was chewing on a Harley. There wasn't anything I could do for the biker, or what little was left of her, so I dropped a rack of AV cluster bombs on the jugger. I think that hurt it, but it sure didn't kill it. And AV clusters are designed to shred panzers. Still want to take on the bounty, Greyhawk?)<<<<<
—Candice (23:12:01/2-24-51)

GAME INFORMATION

	B	Q	S	C	I	W	E	R	Attacks
Juggernaut	15/4	4 x 3	42	–	1/3	9	7	4	9D3

Powers: Enhanced Physical Attributes (Quickness, once per day, for (Essence x 2)D6 turns), Enhanced Senses (Improved Hearing and Smell, Motion Detection), Fear, Immunity to Cold, Immunity to Fire, Immunity to Pathogens, Immunity to Poisons

JUGGERNAUT
Dasypus praegrandis

HABITAT
Any

RANGE
Southern regions of North America, slowly spreading north

RANGE

SIZE COMPARISON

LAMBTON LIZARD
Salamandra lambtoni

IDENTIFICATION

The lambton lizard is an Awakened salamander that can grow to a length of 6.25 meters. It is covered with plates of dermal bone that overlap to form natural armor. Its legs are short, keeping its movement slow on land. In the water, however, the lizard is fast for its size.

The lambton lizard's mouth is surrounded by barbels like those of a catfish. These are sensory organs, but they also secrete a substance that causes temporary paralysis.

The lambton lizard is dull gray, shading to a dull white ventrally. Its small eyes are black.

MAGIC CAPABILITY

Parabiological.

HABITS

The lambton lizard is a carnivore. It normally feeds on large fish, but will also eat animals or birds that come within range. The creature has been known to stray a kilometer or more from water to hunt, but only if the water lacks suitable prey.

The touch of a single barbel is enough to induce temporary, local paralysis. Multiple touches can cause respiratory arrest and death. In addition, the creature can spray the paralyzing substance from ducts near its mouth. This attack form is usable only when the creature's head is above water.

Lambton lizards are solitary creatures, no doubt because of the large amounts they must eat. Few areas have sufficiently abundant prey to support more than one lizard.

COMMENTARY

Certain paranaturalists speculate that creatures similar to the lambton lizard existed in medieval times, and served as the model for the period's many legends of monstrous lizards and serpents. They point to the creature's paralyzing spray as a possible analog to the poison breath often attributed to the big lizards of legend.

POWERS

Paralyzing Touch.

WEAKNESSES

None.

>>>>>(Hey, Clifton, you out there? Where does the name come from, buddy?)<<<<<
—Thud (17:42:56/1-7-51)

>>>>>(It's named after a famous paranaturalist, Ward Lambton. He was the first person to study the thing, and the first to be geeked by one.)<<<<<
—Clifton (16:30:43/1-8-51)

>>>>>(What's it like when they spray venom? A jet, a glob, what?)<<<<<
—Hellcat (10:38:33/2-1-51)

>>>>>(More like a mist of fine particles in suspension.)<<<<<
—Tank (15:46:39/2-1-51)

>>>>>(Do you have to inhale the stuff?)<<<<<
— Hellcat(13:37:48/2-2-51)

>>>>>(No such luck. It absorbs through the skin, through clothes, and even through some plastics. Your best bet is full chem-bio gear: chemsuit, bottled air, the whole shot. And wash yourself down before you take the suit off. The stuff remains active for hours. If there's any on the outside of the suit and you touch it while you're stripping off, it's just as bad as a direct hit.)<<<<<
—Tank (13:44:27/2-2-51)

GAME INFORMATION

	B	Q	S	C	I	W	E	R	Attacks
Lambton Lizard	7/2	4 x 2	5	—	1/4	3	5	3	3S3, +1 Reach

Powers: Paralyzing Touch
Note: Swimming multiplier is 4.

This paralyzing spray has the same effects as a touch from the creature's barbels, with a maximum range of 3 meters. Use the creature's Reaction Rating as its Combat Skill, and treat anything within range as Short Range. A successful hit means that the victim suffers the effect of the creature's Paralyzing Touch. The creature's ducts contain enough substance to attack four times, after which it needs one hour to replenish the ducts.

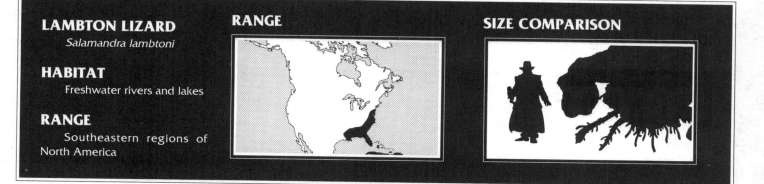

LAMBTON LIZARD
Salamandra lambtoni

HABITAT
Freshwater rivers and lakes

RANGE
Southeastern regions of North America

RANGE

SIZE COMPARISON

IDENTIFICATION

The lesser roc is a large, migratory seabird similar in appearance to the albatross (*D. exulans*, its progenitor species), achieving a wingspan of more than 6.0 meters and a body length of 2.0 meters. Its plumage is mainly white, with black head coloration and black along the leading and trailing margins of its wings. Its beak is sharp and hooked. Instead of the albatross's webbed feet, the lesser roc has the grasping talons of a bird of prey.

MAGIC CAPABILITY

Parabiological.

HABITS

The lesser roc is a carnivore, living on smaller birds that it seizes on the wing and on fish that it catches by diving. It is also a scavenger, eating any carrion or waste. Despite its size, the lesser roc is fast and agile. Particularly in a dive, it is fast enough to overtake and catch almost any other seabird.

Lesser rocs are migratory, traveling up and down a coastline for thousands of kilometers. They fly at great altitude, gliding above weather systems, and can remain airborne almost indefinitely (assuming, of course, that they can catch airborne prey).

They nest in guano-encrusted colonies on sheer oceanside cliffs. Such a colony may be home to as many as 100 rocs.

Lesser rocs can be aggressive when scavenging. There are reports of them swooping down on ocean fishing vessels, trying to scare the crew away from particularly tasty morsels.

COMMENTARY

Lesser rocs have such acute eyesight that they can see well in conditions of almost no light. They have an unerring ability to find their home colonies. (Some researchers speculate that this is a magical ability, while others believe it is the result of attunement to the earth's magnetic field.) Lesser rocs are immune to poisons.

POWERS

Enhanced Senses (Improved Vision, Low-Light Vision), Immunity to Pathogens, Immunity to Poisons.

WEAKNESSES

None.

>>>>>(Hey, I'm one of the guys who reported being attacked by lesser rocs while I was trying to throw garbage over the side of the boat. Let me tell you, those things are big, loud, and scary when they swoop down on you.)<<<<<
— Naf (19:47:28/1-2-51)

>>>>>(These things will eat anything. I knew a guy, a real twisted drekhead, who used to throw lighted firecrackers into the air when he saw lesser rocs nearby. The rocs'd pick them off and swallow them, and then go boom. Sick.)<<<<<
—Greyhawk (19:49:03/1-2-51)

>>>>>(Something else. Don't go near their nesting colonies. They'll scrag you before you can even blink.)<<<<<
—Naf (19:52:29/1-2-51)

>>>>>(Just be glad we don't have the greater roc in our neck of the woods. I seen vids of greater rocs killing and eating elephants!)<<<<<
—Zapper Weisman (23:56:45/1-3-51)

>>>>>(Do not kill the lesser roc. Like the albatross, they are birds of good omen, and killing one will bring ill luck down upon you.)<<<<<
—Cat Dancing (20:52:57/1-14-51)

>>>>>(Oh, drek. If you're a shaman, you think everything's good omen or bad omen. They're just big fragging birds.)<<<<<
—Tango (21:00:42/1-14-51)

GAME INFORMATION

	B	Q	S	C	I	W	E	R	Attacks
Lesser Roc	4	5 x 4	4	—	2/4	2	6	4	3M2

Powers: Enhanced Senses (Improved Vision, Low-Light Vision), Immunity to Pathogens, Immunity to Poisons

LESSER ROC

Diamedia roc

HABITAT

Oceans and shoreline cliffs

RANGE

Coastlines of North America

RANGE

SIZE COMPARISON

LESSER THUNDERBIRD
Avesfulmen minori

D.K.

IDENTIFICATION

The lesser thunderbird resembles a red-brown eagle. It has a wingspan of up to 3.0 meters, a large, hooked beak, and pronounced talons. The creature's large eyes are bright gold in color.

MAGIC CAPABILITY

Innate.

HABITS

Like its cousin, the common thunderbird (*A. splendidus*), the lesser thunderbird is usually active during the day. Its large eyes also endow it with excellent low-light vision, so it is equally capable of nocturnal activity. Lesser thunderbirds hunt small ground animals such as young antelope and deer, and are efficient fishers. They will scavenge carrion when available. They nest in sheltered spots near mountain peaks and may travel hundreds of kilometers from their nests in search of prey.

The lesser thunderbird relishes storm activity, particularly electrical storms. When such storms play around the mountaintops, lesser thunderbirds can be seen flying in and out of the cloud cover, enjoying the static-charged air. It seems unlikely that the lesser thunderbird can somehow summon these storms, as has been claimed by some researchers.

Like *A. splendidus*, the lesser thunderbird can project an electrical field. This field is of shorter duration than the field effect of *splendidus*, and resembles an electromagnetic pulse (EMP) rather than a lightning strike. This EMP seems to have little effect on living creatures, but has devastating consequences for intricate electronics.

COMMENTARY

The origin of the lesser thunderbird's EMP power is unknown. From an evolutionary standpoint, it is inexplicable because it is not a useful defense against potential predators, unless those predators are dependent on electronics (i. e., humans and metahumans). One unproven yet plausible theory is that the EMP is intended to "scramble" the direction sense of creatures that use magnetic effects for homing and location. (Homing pigeons and many other creatures are presumed to use this effect.) The EMP would, theoretically, disorient such creatures so severely that they would be prevented from escaping the lesser thunderbird.

It seems likely that at least some of the lesser thunderbird's body mass is made up of electrical cells like those found in the electric eel (*Electrophorus electricus*). This has not been proven, however, because of the lesser thunderbird's disconcerting tendency to blow up when it dies. (Presumably, at the moment of death, the electrically active tissues discharge simultaneously, blowing the creature apart.)

Respected biologist Juli Francis attempted to circumvent this problem through vivisection. Unfortunately, she must have touched some highly charged tissue with her scalpel during the procedure. The massive discharge killed her instantly and destroyed the specimen.

POWERS

Electrical Projection (EMP), Enhanced Senses (Low-Light Vision), Weather Control (Electrical Storms).

WEAKNESSES

None.

>>>>>(Watch out for these things. They're real nasty when riled.)<<<<<
—Nuke (10:20:44/1-14-51)

>>>>>(Why? That EMP drek can't hurt me. All my chips are optical.)<<<<<
—Slag (19:18:38/1-14-51)

>>>>>(Your chips might be safe, but does any of your cyberware have electronics, Slag? Eyes that use electrons for imaging, maybe? Or how about wired reflexes or a smartgun link? Are you sure all your cyberware is fully optical?)<<<<<
—Nuke (08:47:57/1-15-51)

>>>>>(You mean this thing can crash my head?)<<<<<
—Deckhead (10:27:39/1-15-51)

>>>>>(You got it, chummer, especially if you got the cheap stuff. A lot of interfaces still use electrons and copper wire rather than light photons and optical cable.)<<<<<
—Nuke (14:28:39/1-15-51)

>>>>>(If a bunch of these things got together and pulsed at once, I wonder if they'd reinforce each other or cancel each other out? I guess it depends on the phase and cycle. Anybody out there ever seen it happen?)<<<<<
—Straight Gain (10:29:14/1-28-51)

>>>>>(Yeah, I think so. I saw a small flock of thunderbirds blow a bald eagle out of the sky. There were four of them, and they surrounded the eagle, sort of like formation flying. Then the eagle just kind of convulsed, and dropped like a stone. What do you figure? When a bunch of these things pulse at once, maybe the EMP's powerful enough to mess up neural currents?)<<<<<
—Holly (13:07:08/1-28-51)

>>>>>(I don't know. And I don't really want to get close enough to find out. I value my headware.)<<<<<
—Straight Gain (13:46:43/1-28-51)

GAME INFORMATION

	B	Q	S	C	I	W	E	R	Attacks
Lesser Thunderbird	3	6 x 2	3	—	2/5	3	(6)	6	6L2

Powers: Electrical Projection (EMP), Enhanced Senses (Low-Light Vision), Weather Control (Electrical Storms)

Note: Flying multiplier is 4.

The thunderbird's EMP will affect any cheap electronic equipment (page 100 of the **Street Samurai Catalog**) within 5 meters of the creature. The rating of the EMP attack is the creature's Essence. The Target Number to affect a piece of equipment is 10. If the equipment is Hardened (as in the case of a cyberdeck), add the level of Hardening to the Target Number. (Thus, the Target Number to crash a Fuchi Cyber-6 is 16.)

If the thunderbird achieves 1, 2, or 3 successes against the item, the piece of equipment is inoperative or unstable for 2D6 turns. If the thunderbird wins 4 or more successes, physical damage has resulted. The nature of this damage is up to the gamemaster. A decker using a cyberdeck that is affected by the EMP is immediately dumped.

Note that the EMP ability can affect cyberware. Make only one EMP roll for the wearer. If any successes result, roll randomly for which piece of cyberware is damaged.

The lesser thunderbird can generate as many pulses per day as it has points of Essence.

At the moment of death, the lesser thunderbird's body explodes, inflicting an attack of 3L3 on anyone within 3 meters.

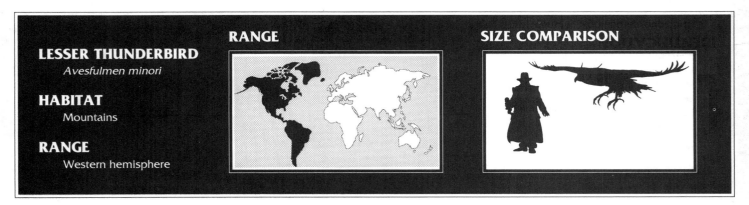

LESSER THUNDERBIRD
Avesfulmen minori

HABITAT
Mountains

RANGE
Western hemisphere

RANGE

SIZE COMPARISON

LEVIATHAN
Grampus immanis

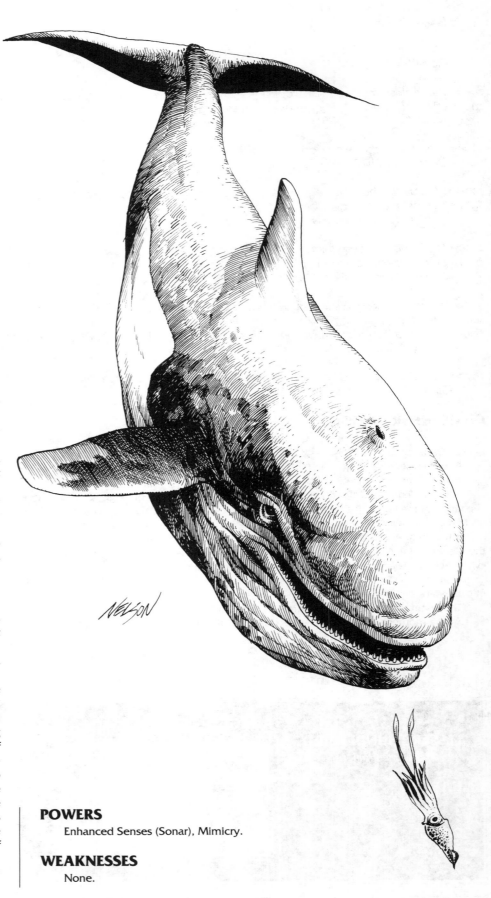

IDENTIFICATION

The leviathan is a large, carnivorous whale that regularly achieves a length of 19.0 meters, with exceptional specimens exceeding lengths of 22.0 meters also on record. The leviathan resembles the killer whale (*Grampus orca*, its progenitor species), but has a broader, flatter body. Like all marine mammals, its tail is oriented horizontally. The leviathan's color is light gray, with amorphous dark patches and markings down its flanks. (These markings change over time, and so cannot be used to identify individuals.)

MAGIC CAPABILITY

Parabiological.

HABITS

The leviathan is an aggressive predator that feeds on smaller whales (even killer whales), walruses, seals, and so on. It can remain underwater for as long as an hour without needing to come up for air, and is reputed to dive as deep as 2,000 fathoms (3.7 kilometers). The leviathan frequently hunts beneath the arctic ice cap.

Leviathans have the ability to mimic the calls of other whales, both to attract prey and to discourage attackers. Leviathans have only three natural enemies: krakens, megalodons, and humans.

Leviathans congregate in pods of up to eight individuals. Multiple pods sometimes hunt cooperatively.

COMMENTARY

Debate continues over the leviathan's level of intelligence. Some argue that because it has one of the largest brain masses on the planet, it must have a correspondingly high level of intelligence. This camp also points to evidence of the leviathan's well-developed playfulness. Because leviathans have been observed in activities such as balancing floating logs on their backs or draping fronds of seaweed over their heads, some researchers have generalized this to intelligence. (They conveniently ignore the fact that several non-Awakened whale species engage in similar behavior.) This cataloguer has yet to see conclusive evidence of intelligence among any of the cetaceans.

POWERS

Enhanced Senses (Sonar), Mimicry.

WEAKNESSES

None.

>>>>>(I've heard stories of leviathans saving shipwrecked sailors and all that drek. Doesn't that imply some intelligence?)<<<<<
—Tapley (10:56:37/1-17-51)

>>>>>(And I've heard stories about them eating scuba divers.)<<<<<
—Sato (16:36:59/1-17-51)

>>>>>(They overturn small boats. I don't know if they mean to, but it's still not a good habit.)<<<<<
—Trudy (09:37:00/1-18-51)

>>>>>(The guide doesn't say it, but I think they might be migratory. I've seen leviathans as far south as Cannon Beach in Tir Tairngire, but only in the fall.)<<<<<
—Sato (13:15:48/1-18-51)

>>>>>(Hey, Sato, I've been thinking about your diver story. Remember what these things eat? Now, doesn't a guy in a black wetsuit look a lot like a nice, shiny, succulent seal?)<<<<<
—Alexander (20:03:49/1-20-51)

>>>>>(Makes sense, maybe.)<<<<<
—Sato (23:11:04/1-20-51)

GAME INFORMATION

	B	Q	S	C	I	W	E	R	Attacks
Leviathan	11/2	5 x 3	10	—	2/4	3	6	5	9D3

Powers: Enhanced Senses (Sonar), Mimicry

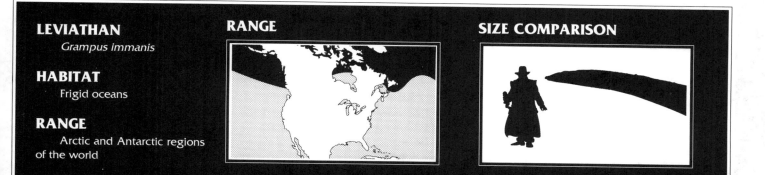

LEVIATHAN
Grampus immanis

HABITAT
Frigid oceans

RANGE
Arctic and Antarctic regions of the world

RANGE

SIZE COMPARISON

LOUP-GAROU
No accepted taxonomy

IDENTIFICATION

The loup-garou looks human, but like one whose form is twisted and contorted in horrible pain. Short, gray-black fur covers the creature's body. Because its lips are drawn back from the teeth and the gums have receded, the loup-garou's teeth resemble fangs, while its bloodshot eyes seem to express either severe pain or malice.

A loup-garou would stand 1.7 meters high (on average), but its twisted posture makes it appear shorter. A loup-garou can move bipedally, but seems to prefer travel on all-fours.

MAGIC CAPABILITY

Parabiological.

HABITS

The loup-garou is an urban predator, feeding on rats and other city-dwelling animals. They will also hunt humans and metahumans, but only the weak, injured, or infirm. If threatened or attacked, the loup-garou defends itself ferociously.

Loup-garous are nocturnal, and sunlight seems to cause them intense pain. In sunless environments, they may be active at any time. Loup-garous have a malign cunning, and are capable of planning effective ambushes and even setting simple traps. Loup-garous are solitary hunters.

The activity of the loup-garou is keyed to a 28-day cycle. (This cycle is not, as sometimes proposed, linked to the lunar cycle, and the cycles of different individuals are rarely aligned.) For most of the cycle, the creature is cunning and aggressive, but intelligent enough to recognize when a foe is too powerful to challenge.

During the four-to-six-day peak of the cycle, however, the loup-garou becomes a ravening monster, attacking and killing anything that moves, whether it needs to feed or not. During this peak, the loup-garou is considerably stronger (mainly because the normal subconscious instincts against self-inflicted damage are overcome), and almost totally immune to pain.

COMMENTARY

Though classified as an independent species by some taxonomists, the loup-garou is not one. These individuals are human, but have been afflicted with a viral infection. (The exact nature of the

virus has yet to be determined, but virological studies seem to indicate a retrovirus similar to HMHVV, possibly the same one that infects the bandersnatch). Loup-garous do not breed true (indeed, do not breed at all), and so cannot be classed as a species.

The trauma of infection seems to destroy the higher cerebral functions of the victim. Loup-garous possess no abstract reasoning power and display no language use. No treatment or vaccine exists to combat the virus they suffer, and

so no cure. (Even if there were, physiological and neurological damage done by the virus appears to be irreversible.)

POWERS

Enhanced Physical Attributes (Strength, once per day, for (Essence)D6 turns), Enhanced Senses (Thermographic Vision).

WEAKNESSES

Allergy (Sunlight, Severe), Allergy (Aconite or Horseradish, Severe).

>>>>>(These things really sound like old-time werewolves, don't they?)<<<<<
  —Casper (15:36:33/3-5-51)

>>>>>(I met a loup-garou last night. It spoke to me.)<<<<<
  —Cindy (07:37:08/3-7-51)

>>>>>(What? Where?)<<<<<
  —Dyson (07:37:40/3-7-51)

>>>>>(In the service tunnels near the Aztechnology compound. Something rushed me from the shadows, and I thought it was attacking. Just as I was about to shoot, it stopped. Just stood there, kind of shifting from foot to foot, snarling. I could see that part of it wanted to attack me, but part of it didn't. Then it spoke to me. "Help me," it said. "For god's sake, help me." Then its control broke and it leaped at me. It was horrible. The best I could do was to kill it painlessly. I still feel like drek.)<<<<<
  —Cindy (07:38:10/3-7-51)

>>>>>(Did you touch it?)<<<<<
  —Dyson (07:42:32/3-7-51)

>>>>>(I rolled it over after it was dead. Dyson, you're not saying what I think you're saying?)<<<<<
  —Cindy (07:43:01/3-7-51)

>>>>>(Cindy. Get to a doctor. Now. Get a broad-spectrum anti-viral.)<<<<<
  —Dyson (07:44:38/3-7-51)

>>>>>(Will that help?)<<<<<
  —Cindy (07:46:09/3-7-51)

>>>>>(Dyson, is that going to help?)<<<<<
  —Cindy (08:48:48/3-7-51)

>>>>>(DYSON!)<<<<<
  —Cindy (09:51:13/3-7-51)

GAME INFORMATION

	B	Q	S	C	I	W	E	R	Attacks
Loup-Garou	4(6)	4 x 4	7(9)	—	3/4	4	5	4(6)	3M2(6M2)

Powers: Enhanced Physical Attributes (Strength once per day, for (Essence)D6 turns), Enhanced Senses (Thermographic Vision)
Weaknesses: Allergy (Sunlight, Severe), Allergy (Aconite or Horseradish, Severe).
Note: Statistics in parenthesis refer to the creature at peak power.

LOUP-GAROU
  No accepted taxonomy

HABITAT
  Urban areas

RANGE
  Throughout the world

RANGE

SIZE COMPARISON

MAN-OF-THE-WOODS

Anima praestantiae

IDENTIFICATION

The "man-of-the-woods" is not an animal but a rare form of forest spirit. When it manifests, it usually appears as a slender human (male or female), usually clad in the garments of a tribal shaman and carrying many shamanic accouterments. Other reports include manifestations as deep patches of shadow in the forest, motile trees, talking woodland animals, and so on. When assensed astrally, the man-of-the-woods appears as a flickering, shimmering humanoid form.

MAGIC CAPABILITY

Innate.

HABITS

Men-of-the-woods are said to be protectors of the forest. More free-willed than the usual nature spirits, they can wander out of their territory, but they rarely do so voluntarily because their powers are keyed to the forest terrain. They are highly intelligent, but their thought-patterns and motives are completely alien (indeed, incomprehensible) to humans.

It is rumored that sufficiently powerful shamans can summon and control a man-of-the-woods. Conflicting accounts state that shamans cannot summon one, but must strike a bargain for its services. These transactions normally entail some form of payment, reputedly a piece of one's soul or a part of one's "past self." Such claims have never been authenticated, however.

COMMENTARY

The man-of-the-woods is analogous to the "manitou" of Algonquin legends. Debate continues on the significance of this similarity.

POWERS

Accident, Alienation, Concealment, Confusion, Fear, Magical Guard, Manifestation, Movement.

WEAKNESSES

None.

>>>>>(I once met a shaman who said he'd conjured one of these things. Called himself Man-of-Many-Names. I think he was Wolf Totem.)<<<<<
—Peterbilt (12:27:06/1-26-51)

>>>>>(Many-Names? Think I know him, too. Young guy with snow-white hair? Doesn't boast, but all the more impressive for that?)<<<<<
—Fran (14:35:25/1-26-51)

>>>>>(That's him. Told me his hair turned white the day he conjured a man-of-the-woods.)<<<<<
—Peterbilt (10:36:45/1-27-51)

>>>>>(Yeah, sure. Anyone can say anything. I can say I conjured a water elemental the size of Lake Union.)<<<<<
—Rhiannan (11:19:46/1-27-51)

>>>>>(I know he summoned one of those spirit things. Saw it with my own eyes.)<<<<<
—Hangfire (20:33:55/1-29-51)

>>>>>(Details?)<<<<<
—Rhiannan (20:34:17/1-29-51)

>>>>>(I used to be a company man. Private expediter for a guy called Teague in one of MTC's subsidiaries. Teague had some kind of action going on the side, but I didn't know it at the time. All I knew was that Teague was trying to squeeze this street-shaman guy, Many-Names, but Many-Names wasn't being squeezed. I was passing Teague's door, and I heard the two of them one day. Death threats from Teague, and Many-Names just tells him quietly to reconsider before it's too late. (He had bone-white hair, all right, and was dressed like a shaman, but everything's real top-drawer stuff. I bet those moccasins were ostrich and made by Gucci.) Anyhow, after the shaman guy leaves, Teague orders me to put a contract out on Many-Names. Well, the hit fell through, and I never saw the hatchet-man again.
Next day, all hell breaks loose. Something busts its way into the compound and comes crashing into the building, looking for Teague. It's this little guy dressed like a shaman, but you can see through him, sort of. And he's backed by something resembling a person made up of garbage. Slotting freaky. One of my sec-guards tries to cut them down with his Uzi, but it blows up in his face. I keep my heat in my holster and just watch.
The little transparent guy and the garbage monster bash into Teague's office. Teague's armed to the teeth, and he unloads all he's got into them, but it doesn't even faze them. Then the little guy says, "I come from Man-of-Many-Names." And that's when I take off, close my ears to Teague's screaming, and just run. I quit MTC, and decided to run the shadows. It's safer.)<<<<<
—Hangfire (20:34:58/1-29-51)

>>>>>(That garbage thing: a city spirit?)<<<<<
—Harvey (21:15:10/1-29-51)

>>>>>(Guess so.)<<<<<
—Peterbilt (21:17:02/1-20-51)

GAME INFORMATION

	B	Q	S	C	I	W	E	R	Attacks
Man-of-the Woods	10	6 x 2	7	5	5	5	5 A	10/15	4S2

Powers: Accident, Alienation, Concealment, Confusion, Fear, Magical Guard, Manifestation, Movement.
*Manifest/Astral Reactions

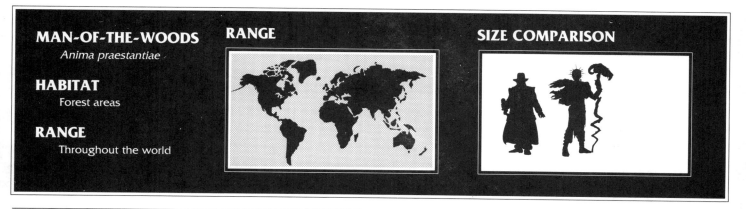

MAN-OF-THE-WOODS
Anima praestantiae

HABITAT
Forest areas

RANGE
Throughout the world

RANGE

SIZE COMPARISON

MARTICHORAS
Martichoras hastae

IDENTIFICATION

Growing to a length of 2.2 meters and to a height of 1.1 meters at the shoulder, the martichoras resembles a lion, but with longer fur. Its wide mouth has multiple rows of teeth, similar to a shark's. Growing from the tip of its tail is a bunch of spines, similar to a porcupine's. Its color is medium brown, with diffuse, darker patches on its flanks, presumed to be a minimal form of camouflage.

MAGIC CAPABILITY

Parabiological.

HABITS

The martichoras is an aggressive carnivore. It is a good climber who occasionally lurks in tree branches until its prey wanders by. It is fast enough to simply run down many forms of prey, however, and prefers this more direct method of hunting.

Martichoras form groups similar to lion prides, except that the group usually consists of one dominant female and up to four adult males. The female martichoras is insatiable for both sex and for prey, and the males spend most of their waking hours satisfying her appetites. Females do not hunt.

A hunting martichoras rarely uses its tail spines except in self-defense. The spines are barbed and venomous. Indeed, a martichoras will not eat a victim that it has slain with the spines. Though the venom does not harm the martichoras, perhaps it has the effect of spoiling the meat.

Though ferocious and merciless toward weaker creatures, a hunting martichoras often backs down from a creature near its own strength. A retreating martichoras will use its tail spines to cover its escape.

COMMENTARY

The martichoras is also referred to as a manticore, a mythical, spike-tailed creature.

The martichoras prefers an unspoiled and untainted environment. Typical pollutants seem to irritate the creature.

POWERS

Enhanced Senses (Low-Light Vision), Venom.

WEAKNESSES

Allergy (Pollution, Mild).

>>>>>(Stay away from these things. It can shoot its tail spines.)<<<<<
   —Suni (12:43:57/2-18-51)

>>>>>(No it can't. It does have some muscular control of the spines, like the porcupine, and can change their angle quite quickly. Maybe that gives the impression it's flipping them or throwing them.)<<<<<
   —Holmes (21:38:37/2-18-51)

>>>>>(The spines are bad news anyway, even if it can't throw them. You know they're barbed? That means it's a bitch to pull them out again. And if you don't, movement will make them burrow in further. Sometimes it takes surgery to remove the slotting things.)<<<<<
   —Shade (18:37:45/2-19-51)

>>>>>The Martichoras are fragging cowards. Just yell at them, and they'll run away.)<<<<<
   —Big Solly (16:37:12/2-29-51)

>>>>>(Don't bet on it.)<<<<<
   —Scalliwag (16:38:19/2-29-51)

>>>>>(Oh yeah? I yell at anything, it runs away.)<<<<<
   —Big Solly (16:40:22/2-29-51)

GAME INFORMATION

	B	Q	S	C	I	W	E	R	Attacks
Martichoras	8	6 x 4	8	—	3/4	3	6	6	7S2, +1 Reach

Powers: Enhanced Senses (Low-Light Vision), Venom
Weaknesses: Allergy (Pollution, Mild)

MARTICHORAS
   Martichoras hastae

HABITAT
   Forest areas

RANGE
   Central and northern regions
of North America

RANGE

SIZE COMPARISON

MEGALODON
Carcharodon neomegalodon

IDENTIFICATION

The megalodon is a huge pelagic shark, growing up to 16.0 meters long. Its dorsal side is slate-gray, shading to white ventrally. Its dorsal fin is highly prominent.

MAGIC CAPABILITY

Parabiological.

HABITS

The megalodon is a fearsome predator, even when compared to other sharks. It will attack anything that swims, from mackerel and tuna on up to blue whales. A pack of megalodons has even been observed harrying a pod of leviathans. Moreover, megalodons will eat almost anything else, including garbage, metal scraps, and so on. (License plates have been found in the stomachs of some shark species, while one megalodon specimen was discovered to have swallowed an entire motorcycle.)

Like many other sharks, megalodons are attracted by the scent of blood, which they can detect as far as several kilometers away. The blood scent will sometimes drive megalodons into a feeding frenzy, during which they will attack anything, including one another.

The megalodon usually hunts alone, but it is not unusual to see the creatures congregate into a pack of three to five individuals.

Megalodons are among those sharks that cannot pump water over their gills while stationary. Thus, they must move continuously or drown. They also have a slight negative buoyancy, which means they must keep swimming or else slowly sink to the bottom.

Megalodons prefer the pelagic depths, in excess of 400 fathoms (738 meters).

COMMENTARY

The name "megalodon" comes from a genera name for large pelagic sharks that became extinct several million years ago. Differences between the modern-day megalodon and fossil records of the earlier type indicate that the current species is an Awakened one. Genetic mapping indicates that the best candidate for the megalodon's progenitor is the great white shark (Carcharodon carcharias). Nevertheless, the strong similarities between this species' teeth and the fossilized teeth of the prehistoric megalodon have resulted in the species name of neomegalodon.

It is difficult to kill a shark, and even harder to kill a megalodon. The only chance is a direct hit to the very small brain or to the brain stem.

POWERS

Enhanced Senses (Improved Smell), Regeneration.

WEAKNESSES

None.

>>>>>(The megalodon may prefer the depths, but that does not mean it avoids coming to the surface. I've seen one chasing a marlin near the surface. And you hear stories of attacks on small boats.)<<<<<
　　—Lu (20:27:16/4-17-51)

>>>>>(These things eat motorcycles?)<<<<<
　　—Himem (13:26:46/4-21-51)

>>>>>(They're easy to kill, though. Stuff a depth charge or a few kilos of plastic explosive inside a dead tuna or something, and troll it at high speed behind your boat. When the shark hits it, boom!)<<<<<
　　—Mad Merc (14:38:30/4-21-51)

>>>>>(Doesn't sound like there's much sport in that.)<<<<<
　　—Naf (14:40:53/4-21-51)

>>>>>(Are you after sport or bounty money?)<<<<<
　　—Mad Merc (14:41:48/4-21-51)

GAME INFORMATION

	B	Q	S	C	I	W	E	R	Attacks
Megalodon	15/2	5 x 4	13	—	1/3	3	6	5	10D2

　　Powers: Enhanced Senses (Improved Smell), Regeneration

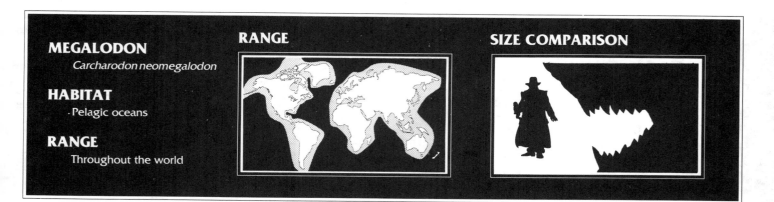

MEGALODON
　　Carcharodon neomegalodon

HABITAT
　　· Pelagic oceans

RANGE
　　Throughout the world

RANGE

SIZE COMPARISON

MERMAID
Merhomo illecebrae

IDENTIFICATION

This marine mammal has two humanoid arms. Its body resembles a sea lion's, but is slightly larger. Its color shades from black near the tail to pale pink around the upper torso and head. Its face resembles a foul-tempered sea lion's, but a shock of long dark hair on its head lends a vaguely human appearance from a distance. Both males and females have pronounced mammae. The mermaid's four fingers (no opposable thumb) have rending claws. It reaches a length of 2.1 meters, and can weigh as much as 350 kilograms.

MAGIC CAPABILITY

Parabiological.

HABITS

The mermaid is a fast-moving predator that normally feeds on fish and mollusks of the coastal waters. It catches and rends its prey using its strong hands.

Like merrows, to which these creatures are distantly related, mermaids congregate in polygamous family groups and associations. It swims with an undulating motion, achieving remarkably high speeds and using its limbs for fine directional control. Though it is a mammal, and thus an air-breather, the mermaid can remain underwater for up to an hour, even during extreme exertion.

Unlike the merrow, the mermaid is neither sentient nor even intelligent. It does exhibit a sly and malign instinctive cunning, however.

Mermaids frequent coastal fishing grounds, mainly because fish congregate there. These areas also offer the possibility of other prey. Mermaids have been known to attack swimmers, particularly fishboat crew who have fallen overboard. When a mermaid hunts mammals, it prefers to drown its prey by dragging it underwater rather than trying to kill it in mortal combat.

There are reports of mermaids frequenting dangerous shorelines, particularly during storms, when they may feed on swimmers trying to escape from foundering vessels.

COMMENTARY

Gene typing shows that the mermaid is an Awakened species derived from the California sea lion (*Zalophys californicus*), though the physiological changes are so profound as to warrant a new taxonomic classification.

The mermaid's metabolism seems to require fairly high levels of mercury. Unless the creature obtains trace levels of this metal in its diet, it weakens and dies within days.

POWERS

Enhanced Physical Attributes (Quickness, once per day, for (Essence x 2)D6 turns), Enhanced Senses (Improved Hearing).

WEAKNESSES

Dietary Requirement (Mercury).

>>>>>(A whole drek-load of these things lives in the Sargasso Sea, in and among the water weeds. I guess they're waiting for something to get caught in the weeds. I saw them there, couple of years back. Real nasty fraggers. Some guys told me you have to keep a lookout on deck at night in case one of these mermaids tries to climb on board for a midnight snack. I think I may have seen one in the Mississippi, too, which means they don't mind fresh water.)<<<<<
 —Macintosh (17:21:19/1-28-51)

>>>>>(Are the mercury levels in the Sargasso that high? I know that mermaids hang around near the outlets from mills and chemical plants, too. Guess they like the chemical waste and effluents. Yum.)<<<<<
 —Tarquin (23:10:08/1-30-51)

>>>>>(Something is strange here, though. How could this animal evolve into its present state? The existence of other paranormal animals could be the result of millions of years of evolution, with the animals adapting to the coming and going of magic. But mercury contamination is a recent phenomenon. There is no way a species could evolve so quickly to a point where the lack of that substance would kill it. So if it wasn't a typical evolutionary process that caused the development of the mermaid, what was it?)<<<<
 —Zapper Weisman (19:00:04/2-6-51)

>>>>> (Maybe they're like the hellbender. Pollution screwed up their Awakening so that they can't live without it?)<<<<<
 —Tarquin (19:48:01/2-6-51)

GAME INFORMATION

	B	Q	S	C	I	W	E	R	Attacks
Mermaid	4	6 x 4	6	—	2/4	3	6	4	4S4

 Powers: Enhanced Physical Attributes (Quickness, once per day, for (Essence x 2)D6 turns), Enhanced Senses (Improved Hearing)
 Weaknesses: Dietary Requirement (Mercury)

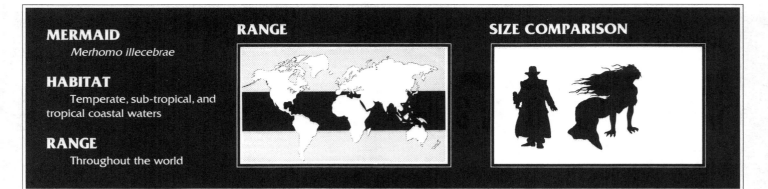

MERMAID
 Merhomo illecebrae

HABITAT
 Temperate, sub-tropical, and tropical coastal waters

RANGE
 Throughout the world

RANGE

SIZE COMPARISON

MIMIC SNAKE
Serpentes fistulae

IDENTIFICATION

The mimic snake grows as long as 4.0 meters. It is a large, powerful, boa-like snake with green and black markings that provide excellent camouflage in the woods. Like a boa constrictor, the mimic snake can unhinge its jaws in order to swallow large prey.

MAGIC CAPABILITY

Parabiological.

HABITS

The mimic snake is a carnivore that uses an innate mimicry ability to attract its prey. It is reputedly able to imitate the calls of many woodland animals, particularly the wild turkey, which makes up a major part of its diet. The snake can mimic the call of highly dangerous creatures also, presumably to scare off an attacker. Once the prey is within range, the mimic snake wraps itself around its victim and constricts until the creature suffocates. It can also inflict a damaging, but non-venomous, bite. Like other boas, it swallows its prey whole. Its rearward-pointing teeth prevent its prey's escape, should it still be alive.

Mimic snakes are terrestrial by preference, but they have been known to hide in trees and drop down onto their prey. They are usually diurnal, but are able to operate with full efficiency at night.

COMMENTARY

The mimic snake is sometimes called the whistling snake, and the Chippewa Indians know it as the turkey snake.

Indications are that the mimic snake is a species derived from the common boa constrictor (*Constrictor constrictor*). These progenitor creatures might have escaped (or been released) from zoos, experimental labs, or perhaps even pet shops.

POWERS

Enhanced Senses (Low-Light Vision), Mimicry.

WEAKNESSES

None.

>>>>>(I met this guy in a bar, and he told me about some old hermit who had a mimic snake as a pet. Said the snake would call prey to the old guy's trap line. Sounds like a load of drek to me.)<<<<<
—Crag (15:19:18/1-27-51)

>>>>>(Why? I got me a pet boa. Me and my snake, we get on just fine.)<<<<<
—Stig (17:28:12/1-27-51)

>>>>>(No wonder you're a loner, Stig.)<<<<<
—Carol (16:38:00/1-29-51)

>>>>>(I saw a mimic snake just south of Portland. Guess they're spreading. It was hanging from a branch, and we just kinda stared at each other for a bit. I don't know, but the feeling I got was that we were both just about as startled by the encounter. I don't think these things are dangerous to humans unless you do something to rile them up. Why should they be? We're just too big to eat.)<<<<<
—Sheldon (08:38:45/1-30-51)

GAME INFORMATION

	B	Q	S	C	I	W	E	R	Attacks
Mimic Snake	4	4 x 3	8	—	2/4	2	6	4	5M1

Powers: Enhanced Senses (Low-Light Vision), Mimicry

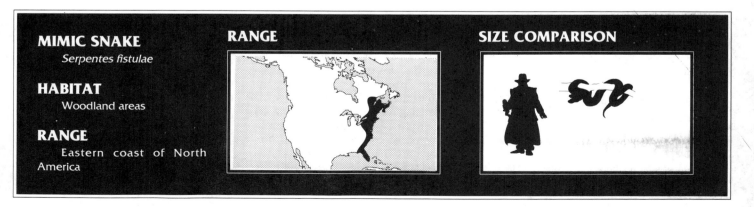

MIMIC SNAKE
Serpentes fistulae

HABITAT
Woodland areas

RANGE
Eastern coast of North America

RANGE

SIZE COMPARISON

MIST LYNX
Lynx caligae

IDENTIFICATION

The mist lynx is an Awakened species of wildcat derived from the Canada lynx (*Lynx canadensis*). It grows up to 1.4 meters long, with a hunched back and limbs proportionately longer than those of the non-Awakened species. The animal's tail is short and its ears tufted. Its fur is smoky gray, marked with white. Its eyes are a cold steel-gray.

MAGIC CAPABILITY

Innate.

HABITS

Like its progenitor, the mist lynx is a predator that feeds on small woodland mammals and birds. There are no confirmed reports of unprovoked attacks against humans or metahumans. Indeed, the mist lynx often appears to be fascinated by the actions of humans, often watching their behavior from a perch in some tree.

Mist lynxes live in small family groups, but are solitary hunters. Females are ferocious in defending their kits, even to the extent of sacrificing their own lives.

The mist lynx's name comes from its innate magical ability to transform its body into a mist, apparently by controlling the molecular cohesion of its cells. The animal uses this ability defensively to escape attack, though some observers have reported the mist lynx waiting in mist form for prey to approach.

Mist lynxes can be active at all hours.

COMMENTARY

At night and in its woodland terrain, a mist lynx in mist form is difficult to detect.

The creature shows no signs of intelligence.

POWERS

Enhanced Senses (Low-Light Vision), Mist Form.

WEAKNESSES

None.

>>>>>(This drekking guide isn't worth the RAM its stored in! No attacks on humans, like frag. I got bounced by a mist lynx on slotting Galiano Island. Like to ripped me apart before my back-up could get a clean shot into it. Bloody near cost me an arm.)<<<<<
 —Garth (15:58:40/3-15-51)

>>>>>(Brother Garth is correct. I lost a very close friend to the attentions of a mist lynx. Since that time, I have heard almost a score of other similar stories. If the mist lynx shows an interest in the activities of metahumanity, it is an extremely malign interest.)<<<<<
 —Lethe (16:03:12/3-15-51)

>>>>>(You ever seen these things at night? Like, they're weird, man. With those long legs, they look a lot like a man crawling on all fours. You see that and decide not to geek it until you can tell who it might be. And by the time you can see, the bleeder's close enough to pounce.)<<<<<
 —Blaster (10:04:21/3-17-51)

>>>>>(Mist form, huh? So if that thing wants you, it can get to you even if you're shut up inside a car or something.)<<<<<
 —Devon (08:17:03/3-24-51)

>>>>>(Never though of it like that. And drek, I don't like the idea much.)<<<<<
 —Garth (16:35:27/3-24-51)

GAME INFORMATION

	B	Q	S	C	I	W	E	R	Attacks
Mist Lynx	4	5 x 4	5	—	2/4	3	(6)	4	4S2

Powers: Enhanced Senses (Low-Light Vision), Mist Form

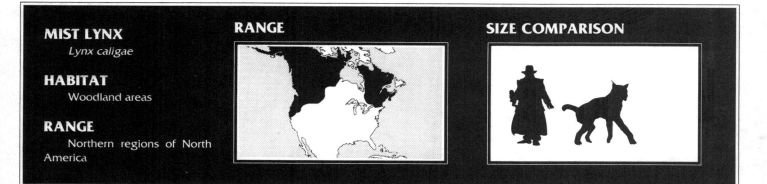

MIST LYNX
 Lynx caligae

HABITAT
 Woodland areas

RANGE
 Northern regions of North America

RANGE

SIZE COMPARISON

MUNCHKIN
Simiidiabolus hibernicus

IDENTIFICATION

The munchkin is a short, squat hominid, approximately 0.9 meter tall, covered in brown fur. Its limbs are powerful, and its jaws broad and full of a carnivore's teeth. Observers describe its expression as both intelligent and sinister. Its clawed fingers and toes are designed for rending. Munchkins are bipedal and can move rapidly through the trees via brachiation. Their tails are vestigial.

MAGIC CAPABILITY

Parabiological. (Unsubstantiated reports continue to assert the existence of magically active individuals.)

HABITS

Munchkins are fast-moving predators that normally feed on squirrels, owls, newborn deer, and the like. Though normally solitary creatures, groups of up to four individuals have also been reported.

Attempts to study munchkins in captivity have come to naught because the creatures either died or managed to escape.

Munchkins are reported to have a rudimentary language. So far, field studies have not discovered any language usage greater than that of chimps and other primates. The creatures use grunts and howls to express anger, enjoyment, or fear. Munchkins are tool-users, but again, in ways similar to chimps in the wild (e.g., stripping leaves from twigs to extract termites from a small hole in a tree).

There are reports of attacks by small groups of munchkins against both humans and metahumans.

COMMENTARY

Genetic analysis has shown a relationship between the munchkin and the spider monkey (genus *Ateles*), but the nature of the relationship is puzzling. Some portions of the munchkin's genetic code are identical to the spider monkey's, but these are interspersed with inserted segments ("introns") of totally alien content. No theories adequately explain this fascinating fact, and the creature's inability to live in captivity has seriously handicapped further research.

One researcher, Dr. Derek Maclean of Berkeley, California Free State, claims to have studied a group of munchkins in captivity, during which time they proved easily amenable to training. Dr. Maclean's general uncommunicativeness and his refusal to allow other researchers into his facilities tend to cast doubt on the credibility of his findings, however.

The name munchkin derives from a race of small humanoids described in children's fiction of the early 20th century.

POWERS

Enhanced Senses (Thermographic Vision).

WEAKNESSES

Dietary Requirement (Molybdenum).

>>>>>(The guide is wrong about the munchkin's language use. I know because I've been studying it. I have yet to understand it fully, except to know that it isn't just a simplistic expression of emotion. Brute-force mathematical analysis begins to show patterns in its morphology, syntax, and grammar. I'm almost certain that this language is a degraded form of another language, not something developed a priori. Unfortunately, it falls into no known linguistic group.)<<<<<
    —Marcus (16:34:14/1-21-51)

>>>>>(Language aside (and there is no evidence of it yet, as Marcus refuses to publish his data), the genetic studies are intriguing. If you take a look at the stretch between loci int_1 and tel_a, you'll see what I mean.)<<<<<
    —Doc (16:47:58/1-21-51/)

>>>>>(Are you saying the munchkin was engineered?)<<<<<
    —Sagan (16:51:22/1-21-51)

>>>>>(Don't really want to say. Contact me offline here. Give me your access code and I'll dump you my analysis.)<<<<<
    —Doc (16:53:46/1-21-51)

>>>>>(But if it was, then who engineered it?)<<<<<
    —Scott (16:56:55/1-21-51)

>>>>>(That would be the mystery, of course. The techniques needed are beyond the current abilities of anyone in the field.)<<<<<
    —Doc (16:57:39/1-21-51)

>>>>>(Except for maybe old wacko Maclean. He's cracked, but if there's a better chimeric gene-splicer alive, I don't know him.)<<<<<
    —Hal (17:03:25/1-21-51)

>>>>>(If these things are sentient, why isn't there some plan to protect them?)<<<<<
    —Suki (17:38:18/1-21-51)

>>>>>(Because they're mean, that's why, and they hide well. The only time you'll ever see them is when they want you to, and then it means that they're coming to rip you up. I know it's an unfashionable concept, but I think these things are actively evil.)<<<<<
    —Harry (17:39:16/1-21-51)

GAME INFORMATION

	B	Q	S	C	I	W	E	R	Attacks
Munchkin	3	4 x 4	6	—	4/5	5	5	5	3M2 or Humanoid

Powers: Enhanced Senses (Thermographic Vision)
Weaknesses: Dietary Requirement (Molybdenum)

MUNCHKIN
    Simiidiabolus hibernicus

HABITAT
    Woodland areas

RANGE
    Great Lakes region of North America, spreading westward

RANGE

SIZE COMPARISON

NEW BOAR
Sus singulàris

IDENTIFICATION

This paraspecies is a larger, more aggressive version of the wild boar (*Sus scrofa*) commonly hunted for sport. It has black or brown grizzled fur, with lighter brown hackles and sharp, upward-curving tusks. Its small trotters are black, with sharp, bony ridges along the front. The creature reaches a length of 1.7 meters and a height of 1.1 meters at the shoulder. A full-grown specimen can weigh well over 200 kilograms.

MAGIC CAPABILITY

Parabiological.

HABITS

The new boar is an omnivore. It spends most of its time digging up succulent roots and tubers, though it eats mice, rabbits, and other small animals when it can catch them. When these small prey hibernate in winter, the new boar digs them out of their burrows, perhaps detecting their hiding places by smell.

The new boar is so territorial that it will charge any creature, regardless of size, that enters its territory. A new boar will also attack and attempt to kill any other new boar that intrudes, except when a female in estrus enters the territory of a male. (Females, regardless of season, will attack one another on sight.) Unlike most other animals, the new boar will not give up the attack even when severely wounded, and will fight to the death.

For obvious reasons, new boars are solitary creatures.

COMMENTARY

The new boar is one of the most aggressive and one of the least intelligent of all Awakened species.

POWERS

Enhanced Physical Attributes (Strength, once per day, for (Essence x 3)D6 turns), Enhanced Senses (Improved Hearing and Smell).

WEAKNESSES

None.

>>>>>(Them's good eating.)<<<<<
   —Lurch (17:04:20/2-28-51)

>>>>>(Hey, a new marketing concept. New boars, fast food for trolls. Death on a bun.)<<<<<
   —Bung (17:06:02/2-28-51)

>>>>>(Very funny, shorty.)<<<<<
   —Lurch (17:07:28/2-28-40)

>>>>>(Where I grew up, we used to play a game of hiding in the trees till a new boar came along. Someone would have a garbage can or something, which he'd let drop as soon as the boar appeared. Seeing something moving, the boar would charge the can, dent the hell out of it, and send it flying. Of course, when the can hit, it was usually rolling, and so it kept on moving. Well, the boar just hit it again. And on and on until it was exhausted. Then maybe we'd spear it to take home for dinner.)<<<<<
   —Taylor (18:36:18/2-28-40)

>>>>>(And I thought I came from a tough neighborhood.)<<<<<
   —Suki (18:43:26/2-28-40)

>>>>>(These things sound like pigs from hell. I think I'm going to stay in the city, where it's nice and safe.)<<<<<
   —Gilley (18:44:03/2-28-40)

GAME INFORMATION

	B	Q	S	C	I	W	E	R	Attacks
New Boar	4	4 x 6	4	—	2/3	3	6	4	(Str)M2

Powers: Enhanced Physical Attributes (Strength, once per day, for (Essence x 3)D6 turns), Enhanced Senses (Improved Hearing and Smell).

NEW BOAR
   Sus singularis

HABITAT
   Woodlands and hills

RANGE
   Northwestern regions of North America

RANGE

SIZE COMPARISON

NEW LEATHERBACK
Dermochelys novalis

IDENTIFICATION

The new leatherback is a large sea turtle, growing to a length of 3.0 meters and achieving a mass of more than 540 kilograms. It is an Awakened version of the common leatherback turtle (Dermochelys coricea) and is the largest sea turtle in the world. Its back is covered with a flexible carapace composed of a mosaic of small bones embedded in a thick, leathery skin. The turtle has a sharp, bony "beak" similar to a snapping turtle's. Its body is muddy green, while its carapace is brown (the bones are a slightly lighter brown).

MAGIC CAPABILITY

Innate.

HABITS

The new leatherback is an aggressive predator, feeding on fish, small aquatic mammals, and other turtles. It is a rapid swimmer.

Like other sea turtles, the female returns to the same beach year after year to dig a nest in the sand, where she will lay her eggs. Unlike other turtles, the new leatherback male and female remain to protect the nest and to defend the hatchling turtles during their dash toward the ocean. Because of this protective behavior, the infant mortality among new leatherbacks is an order of magnitude lower than among other species of turtle; thus is the new leatherback population increasing more rapidly than other species.

During the season of nesting and hatching, new leatherbacks will attack anything that approaches their nesting site. At other times, they will attack non-prey only when threatened.

COMMENTARY

The Awakening has endowed the new leatherback with magical abilities that make it a formidable opponent. The most important of these is the ability to compel an enemy to immerse itself in the ocean. Thus, anyone approaching a leatherback nesting site may suddenly feel a compulsion to sink himself in the ocean.

The appearance of the new leatherback coincides well with the decline and disappearance of the Mexican turtle.

D. potami, the freshwater species of the new leatherback, is exceptionally rare.

POWERS

Engulf, Magical Resistance, Movement.

WEAKNESSES

Allergy (Mercury, Extreme), Vulnerability (Mercury).

>>>>>(You're slotting me. Engulf?)<<<<<
— Klaatu (18:12:18/3-17-51)

>>>>>(No kidding, Klaatu. Come too near these guys, and you get a sudden urge to go soak your head. Wiz defense, huh?)<<<<<
— Ballhog (21:12:38/3-17-51)

>>>>>(Wiz until it happens to you. Worse, you don't have to threaten the turtle. It just has to think you might. I was crewing on a skimmer out of San Diego couple of years ago, doing some "free trading." We blew it somewhere, and got a patrol boat on our butts. Just about then, half the crew suddenly decides they're going to jump overboard. All I can figure is that we came too near some bloody, fragging leatherback and it got worried.)<<<<<
— NAF (10:36:16/3-18-51)

>>>>>(If you ever need to take out a leatherback, the round of choice is a kinetic-explosive, mercury-filled round. That does them real good.)<<<<<
— Mad Merc (09:00:01/3-24-51)

GAME INFORMATION

	B	Q	S	C	I	W	E	R	Attacks
New Leatherback	8/3	3 x 2	5	—	2/4	3	(6)	3	3M2

Powers: Engulf, Magical Resistance, Movement
Weaknesses: Allergy (Mercury, Extreme), Vulnerability (Mercury)
Note: Swimming multiplier is 5.

NEW LEATHERBACK
Dermochelys novalis

HABITAT
Tropical oceans

RANGE
Gulf of Mexico, western coast of Aztlan

RANGE

SIZE COMPARISON

NOMAD
Umbra mortis

IDENTIFICATION

The nomad is an astral being presumably responsible for many tales of possession. Manifesting as an amorphous patch of darkness about 0.5 meter across, it appears on the physical plane only when attacking a potential host. When assensed on the Astral plane, however, the nomad appears as an amoeboid creature of impenetrable blackness that is perhaps 1.5 meters across.

MAGIC CAPABILITY

Innate.

HABITS

A form of mental parasite, the nomad dwells on the astral plane until it can find a suitable host. Finding one, it manifests on the physical plane and tries to gain entry into the victim's mind. Upon entering, the nomad simply seems to disappear, leaving the new host apparently unaffected. Within hours, however, the nomad's host undergoes uncontrollable periods of homicidal mania, when it attacks any creature within range, fighting to the death in the attempt to kill its victim. The precursor symptoms to such a homicidal rage are indistinguishable from symptoms of extreme psychosis (feelings of paranoia, voices—often the host's own—urging him or her to kill, and so on). The nomad-controlled host will use the most efficient killing method available to it, but will also attempt to be in physical contact at the actual instant of death. In some way, the nomad absorbs the life essence of the dying prey, on which it feeds.

Having possessed its host, the nomad is detectable only through astral assensing. Then it appears as a dark blight on the host's form.

A nomad is rarely encountered without a host of some kind, which might be virtually any corporeal creature, intelligent or non-intelligent. If the creature's current host dies, it transfers instantly to the astral plane, and immediately attacks another creature. A nomad without a host can survive on the astral plane for no more than five minutes. If unable to possess another host within that time, the nomad dies.

It is possible to attack the parasite through astral combat without also attacking its current host. The host does reportedly suffer some collateral damage from such an attack, however.

Nomads require the life energy of other creatures to live and reproduce, but they are not to be confused with vampires, who drain life force. As a creature dies, its life force leaves its body, and the nomad somehow absorbs it. This is why the nomad generates homicidal mania in its host: to drive the host to kill other creatures, so the parasite can feed off the ebbing life force. They can parasitize any carbon-based life form, from small rodents to humans, metahumans, and even up to dragons (theoretically). Because nomads feed on the ebbing life force of dying creatures, they prefer carnivorous hosts. Nomads can generate homicidal mania no matter what the host's species, turning even the most timid creature into a raging killer.

Eventually, a host will be driven into combat with something it cannot defeat; a maniacal rabbit attacking a wolf, for example. If the host is killed, the nomad simply absorbs its life force and immediately transfers to the creature that killed the host. Thus do nomads tend to "migrate" to the most lethal creatures in a region.

Nomads have no need to communicate with one another or with their hosts, and so have no language.

Nomads are well-adapted to their parasitical life. They have no natural enemies.

COMMENTARY

Though the symptoms of nomad possession are similar to those of deep psychosis, no treatment normally effective against such mental disorders has any effect.

It should be noted that this information comes from an interview with the Great Dragon Dunkelzahn. For obvious reasons, it has been impossible to totally corroborate his statements.

POWERS

Compulsion (Homicidal Mania), Essence Drain (Modified), Immunity to Normal Weapons, Manifestation.

WEAKNESSES

None (see above).

>>>>>(I've never heard of these things before. Frag, they're terrifying.)<<<<<
—Raider (18:01:58/2-13-51)

>>>>>(Yeah, but think of the movie you could make about them.)<<<<<
—Bladerunner (8:36:40/2-13-51)

>>>>>(Some people say that nomad possession explains a lot of the random violence in the inner city. This is an interesting thesis.)<<<<<
—Doc (11:51:09/3-01-51)

>>>>>(How the frag can you talk so calmly about these buggers? If you'd ever felt what it's like to have something inside your head, controlling your behavior, you'd wake up screaming every night, chummer. And I oughtta know.)<<<<<
—Rainbow (14:04:04/3-02-51)

GAME INFORMATION

	B	Q	S	C	I	W	E	R	Attacks
Nomad	6	3 X 3	0	6	1/6	6	9A	5	Special

Powers: Compulsion (Homicidal Mania), Essence Drain (Modified), Immunity to Normal Weapons, Manifestation

Note: To make an attack, the nomad must be at melee range. Make an Opposed Test using the nomad's Essence and the victim's Body or Willpower Rating, whichever is greater (always use the Body Rating for animals). Neither armor nor dermal plating are protection against this kind of attack. For each net success that the nomad achieves, apply 1 point of damage to the victim's Mental Condition Monitor. When all spaces on this track have been filled in, the character does not fall unconscious; instead, he or she is parasitized by the nomad.

Every 2D6 hours, the nomad makes one attack on its host, using the same procedure. If the Nomad wins this Opposed Test, the host flies into a homicidal rage, attacking the nearest creature or creatures in the most effective manner. As the nomad's host kills other creatures, the nomad absorbs their Essence (in a manner similar to Essence Drain power). When the nomad reaches a total Essence Rating of 18, it splits into two nomads, each with an Essence Rating of 9.

If a nomad host is prevented from killing while in a homicidal rage, the rage continues for 2D6 minutes, after which the host returns (apparently) to normal.

Nomad hosts are able to cast spells while under the effect of homicidal mania. Add +1 to all Target Numbers to reflect the distracting effects of the rage.

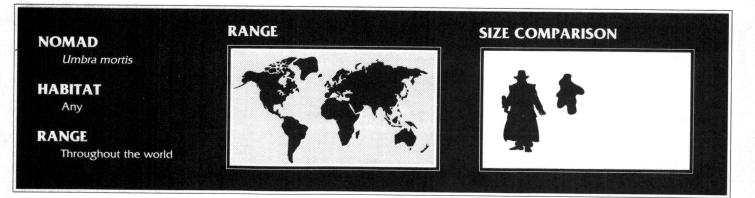

NOMAD
Umbra mortis

HABITAT
Any

RANGE
Throughout the world

RANGE

SIZE COMPARISON

NOVOPOSSUM
Didelphis ericae

IDENTIFICATION

The novopossum is an Awakened species derived from the North American opossum (*Didelphis marsupialis*). At 0.75 meter in length, it is slightly larger and somewhat more aggressive than its progenitor. The typical novopossum is light gray, with small red eyes. Its snout is long and sharply pointed. Its canine teeth are enlarged into fangs.

MAGIC CAPABILITY

Parabiological.

HABITS

Like *D. marsupialis*, the novopossum is an omnivore, but seems to prefer Awakened insects of the class *Diplopada*, or Metapedes, as they are commonly known.

The saliva of the novopossum is corrosive, though it does not seem to affect the animal itself. This feature is apparently an adaptation to the defense tactics of various Metapedes. When threatened, many Metapedes roll up into a ball or spiral, protected by their phenomenally hard exoskeletons. When curled up, a typical Metapede is more than 25.0 centimeters in diameter, much too large to swallow whole. The novopossum uses its corrosive saliva to melt the insect's hard shell. Once softened, the novopossum then eats the insect normally.

The novopossum's broad-based saliva can react with a wide range of chemical compounds, including those composed of hydrocarbons, ferrous-metals, and even ceramics. This is probably in direct response to the range of variations present in the chemical makeups of the various Metapede exoskeletons.

The novopossum rarely attacks a larger creature, but will defend itself with ferocity. When so threatened, the novopossum salivates profusely, splattering its attacker with saliva, even if unable to bite. The saliva can cause serious burns, and just a few drops usually deters even the hungriest attacker. Because of this ability, novopossums have no natural enemies.

Novopossums are predominantly nocturnal, but may sometimes be active during daylight hours. They are not by nature arboreal, but can climb well.

COMMENTARY

The novopossum's taxonomic classification comes from the name of its discoverer, respected naturalist Erica Maclean, who is married to Dr. Derek Maclean of Berkeley.

POWERS

Corrosive Saliva, Enhanced Senses (Low-Light Vision).

WEAKNESSES

None.

>>>>>(Metapedes? Are those things dangerous?)<<<<<
—Bobby (13:31:3/3-3-51)

>>>>>(No. Just look at them funny and they curl up tight. But they do make great substitute baseballs.)<<<<<
—Dahlia (17:46:23/3-3-51)

>>>>>(Just don't get into a tussle with a ticked-off novopossum. Even if you're armored from head to foot and laugh off assault cannon rounds, a few slobbers from this critter and you're definitely S.O.L.)<<<<<
—Hoffer (19:27:01/3-5-51)

>>>>>(Assuming you can beat one in a fight, don't ever eat a novopossum, no matter how desperate you are for food. Their flesh is poisonous. I found that out the hard way. I almost died, and was flat on my back for a week.)<<<<<
—Travis (18:44:16/3-19-51)

>>>>>(You probably just didn't cook it enough, or got one that was sick.)<<<<<
—Cameron (19:03:59/3-19-51)

>>>>>(Whatever. I just wouldn't risk it. And if you see one, don't make loud noises. I think they perceive loud noises as a direct threat.)<<<<<
—Travis (19:34:44/3-19-51)

GAME INFORMATION

	B	Q	S	C	I	W	E	R	Attacks
Novopossum	3	4 x 4	3	—	2/4	2	6	4	6L1

Powers: Corrosive Saliva, Enhanced Senses (Low-Light Vision)

NOVOPOSSUM
Didelphis ericae

HABITAT
Woodland areas

RANGE
Eastern and southern regions of North America

RANGE

SIZE COMPARISON

PIASMA
Ursus piasma

IDENTIFICATION

The piasma is a well-adapted predator derived from the North American black bear (*Ursus americanus*). It has a stout body, which favors strength over speed. The piasma's ears are short and its large head is equipped with the thick, short tusks of a boar. It has typical bear feet with large, rending claws, and a bushy tail 0.2 meter long. It is iron-gray in color, except for lighter patches spreading down its flanks.

A male adult piasma reaches a height of 1.5 meters at the shoulder, is approximately 3.0 meters long, and can weigh more than 600 kilograms.

MAGIC CAPABILITY

Parabiological.

HABITS

Unlike its omnivorous progenitor, the piasma is a carnivore. It may appear to be slow, but can display bursts of exceptional speed that permit it to run down even swiftly fleeing prey. The piasma prefers live prey if it can be obtained without major risk, but it often subsists by scavenging, seeming to prefer the leavings of humans and metahumans. For this reason, the creature sometimes dwells on the fringe of human settlements.

The piasma is nocturnal, lairing in caves. The animal is not territorial, however, an innovation that may have evolved because extreme territoriality near human settlements would soon lead to detection and eventual extermination. For the same reason, it is usually a solitary creature, except during the mating season in late summer.

Piasma will sometimes attack a solitary human, dragging the body back to its lair. If attacked or threatened, piasma are ferocious fighters with phenomenally strong jaws.

COMMENTARY

Piasma are an Awakened species derived from the North American black bear. Unlike other Awakened species, the piasma has not extended its range beyond that of its progenitor.

It is also interesting to note reports that some European entertainers have been able to train piasma to perform tricks, just as trainers achieved with the Russian *U. arctos*, in the 20th century.

NELSON

POWERS

Enhanced Physical Attributes (Strength or Quickness, once per day each, for (Essence x 2)D6 turns), Enhanced Reactions, Enhanced Senses (Thermographic Vision, Wide-Band Hearing).

WEAKNESSES

Allergy (Sunlight, Nuisance).

>>>>>(I lived in a little mining community in Idaho for a while, and it sounds like we had at least one piasma on the outskirts of town. It couldn't have been raccoons or bandits demolishing those steel-sheet Duro-Cans—you know, the ones you see on the vid—that could take a full clip from an Uzi III without damage. Those cans had teeth marks through them.)<<<<<
—Tarquin (19:06:08/2-11-51)

>>>>>(If it's true piasma are trainable, somebody ought to be using them like dogs.)<<<<<
—Big Solly (14:05:33/2-15-51)

>>>>>(You can try training a fraggin' metabear, chummer. I'll watch.)<<<<<
—Hangfire (09:36:40/2-15-51)

>>>>>(MTC already uses them as guard animals at their Military Contracts division. I've seen a couple of them patrolling inside the wire at their research lab near Everett.)<<<<<
—Blacknight (15:40:52/2-15-51)

>>>>>(Everett? Inside the wire? Chummer, that whole place is classed as a corp zero-zone. Nothing should be able to get close enough to even see the wire. Drek, how'd you manage that?)<<<<<
—Hangfire (15:43:22/2-15-51)

>>>>>(You think I'm going to tell you just for the asking? I might have to do it again.)<<<<<
— Blacknight (15:46:23/2-15-51)

>>>>>(If you ever have to get past those nice doggies, Blacknight, I've got an idea for you. Heard it from someone who should know. (I mention no names, but Hangfire probably knows him.) Sonics, real loud at about 36 Khz. You can't hear it (or you can set your cyberears to filter it out), but it slotting near kills those metabears. Hurts them so much they can't even think to growl. Come to think of it, that's probably how they train them.)<<<<<
—Straight Gain (03:35:51/2-16-51)

GAME INFORMATION

	B	Q	S	C	I	W	E	R	Attacks
Piasma	11/2	4 x 5	13	—	2/4	4	6	4	9D2, +1 Reach

Powers: Enhanced Physical Attributes (Strength or Quickness, once per day each, for (Essence x 2)D6 turns), Enhanced Reactions, Enhanced Senses (Thermographic Vision, Wide-Band Hearing)

Weaknesses: Allergy (Sunlight, Nuisance)

PIASMA
Ursus piasma

HABITAT
Woods and forested mountains

RANGE
Northern and mountainous regions of North America, Great Lakes, and Gulf of Mexico

RANGE

SIZE COMPARISON

PRICURICU
Hylocichla cynophilus

IDENTIFICATION

The pricuricu is a small bird shaped like a thrush, but with an owl's large, night-adapted eyes. It grows to a length of 0.2 meter, with a wingspan of approximately 0.3 meter.

MAGIC CAPABILITY

Parabiological.

HABITS

Pricuricu are insectivores, flying by night in flocks of up to 100 individuals. Their diet consists of moths, mosquitos, and other nocturnal insects. By day, they remain in enclosed nests formed from tree sap and grass and bound together with saliva. The nests are similar to those of bowerbirds.

Pricuricu are migratory, spending the summer in the northern reaches of North America and wintering in South America. Some primitive tribes in what is now called Amazonia attribute great religious significance to the pricuricu.

COMMENTARY

The call of the pricuricu is pitched at about 30 kilohertz, well above the range of most human and metahuman hearing. Creatures such as dogs can hear sounds of this frequency, however. The sound produced by large flocks of pricuricu can be acutely painful to creatures able to perceive their cries.

Gene typing has shown that the pricuricu is an Awakened species derived from the common thrush (*H. mustelina*).

POWERS

Enhanced Senses (Low-Light Vision), Sonic Projection (High-Frequency).

WEAKNESSES

Allergy (Sunlight, Mild).

>>>>>(People with cyberware take note. When these peckers fly over, it hurts like all hell. If you've got damping, use it. It'll mess you up otherwise.)<<<<<
—Lolita (17:45:35/1-3-51)

>>>>>(Hey, Straight Gain. Those metabears of yours must just love these things.)<<<<<
—Blacknight (03:29:32/2-16-51)

>>>>>(I don't think the frequency's high enough to incapacitate them, but it sure must give them something to think about.)<<<<<
—Straight Gain (10:30:03/2-16-51)

>>>>>(Pricuricu play merry bleeding hell with sonar. Random noise, phantom images, the whole enchilada.)<<<<<
—Reaver (19:37:39/2-19-51)

>>>>>(They put bats out of business, too. Those buggers start running into trees and stuff when pricuricu decide to sound off.)<<<<<
—Mallonson (19:38:35/2-19-51)

GAME INFORMATION

	B	Q	S	C	I	W	E	R	Attacks
Pricuricu	1	4 x 4	0	—	1/4	1	6	4	1L1

Powers: Enhanced Senses (Low-Light Vision), Sonic Projection (High-Frequency)
Weaknesses: Allergy (Sunlight, Mild)

PRICURICU
Hylocichla cynophilus

HABITAT
Woodlands and parklands

RANGE
Northern regions of North America (summer); northern regions of South America (winter)

RANGE

summer only

SIZE COMPARISON

ROCK LIZARD
Phrynosoma caliburni

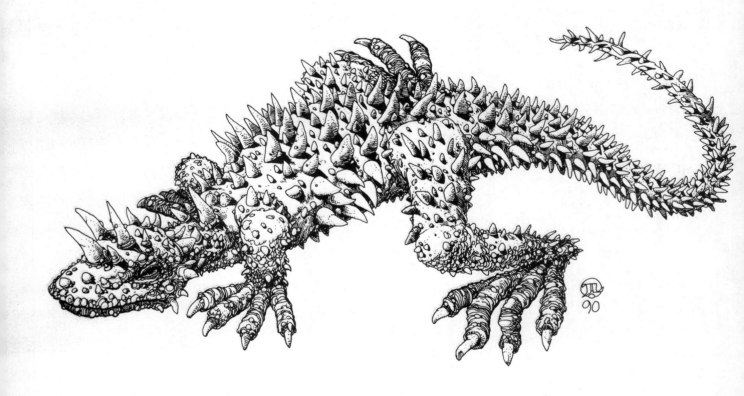

IDENTIFICATION

The rock lizard is a large, desert-dwelling reptile whose appearance is similar to a horned toad. Its rough-textured skin can change from light tan to dark brown or even gray-black. It has a long, prehensile tongue that is forked like a snake's. Its toes have sharp, curved claws. The rock lizard can grow to a length of 1.0 meter, with an additional 0.5 meter for the tail.

MAGIC CAPABILITY

Parabiological.

HABITS

The rock lizard is a carnivore that preys on kangaroo rats and other small desert mammals. Using its natural camouflage, it remains motionless until its prey comes within range, then it flicks out its tongue, attempting to kill or incapacitate with its venomous saliva. The rock lizard swallows its prey whole. Though the animal is normally solitary, some observers have reported small family groups on cooperative hunts. When such groups hunt, several members will "herd" their prey toward where others lie in wait, motionless and concealed.

Rock lizards are diurnal. During the hours of darkness, they lair in burrows or under rocks.

Perhaps because they are venomous, rock lizards are immune to most toxins.

COMMENTARY

Rock lizards are not aggressive toward creatures that are too large for them to swallow. Even if attacked, they prefer flight to combat.

POWERS

Immunity to Poisons, Venom.

WEAKNESSES

None.

>>>>>(Like drek, they're not aggressive. If they can get away with it, a couple of them will gladly try to dry-gulch a lone man.)<<<<<
—Desert Rat (18:46:37/3-4-51)

>>>>>(Come on, chummer. That isn't something animals do.)<<<<<
—Wendy (18:48:01/3-4-51)

>>>>>(Don't bet on it, Wendy, my gal. I'm with Desert Rat. If you're alone and you see a bunch of these things, high-tail it out fast.)<<<<<
—Digit (18:50:26/3-4-51)

>>>>>(You're talking from experience, I gather?)<<<<<
—Wendy (18:51:58/3-4-51)

>>>>>(Wendy, you're the only person I know who can squeeze sarcasm down a datajack. Yeah, I'm speaking from experience. I had some problems with my sandbike (probably had to do with a couple of steel-jacketed rounds in the engine casing), and so I had to take a hike. I was going down an arroyo, and two rock lizards were going up. I figured they had right of way, so I just hugged the wall to let them by. One of those buggers lets fly with his tongue and gets me in the right leg. The only reason I didn't go down from the poison is because my right leg isn't meat. (I lost the real one in a poker game years back). Let me tell you, I ran so fast and so far, I had curvature on those buggers before I stopped. So, Wendy, why don't you shove your sarcasm right back up your...datajack.)<<<<<
—Digit (18:54:03/3-4-51)

GAME INFORMATION

	B	Q	S	C	I	W	E	R	Attacks
Rock Lizard	3	3 x 4	3	—	1/3	3	6	5	6L2

Powers: Immunity to Poisons, Venom

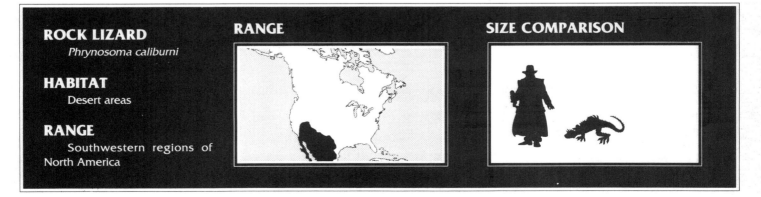

ROCK LIZARD
Phrynosoma caliburni

HABITAT
Desert areas

RANGE
Southwestern regions of North America

RANGE

SIZE COMPARISON

ROCKWORM
Vermes saxi

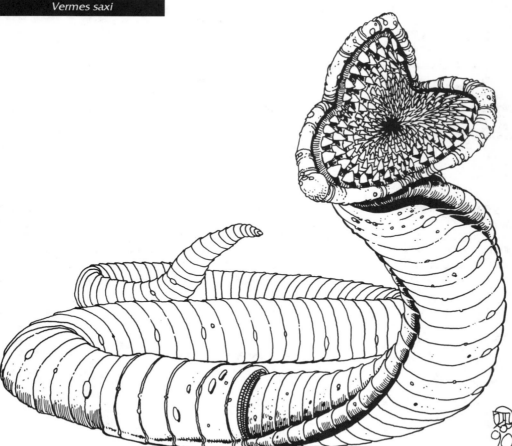

IDENTIFICATION

The rockworm is a pallid, fleshy-looking worm that can reach 2.0 meters in length. It is proportionately thicker and stronger than a nightcrawler, from which it seems to have derived. It has a mouth full of grinding teeth and horny plates, showing trilateral symmetry (an arrangement vaguely resembling a rock drill-bit for drilling oil).

Rock worms have no apparent sensory apparatus. Like night crawlers, they have a "collar" about a third of the way down their bodies.

MAGIC CAPABILITY

Parabiological.

HABITS

The rockworm burrows into, and digests, rock and stone. Its tripartite labial teeth and plates grind the rock into dust, mix it with a corrosive saliva, and then ingests it through the anterior orifice. After extracting the minerals it needs, the rockworm excretes the remainder through its posterior orifice. Rockworms can burrow, albeit slowly, through even the hardest rock.

Rockworms dig large burrows deep into large rock areas, where they dwell in groups. Over the years, these burrows can be enlarged to form caverns, significantly reducing the structural integrity of the rock around them. Rockworm burrows are sometimes responsible for cave-ins and collapses in mines, and rock-falls in mountain canyons.

Unlike most creatures, which operate on a simple carbon-oxygen chemical economy, rockworms metabolize silicon compounds rather than carbon compounds. This is not to say that the rockworm is a silicon lifeform. The length of the DNA/RNA molecule precludes the substitution of silicon for carbon in this all-important building block. The diameter of the silicon atom is so much larger than the diameter of the carbon atom that a silicon atom can only weakly bind a hydrogen atom, making it impossible to build the long, complex DNA/RNA chains. Rockworms still need some carbon intake, but only as trace elements.

Because rockworms also require oxygen, they must dig "ventilation tunnels" into their rock burrows. It is these ventila-tion tunnels that can cause significant structural damage to buildings.

Like earthworms, rockworms are hermaphroditic; however, one rockworm cannot fertilize itself.

If attacked, a rockworm can inflict serious injury with its mouth and the acid excretions it uses to help break up the rocks it ingests.

COMMENTARY

The addition of a silicon metabolism to the standard carbon-oxygen economy may be one of the greatest biochemical changes to result from the Awakening. A number of respected experts deny that such a change could have come about without outside manipulation, but none can even begin to speculate who might have accomplished such manipulation.

POWERS ADD

Corrosive Saliva, Immunity to Pathogens, Immunity to Poisons, Regeneration.

WEAKNESSES

None.

>>>>>(There was some kind of flap a few years back about rockworms possibly getting into dams and highways. Anybody heard more about that?)<<<<<
  —Holden (20:29:27/2-22-51)

>>>>>(Not directly. But—hooboy—does that make sense out of something I couldn't understand before. You know the old Interstate 5 interchange, all those ramps and cloverleaf drek just east of downtown? You know where they built the low-rent housing underneath? Get this. A couple of months ago, I saw exterminators wandering around and spraying the supports and some of the ramps with something. It must have been toxic as all hell, 'cause those guys were wearing full chem-biol warfare chemsuits. Draw your own conclusions.)<<<<<
  —Nighthawk (23:02:43/2-22-51)

>>>>>(Scar-y! You're thinking they've got rockworms in the I-5 interchange, aren't you? And the city knows? Why haven't they told anybody?)<<<<<
  —Stella (23:10:57/2-22-51)

>>>>>(Sure, Stella. The mayor gets on the vid and says, "Sorry for the inconvenience, but something's eating the freeway and it's going to fall on your heads. Please move. 'Where are they going to move to? Besides, the city would have to take responsibility and so pick up the tab. It stands to reason they're not going to broadcast it.)<<<<<
  —Trent (23:13:48/2-22-51)

>>>>>(The old buildings seem to be fair game. Rockworms eat granite. Ferrocrete and (god help us) pre-stressed concrete would be like dessert. But I don't think they can eat compound ceramics, which means they probably leave the newer buildings alone.)<<<<<
  —Doc (23:29:00/2-22-51)

GAME INFORMATION

	B	Q	S	C	I	W	E	R	Attacks
Rock Worm	2/1	4	2	—	1/2	3	3	2	2M2

Powers: Corrosive Saliva, Immunity to Pathogens, Immunity to Poisons, Regeneration
Note: Burrowing multiplier is 0.25 for soft rock; 0.125 for hard rock.

ROCK WORM
Vermes saxi

HABITAT
Mountains, hills, and urban areas

RANGE
Northern regions of North America, and spreading southward

RANGE

SIZE COMPARISON

SABER-TOOTH CAT
Felis novalis

IDENTIFICATION

The saber-tooth cat is an Awakened species derived from the cougar or mountain lion (*Felis concolor*). It reaches a length of 1.8 meters, with its tail adding another 1.0 meter. Two large, curved fangs protrude from its upper jaw. These greatly enlarged canine teeth can grow up to 0.25 meter long. The saber-tooth cat is fast and powerful. Its coat is tawny brown and unmarked.

MAGIC CAPABILITY

Parabiological.

HABITS

Like its progenitor species, the saber-tooth cat is a predator. Unlike its progenitor, it can hunt as effectively by night as by day. Its prey consists of mountain goats and deer, and sometimes includes cattle. The animal would not be likely to attack humans or metahumans without provocation, but a few such instances have occurred.

Saber-tooth cats hunt only when hungry, spending the rest of their time basking in the sun. A typical lair is either a small cave or a nook sheltered by large rocks. During the breeding season in early spring up through late June when the young finally begin to fend for themselves, saber-tooth cats are highly territorial. It is during these periods that attacks on humans and metahumans may occur. During the rest of the year, the cats are not overly territorial or aggressive except in self-defense.

COMMENTARY

In the case of the saber-tooth cat, the only significant physiological changes resulting from the Awakening process are the enlargement of the canine teeth and improved night vision. The most significant changes have been behavioral. Though the progenitor was known for avoiding contact with humans and for hunting animals deer-size or smaller, the saber-tooth cat has become much more aggressive. When hungry, it is likely to prey upon any animal in its territory, seemingly regardless of size. There are even unconfirmed reports of a saber-tooth cat stalking and attacking a juggernaut!

POWERS

Enhanced Senses (Low-Light Vision, Thermographic Vision).

WEAKNESSES

None.

SHADOWTALK

>>>>>(If you ever have the chance, check these creatures out. They're fantastically graceful and fascinating to watch.)<<<<<
—Arnold (09:38:21/2-19-51)

>>>>>(Yeah, check them out—but from a distance.)<<<<<
—Hardbody (09:40:19/2-19-51)

>>>>>(Don't sweat it. They're only dangerous when they've got cubs around.)<<<<<
—Arnold (09:41:03/2-19-51)

>>>>>(Like drek, chummer. Sometimes they'll jump you just for the fun of it.)<<<<<
—Dino (09:43:19/2-19-51)

>>>>>(Now you're talking drek, Dino. They're more scared of you than you are of them. As long as they've got a safe escape route, they'll usually bug out rather than start something. Discretion is the better part, and all that drek.)<<<<<
—Gavin (09:44:08/2-19-51)

>>>>>(Are we all talking about the same critter here?)<<<<<
— Nighthawk (10:38:33/2-19-51)

GAME INFORMATION

	B	Q	S	C	I	W	E	R	Attacks
Saber-Tooth Cat	5	5 x 4	5	—	2/4	2	6	4	5S2

Powers: Enhanced Senses (Low-Light Vision, Thermographic Vision)

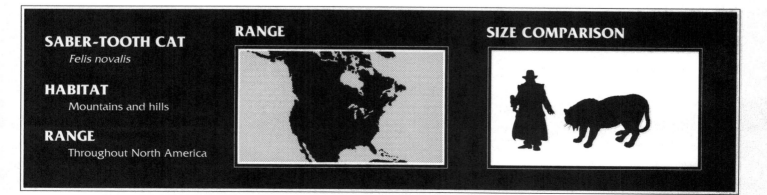

SABER-TOOTH CAT
Felis novalis

HABITAT
Mountains and hills

RANGE
Throughout North America

RANGE

SIZE COMPARISON

SALAMANDER
No accepted taxonomy

IDENTIFICATION

The salamander resembles a small, swirling ball of flame hovering and dancing in mid-air. It is about 12.0 centimeters in diameter, not much bigger than a fist. Sometimes it cloaks itself in diaphanous veils of flame. Salamanders are often seen at large conflagrations, particularly forest fires, drifting among the flames.

MAGIC CAPABILITY

Innate.

HABITS

It is not known whether salamanders eat, and if so, what. Nor do even vague theories exist concerning their reproductive capacities or habits.

Salamanders enjoy fire, seeming totally unaffected by any form of radiant energy. No substantive proof exists, but it seems likely that salamanders sometimes start large fires for the sheer enjoyment of dancing among the flames.

COMMENTARY

Salamanders are almost certainly a form of free-roaming fire elemental, and so dwell predominantly on the astral plane. Reports indicate that they are intelligent, and that they can communicate among themselves and with other creatures. Even though reputed to have caused great destruction, they do not behave in an actively malign manner toward humans or metahumans.

No sightings of free-roaming analogs of the salamander have been reported for the other three elements. It is assumed that they exist, however. Awaiting their discovery, common names have already been chosen for them: Gnome (Earth), Sylph (Air), and Undine (Water).

POWERS

Engulf, Flame Aura, Flame Projection, Guard, Immunity to Fire, Magical Resistance, Manifestation, Psychokinesis.

WEAKNESSES

Allergy (Water, Severe), Vulnerability (Water).

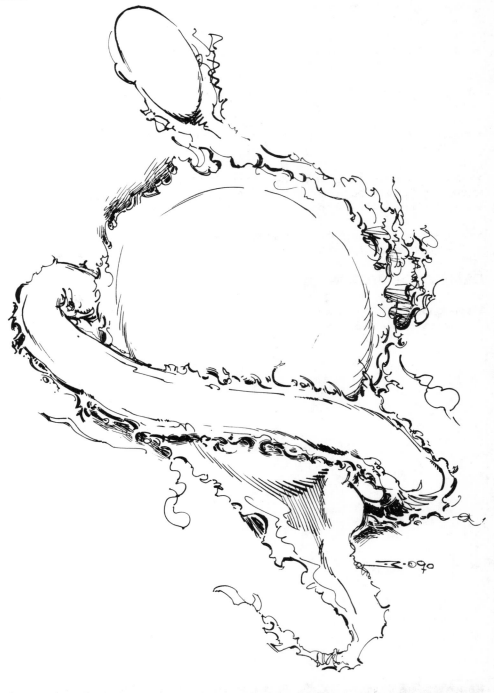

>>>>>(I have assensed the salamander on the astral plane. It appears as a small lizard composed entirely of brilliant flame.)<<<<<
—Tinuviel (09:59:27/1-22-51)

>>>>>(Soon after I quit the corp, some bastard sent a fragging salamander after me. I got away, but it burned down the whole fragging rooming house where I lived. That sounds "actively malign" to me.)<<<<<
—Hangfire (18:36:24/1-27-51)

>>>>>(Hold on just a minute here, Hangfire. You said someone sent a salamander after you. That means these things can be conjured?)<<<<<
—Barre (18:39:01/1-27-51)

>>>>>(I cannot do so, but I know another sorcerer of great and wide-ranging power who says he can. The rite is difficult and intricate, however, and highly dangerous. He told me that conjuring a salamander drained him so much that he was wiped out for a week. Another mage has said that salamanders cannot be conjured, but rather that they will strike a bargain with you. What you might use as a bargaining item, I know not.)<<<<<
—Tinuviel (18-44-38/1-27-51)

>>>>>(If you want to know where to find the Gnome, Sylph, and Undine, look at the entries for Toxic Waste Spirits. We've killed them off. We poison the land, the air, and the water, and then wonder why nature turns against us. The only thing left for us is to purify the planet once again with the only thing we have not tainted: fire. Join with me to cleanse the dens of corruption that taint our very lives. Take up the torch and (7.5 Mp Deleted by sysop).)<<<<<
—Saloman (18-51-09/1-27-51)

>>>>>(Bit hot under the collar, isn't he?)<<<<<
—Hangfire (18-54-00/1-27-51)

GAME INFORMATION

	B	Q	S	C	I	W	E	R*	Attacks
Salamander	5	6 x 3	2	4	4	4	4A	10/15	3M4

Powers: Engulf, Flame Aura, Flame Projection, Guard, Immunity to Fire, Magical Resistance, Manifestation, Psychokinesis.
Weaknesses: Vulnerability (Water)
*Manifest/Astral Reactions

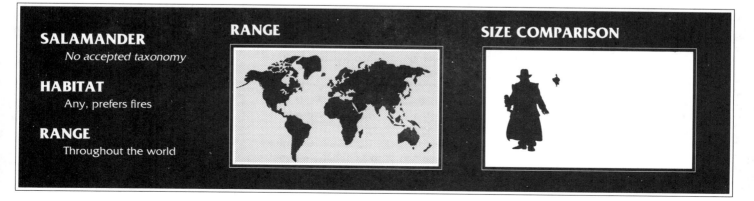

SALAMANDER
No accepted taxonomy

HABITAT
Any, prefers fires

RANGE
Throughout the world

RANGE

SIZE COMPARISON

SEA DRAKE
Neotylosaurus pacificus

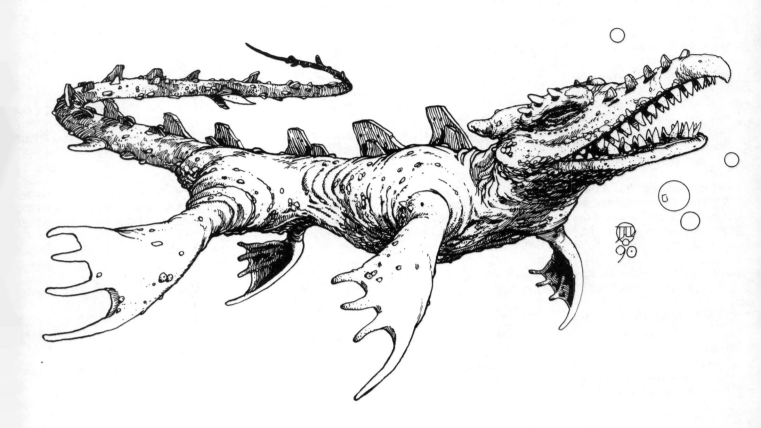

IDENTIFICATION

The sea drake is an ocean-adapted reptile that can achieve a length of 13.5 meters. Its body resembles a lizard's, except that all four limbs have evolved into broad, paddle-like flippers. A saw-toothed, bony ridge runs down its spine, and its head vaguely resembles a western dragon's. The sea drake has a short neck rather than the long or sinuous one of other "sea serpents." The sea drake is lead gray in color.

MAGIC CAPABILITY

Innate.

HABITS

The sea drake is a fast and efficient predator, feeding on fish and aquatic mammals such as seals and dolphins. Sea drakes have been known to attack cetaceans as large as a sperm whale; one

unsubstantiated report tells of a group attacking and killing a small pod of leviathans.

Sea drakes are air-breathers, but can switch to anaerobic metabolism for long periods. This allows them to remain submerged for more than two hours, even under heavy exertion. Sea drakes are as at home in great watery depths as they are at the surface. The Tir Tairngire bathyscaph *Celene* has observed sea drakes at depths of 3,200 fathoms (6.65 kilometers), but the creature was ascending when spotted. No one knows the maximum depth to which a sea drake can descend.

Sea drakes frequently hunt in small packs of two to four individuals. In areas of abundant prey, multiple packs operate cooperatively.

Sea drakes are aggressive enough to attack human or metahuman swimmers and small boats.

COMMENTARY

Though a vociferous faction of taxonomists argued for classifying the sea drake as genus *Draco*, implying a relationship to the dragons, reason prevailed. The name *Neotylosaurus* was selected because the sea drake resembles reconstructions of the extinct tylosaur, not because of any relationship with that aquatic reptile of the Jurassic period. As of this publication, no progenitor species has been determined.

POWERS

Enhanced Physical Attributes (Movement, once per day, for (Essence)D6 turns), Enhanced Senses (Low-Light Vision).

WEAKNESSES

None.

>>>>>(Genetic typing strongly implies that the sea drake is closely related to the ice drake and the fire drake, and distantly related to dragons. Again, Paterson isn't telling the whole story.)<<<<<
—Doc (10:29:52/3-25-51)

>>>>>(Maybe the tylosaur never died off. Maybe sea drakes are them.)<<<<<
—Flash (10:32:39/3-25-51)

>>>>>(No. Somebody would have spotted them before now. They're not like deep-water fish that can remain hidden in deep, watery abysses. These are air-breathers that must surface.)<<<<<
—Doc (10:34:59/3-25-51)

>>>>>(Maybe they hibernate or something.)<<<<<
—Rowan (10:39:35/3-25-51)

>>>>>(There are sea drakes around the San Juan Islands just west of Seattle. And they do attack small boats, but that's not all. One night I was on a midnight run through the islands in an Aztech Nightrunner. Everything was going great. I thought we'd avoided corporate involvement, if you get my drift. Then the boat hit something, like we'd run aground, but the chart said we had a couple of meters of water under the keel. I looked over the side, and something lunged at me, something that was all teeth and scales.
   We were on a run so I was chipped kind of high, and I managed to get out of the way. And that's when this thing starts to attack the boat. It tore off the prop and started to chew on the hull. We put a few rounds into it, but nothing we had was heavy enough to distract it. A couple of hand grenades that we dropped over the side only made it back off for a bit.
   As if that weren't enough, we suddenly heard an engine behind us. I've got enhanced optics, so I could see a Yellowjacket rotorcraft coming up astern. I could also see by its paint job that it was from the corp we were trying to avoid tangling with. We sent a few rounds its way, but we couldn't really give it all our attention in case the sea drake came back.
   The Yellowjacket comes down real low, so it's just skimming the waves, and I know it's lining us up for a strafing run. We're carrying some rather volatile cargo, so it's almost certain the Nightrunner's going to blow. But if we go over the side, we've got the sea drake to worry about. Its just then that the sea drake surges right out of the water and picks the Yellowjacket clean out of the air. Bang, one moment it's there, the next it's gone. I guess the drake was happy with its snack, because it didn't come back.)<<<<<
—Go-Boy (18:37:38/3-28-51)

GAME INFORMATION

	B	Q	S	C	I	W	E	R	Attacks
Sea Drake	4	4 x 4	4	—	2/3	3	(6)	5	3M2, +1 Reach

Powers: Enhanced Physical Attributes (Movement, once per day, for (Essence)D6 turns), Enhanced Senses (Low-Light Vision)

SEA DRAKE
   Neotylosaurus pacificus

HABITAT
   Temperate and subarctic oceans

RANGE
   Throughout the world, especially the Pacific Ocean

RANGE

SIZE COMPARISON

SERPENT, FRESHWATER

Pleuracanthus laci

IDENTIFICATION

The freshwater serpent is an aquatic lizard with a long tail and a long, sinuous neck supporting a small, crested head. Its limbs have adapted into broad, paddle-shaped flippers. The creature can grow to a length of 18.0 meters, much of which consists of tail and neck. The freshwater serpent has a broad jaw, with the flat, grinding teeth of a herbivore. It ranges in color from dark green to muddy brown. Its blunt spinal ridge is usually a shade lighter than the rest of its body.

MAGIC CAPABILITY

None.

HABITS

As its morphology indicates, the freshwater serpent is a herbivore. It feeds on weeds and lake grasses, which it scoops from lake bottoms with its broad lower jaw. The creature is normally slow-moving, spending most of its time near the bottom of deep lakes (it is an air breather, but capable of remaining submerged for up to three hours). It rarely appears during daylight hours, except to raise the tip of its snout above the surface to draw in air. During darkness, however, it sometimes swims with its neck and head raised out of the water.

Though normally placid, the freshwater serpent is a large and powerful creature to be treated with respect. If provoked, it is capable of inflicting considerable damage on its attacker.

Studies indicate that freshwater serpents can live for more than a hundred years. The female lays a single egg every second year, but the chance of the egg hatching is less than 50 percent. Thus, the population of the creature remains low but stable.

COMMENTARY

In 2046, researchers found a freshwater serpent in Scotland's Loch Ness. Though it is tempting to conclude that the Loch Ness "monster" stories of the 20th century were actually sightings of this creature, the freshwater serpent is presumed to be an Awakened species. As Awakening did not occur until the early 21st century, the existence of the freshwater serpent cannot explain "monster" sightings from more than a century earlier.

POWERS

None.

WEAKNESSES

None.

>>>>>(Everybody always concentrates on Loch Ness. Lake Okanagan, in what used to be British Columbia, had its own monster, Ogopogo. It was sighted before the turn of the 20th century, which kind of puts another nail in the idea of "premature" Awakening.)<<<<<
—Hardcore (11:11:46/1-24-51)

>>>>>(The freshwater serpent and the closely related saltwater serpent are dracoforms. Like the drakes, they've got some genetic similarity to dragons, but they evolved differently. I don't think these are Awakened creatures at all. They've always been around.)<<<<<
—Doc (21:38:23/3-28-51)

>>>>>(But where?)<<<<<
—Calvin (21:42:103-28-51)

>>>>>(There's the rub. But I bet some precursor of the dragons, the drakes, and the serpents exists somewhere in the fossil record. We could call it Predraco amandae.)<<<<<
—Doc (21:42:57/3-28-51)

>>>>>(Why "amandae"?)<<<<<
—Calvin (21:45:08/3-28-51)

>>>>>(For Amanda. That's my first name.)<<<<<
—Doc (21:46:49/3-28-51)

>>>>>(The guide's right about serpents being dangerous just because of their size. They're stupid, too, which doesn't help. One surfaced under my boat in Lake Michigan, capsized it, and tossed me into the water. I'm thrashing around trying not to sink, and this big head just sort of cranes over and looks at me, all puzzled like. Like it's saying, what the drek are you doing down there?)<<<<<
—Pavel (16:19:26/3-30-51)

GAME INFORMATION

	B	Q	S	C	I	W	E	R	Attacks
Serpent, Freshwater	12/1	4 x 3	7	—	1/3	3	6	3	4S3, +1 Reach

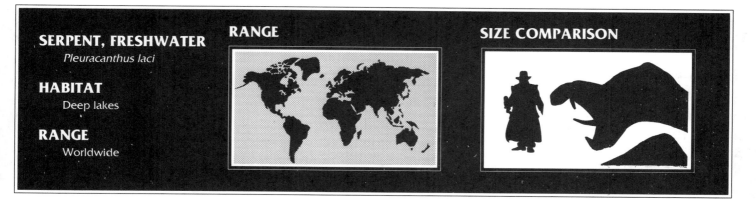

SERPENT, FRESHWATER
Pleuracanthus laci

HABITAT
Deep lakes

RANGE
Worldwide

RANGE

SIZE COMPARISON

SERPENT, SALTWATER
Pleuracanthus oceani

IDENTIFICATION

The saltwater serpent is a larger, more streamlined version of its freshwater brethren. It, too, is an aquatic lizard with a long tail and a long, sinuous neck supporting a small, crested head. Its limbs have adapted into broad, paddle-shaped flippers. The creature attains a length of 25.0 meters, much of it tail and neck. The saltwater serpent has a narrow, pointed jaw with the sharp, tearing teeth of a carnivore. It ranges in color from light to dark green. Its saw-toothed spinal ridge is usually a shade darker than the rest of its body.

MAGIC CAPABILITY

None.

HABITS

The saltwater serpent is an aggressive predator. It feeds on fish and such aquatic mammals as seals and dolphins. Saltwater serpents have been known to attack larger cetaceans like sperm whales, and some reports indicate that the creatures also attack sea drakes. They will also attack swimmers and small boats.

Salt-water serpents are air-breathers, but can switch to an anaerobic cycle for long periods of time, allowing them to remain submerged for more than two hours, even under heavy exertion. Unlike sea drakes, these animals seem to prefer to remain within a few hundred meters of the surface.

Saltwater serpents are highly prolific. A female lays up to 20 eggs, 80 percent of which will hatch. The young are highly aggressive, however, fighting among themselves and even attacking unhatched eggs. For this reason, infant mortality among saltwater serpents is more than 90 percent. The lifespan of these creatures is much shorter than that of their freshwater brethren, averaging about 35 years.

COMMENTARY

The close relationship between the freshwater serpent and its saltwater counterpart cannot be denied. No progenitor species has been discovered for either type, however.

POWERS

Enhanced Physical Attributes (Quickness, twice per day, for (Essence)D6 turns).

WEAKNESSES

None.

>>>>>You could water ski behind one of these things. That's how fast they are. They can leap clear out of the water, too.)<<<<<
—Iris (11:41:00/1-10-51)

>>>>>(I don't know about water-skiing, but when they're swimming just below the surface, they can kick up quite a rooster-tail.)<<<<<
—Telly (11:45:38/1-10-51)

>>>>>(Hey, Go-Boy. Are you sure it was a sea drake you saw in the San Juans? Couldn't it have been a saltwater serpent?)<<<<<
—Iris (13:47:50/3-29-51)

>>>>>(Don't think so, Iris. This one didn't have a long neck, or else it could have picked me and Ghost right up off the deck. The behavior's similar, though. Both critters will eat just about anything, as long as it's moving.)<<<<<
—Go-Boy (13:50:01/3-29-51)

GAME INFORMATION

	B	Q	S	C	I	W	E	R	Attacks
Serpent, Saltwater	10/2	4 x 4	18	—	1/4	4	6	4	7S3, +1 Reach

Powers: Enhanced Physical Attributes (Quickness, twice per day, for (Essence)D6 turns)

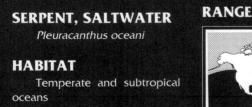

SERPENT, SALTWATER
Pleuracanthus oceani

HABITAT
Temperate and subtropical oceans

RANGE
Throughout the world

RANGE

SIZE COMPARISON

SHADOWHOUND
Canis umbrae

D.K.

IDENTIFICATION

The shadowhound resembles a huge dog, reaching a height of 1.2 meters at the shoulder. Its coat is gray, marked with black patches. These patches can move and shift. (In fact, the hound has a coat consisting of two lengths of hair. The shorter undercoat is black, while the longer hairs are gray. By shifting the muscles under the skin, the hound can make the longer hairs move, displaying or concealing the black undercoat.) This provides it with excellent camouflage at night.

MAGIC CAPABILITY

Parabiological.

HABITS

The shadowhound is a nocturnal predator that hunts in packs of up to a dozen individuals. They feed on rabbits, rats, young deer, and other small mammals, but occasionally attack larger animals.

There are no reported attacks on humans or metahumans.

The shadowhound's eyes are built for low-light vision, making full sunlight or any other bright light painful to the creature. During the day, the shadowhound lairs among the rubble of buildings, in caves, and so on.

When shadowhounds concentrate on stealth, they are almost impossible to detect.

COMMENTARY

Some reports describe the shadowhound as hostile toward humans, to the point of gathering other creatures together to prey on man. Conflicting reports claim that the hounds are protectors of mankind and metahumanity. With no evidence to support either side of the controversy, these rumors remain suspect, at best.

POWERS

Darkness, Enhanced Reactions, Enhanced Senses (Low-Light Vision), Silence.

WEAKNESSES

Allergy (Sunlight, Severe).

>>>>>(These things are bad news. Any time I ever seen one, there was something real nasty around, waiting to tear my head off.)<<<<<
　　—Trasher (04:39:38/1-31-51)

>>>>>(You speak hastily. It is true the shadowhound is often near when fell creatures are afoot, but not for the reason you think. Evil attracts the presence of shadowhounds, but only because they are drawn to fight against it.)<<<<<
　　—Cat Dancing (04:40:33/1-31-51)

>>>>>(That's mystical drek, from both of you. There's no 'evil' in the world. And those things are just animals.)<<<<<
　　—Martin (07:09:52/1-31-51)

>>>>>(I've seen one of these shadowhounds. Or, rather, I didn't see it, which is the point. I knew it was there, just across the alley from me. I could assense it. But even then, I couldn't see it. Wild. Hey, what a pet for a shadowrunner, huh?)<<<<<
　　—Leatherjacket (14:11:02/2-1-51)

>>>>>(Who wants a pet you can't see? It'll run away one day, and you won't know it's gone for a week.)<<<<<
　　—Bung (15:52:34/2-1-51)

>>>>>(Leatherjacket, the hound didn't attack you?)<<<<<
　　—Blacknight (18:04:34/2-1-51)

>>>>>(Nah. It just watched me. Maybe it figured I was too big.)<<<<<
　　—Leatherjacket (18:45:49/2-1-51)

GAME INFORMATION

	B	Q	S	C	I	W	E	R	Attacks
Shadowhound	4	4 x 4	5	—	2/4	3	6	4	5M2

　　Powers: Darkness, Enhanced Reactions, Enhanced Senses (Low-Light Vision), Silence
　　Weaknesses: Allergy (Sunlight, Severe)

SHADOWHOUND
　　Canis umbrae

HABITAT
　　Woods and urban wastelands

RANGE
　　Throughout the world

RANGE

SIZE COMPARISON

SIREN
Siren canori

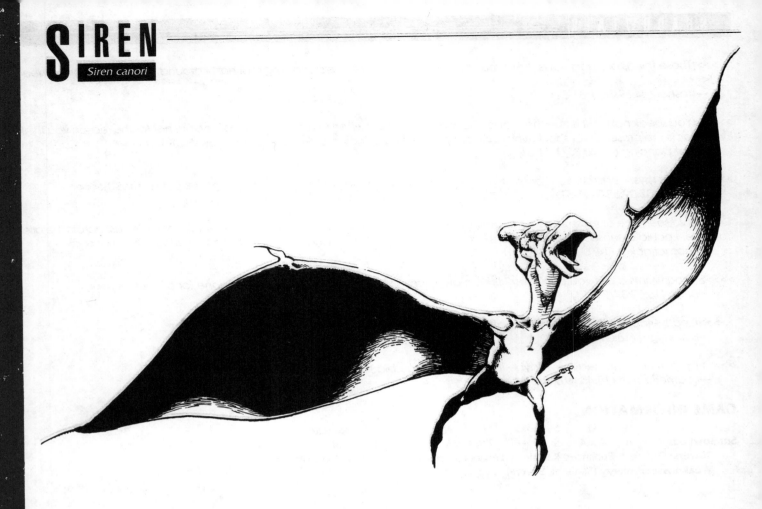

IDENTIFICATION

The siren resembles a small pterodactyl, with a 2.5-meter wingspan, a short, crushing beak like a parrot's, powerful taloned feet, and small, clawed "hands" halfway up the upper portion of its wings. Bony ridges protect its small red eyes. The siren's color ranges from dusty brown on its dorsal side to off-white on its ventral portion. Its beak is light brown near the base, shading to black at the tip.

MAGIC CAPABILITY

Innate.

HABITS

The siren is a ferocious predator that feeds on terrestrial mammals, reptiles, and birds. It is a fast and maneuverable flyer, able to catch and eat birds on the wing. It can swoop down and snatch up smaller land animals, trying to kill them with a single beak-strike to the back of the

neck, then carrying them back to its lair. If unable to kill its prey quickly, the siren will usually drop it from altitude, then retrieve the corpse. They almost never feed at the site of their kill, except in the case of creatures too large to carry off.

Sirens often hunt in flocks, but are observed just as frequently in solitary hunt. Substantiated reports exist of sirens attacking and killing humans.

Siren lairs are usually caves or caverns in desolate mountainsides. A single lair usually contains one or more small family groups, each consisting of a single dominant female, one or two subservient males, and up to three immature sirens. The female is a wide-ranging hunter, while the males usually stay near the lair to protect the eggs and feed the young.

The breeding season is unrestricted. Females lay up to four single eggs per year. The eggs hatch in 40 to 50 days, and the hatchling can fly and hunt within five days of birth. Sirens grow rapidly, reaching full adult size in approximately nine

months.

Sirens have a high-pitched, musical song to which some have attributed a hypnotic effect that makes the listener draw near. Whether or not the siren uses its song to hunt smaller prey is as yet unproven.

Sirens are diurnal by preference, but can function well in darkness.

COMMENTARY

The genetic derivation of the siren is unknown. Though it is obviously an Awakened species, no progenitor species has yet been identified.

POWERS

Enhanced Senses (Low-Light Vision), Hypnotic Song, Immunity to Pathogens, Immunity to Poisons.

WEAKNESSES

None.

>>>>>(Doc and I have been studying the gene map of the siren, and we agree that this is not actually an Awakened species but an engineered strain. Though we can't identify the base strain, it was probably reptilian. There are incontrovertible signs of subtle, elegant genetic manipulation, however. We've sent our findings to Dr. Derek Maclean at Berkeley, but he hasn't responded.)<<<<<
—Sagan (13:02:46/2-18-51)

>>>>>(Sirens are ideal guard animals: highly territorial and very vicious. Could that be what they were bred for?)<<<<<
—Hangfire (11:37:27/2-20-51)

>>>>>(One problem, Hangfire: they'll attack anything. If I'm going to put animals out to guard something, I'd like to be sure it'll be there when I get back.)<<<<<
—Driver (11:40:28/2-20-51)

>>>>>(I've heard a siren sing and it's emotionally evocative, if you know what I mean. Like the way a sound might remind you of your childhood, but orders of magnitude more intense. You just stand there, remembering emotions, images, thoughts, even voices. God, it's almost impossible to shake off.)<<<<<
—Constance (09:16:10/2-24-51)

>>>>>(And you saw the siren?)<<<<<
—Gorgon (09:17:01/2-24-51)

>>>>>(I must have, but I can't remember. My partner saw me just standing there while the siren swooped down toward me. He blew it out of the sky and it landed right at my feet. But I can't remember anything between hearing the song the first time and then seeing the smoking body on the ground.)<<<<<
—Constance (09:17:49/2-24-51)

>>>>>(How come the song didn't get your partner?)<<<<<
—Gorgon (09:21:39/2-24-51)

>>>>>(He knew what to expect. He had his cyberears turned off. I'd plugged my ears (meat ears, damn it, and you can't turn them off), but apparently not well enough.)<<<<<
—Constance (09:22:18/2-24-51)

>>>>>(Sirens are fascinated by music. Play them some, and they'll just sit around and listen.)<<<<<
—Helm (11:13:47/3-4-51)

>>>>>(That's not how those babies act at all. Play 'em a tune and they'll tear your fraggin' head off.)<<<<<
—Slag (13:05:33/3-4-51)

GAME INFORMATION

	B	Q	S	C	I	W	E	R	Attacks
Siren	3	8 x 2	4	—	3/5	5	(5)	5	4M2

Powers: Enhanced Senses (Low-Light Vision), Hypnotic Song, Immunity to Pathogens, Immunity to Poisons

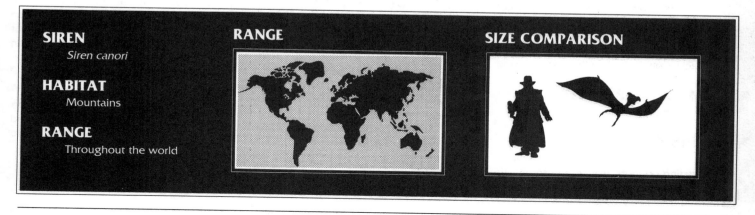

SIREN
Siren canori

HABITAT
Mountains

RANGE
Throughout the world

RANGE

SIZE COMPARISON

SNOW MOOSE
Alces natisis

Nelson

IDENTIFICATION

The snow moose can attain a height of 2.5 meters at the shoulder, and its antlers can reach a spread of 1.6 meters. Its coat is white, with pronounced gray hackles on the back of the animal's neck.

MAGIC CAPABILITY

Innate.

HABITS

The snow moose is a herbivore, feeding on roots, leaves, and shrubs. Its favorite food is new leaf buds.

Though a herbivore, the snow moose can be dangerous. They travel in herds of up to five males and three times as many females, and sometimes with young. The herd leader is a dominant male. Males will defend their females and young, forming a defensive perimeter around them. If anything approaches too closely, it will almost certainly trigger a charge by at least one male.

Snow moose have excellent vision, even at night. When necessary, they can move with a stealth remarkable for creatures their size.

COMMENTARY

Snow moose have few natural enemies. A wolf pack may pull down an old, infirm, or injured snow moose, but only rarely. Able-bodied moose very often defend weaker members of the herd.

POWERS

Enhanced Physical Attributes (Quickness), Enhanced Senses (Improved Vision, Low-Light Vision), Immunity to Cold, Silence.

WEAKNESSES

None.

>>>>>(During the rutting season, snow moose males are mean and aggressive. And you'd be surprised how fast they move. It's slotting freaky seeing something that big bearing down on you. Its head is down, antlers forward. And even if you put a high-velocity round right through the top of its head, you know that sheer momentum will keep it coming at you. It's best just to stay well away from them.)<<<<<
—Move-Softly(18:36:38/3-1-51)

>>>>>(They're not that bad. Just don't let them think you're after their females or their young. If you do, then you're toast.)<<<<<
—Lapis (18:41:31/3-1-51)

GAME INFORMATION

	B	Q	S	C	I	W	E	R	Attacks
Snow Moose	11/1	4 x 4	9	—	2/4	3	(6)	4	6S2

Powers: Enhanced Physical Attributes (Quickness), Enhanced Senses (Improved Vision, Low-Light Vision), Immunity to Cold, Silence

SNOW MOOSE
Alces natisis

HABITAT
Forests and tundra

RANGE
Northern regions of North America

RANGE

SIZE COMPARISON

SNOW SNAKE
Ophidia niphophilia

IDENTIFICATION

The snow snake is a long, slender serpent with pure white fur and non-reflecting scales along the belly. Its eyes are small and ruby-red. Its mouth, too, is proportionately small, with long poison fangs that fold inward when the mouth closes. The snow snake can reach a length of 2.5 meters.

MAGIC CAPABILITY

Innate.

HABITS

Snow snakes feed on small mammals and reptiles. Being active throughout the winter, they are adept at finding and pen-etrating the burrows of hibernating creatures.

Snow snakes excavate extensive burrows in the snow, particularly around coniferous trees. During the summer months, the creatures are torpid. After excavating small lairs among the roots of large trees, they often remain there in a kind of hibernation.

The snow snake is not aggressive toward larger creatures. Detecting the approach of an animal too large for it to swallow, it usually hides in the snow, watching, until the creature has passed by. The snake is venomous, however, and handling one is a certain invitation for it to strike.

The creatures are active around the clock.

COMMENTARY

Some observers claim that the eyes of the snow snake glow faintly at night, appearing as ruby-red pricks of light against the snow. This has not been authenticated, however.

POWERS

Enhanced Physical Attributes (Quickness), Enhanced Senses (Improved Smell, Low-Light Vision), Immunity to Cold, Venom.

WEAKNESSES

Vulnerability (Fire).

>>>>>(Their eyes glow, all right. And it's not just reflection. Sometimes at night you can see them watching as you pass.)<<<<<
—Toni (18:34:07/2-5-51)

>>>>>(If you concentrate, you can smell them, too. It's a sharp, lemon-like smell. If you get a whiff, step carefully.)<<<<<
—Glen (23:21:13/2-5-51)

>>>>>(Snow snakes killed a friend of mine. We were walking through the woods, and Jock's foot went through the crust of the snow. He went in up to his hip, but must have stepped right on top of a snake burrow. He started screaming and thrashing, shouting about something biting his leg. Then he convulsed and died before I could do anything. I pulled him out and then peeped carefully into the hole. There were maybe a dozen of the bleeders in there, all watching me with their beady red eyes. No fragging way I was going to leave them after they'd killed Jock. I fed 'em a thermite grenade. Let 'em chew on that.)<<<<<
—Shag (17:50:46/2-7-51)

GAME INFORMATION

	B	Q	S	C	I	W	E	R	Attacks
Snow Snake	2	3 x 3	2	—	1/4	2	(6)	3	4L1

Powers: Enhanced Physical Attributes (Quickness), Enhanced Senses (Improved Smell, Low-Light Vision), Immunity to Cold, Venom
Weaknesses: Vulnerability (Fire)

SNOW SNAKE
 Ophidia niphophilia

HABITAT
 Woodlands

RANGE
 Northern regions of North America

RANGE

SIZE COMPARISON

STONEBINDER
Myotis saxi

IDENTIFICATION

The stonebinder is an Awakened species derived from the common brown bat (*Myotis lucifugus*). Its front limbs are extended, as are several of its "fingers;" membranous skin joins them to the body, forming wings. The stonebinder has a long tail, with a barb at its tip. It is matte gray in color. Its eyes are tiny, and often are covered with a white film. (The implication is that the eyes are largely vestigial and will probably disappear during the course of evolution.) The stonebinder can achieve a wingspan of 0.7 meter.

MAGIC CAPABILITY

Innate.

HABITS

Like most other bats, the stonebinder is omnivorous, feeding as happily on flying insects as on fruit. It is not aggressive toward other creatures, preferring escape to combat. If unable to flee, however, it can put up a good defense.

The barbed tail is envenomed. Even more dangerous, however, is the creature's saliva, which it can spit accurately to a range of more than a meter. This saliva contains an enzymatic solution that calcifies any living tissue it touches, apparently turning it to stone (hence the creature's name). The condition is irreversible and begins to spread immediately. If the affected area is not excised within a few hours, it will continue to spread and eventually kill the victim. The stonebinder cannot eat calcified tissue, but uses this tactic purely for defense. The calcifying enzyme will penetrate almost all types of clothing.

Stonebinders are nocturnal, traveling in flocks of up to a dozen individuals as they feed on moths and other night insects. They lair by day in dark caves. Like other bats, the stonebinder uses a very precise echo-location system to locate its prey.

COMMENTARY

In areas such as the eastern seaboard of the UCAS, stonebinders are common enough to have become dangerous pests. The government mounts periodic extermination campaigns to eradicate the creature, but the stonebinders seem always to return again in force.

POWERS

Enhanced Senses (Sonar), Immunity to Poisons, Petrification, Venom.

WEAKNESSES

Allergy (Sunlight, Severe).

>>>>>(Frag, these things are dangerous pests no matter how few of them there are.)<<<<<
—Mace (16:15:20/2-19-51)

>>>>>(Is it true they can actually turn someone to stone?)<<<<<
—Hawkmoon (11:04:40/2-20-51)

>>>>>(Not really stone. It's more like calcium carbonate. But the effect's the same.)<<<<<
—Frenchie (11:05:12/2-20-51)

>>>>>(I seen a flock of stonebinders just outside of town. Some kinda bird came along, and it was big. It picked off a couple of stonebinders as it cut right through the flock, then came back for a second pass. That's when a bunch of them little bats let fly that spit of theirs. That giant bird just dropped out of the sky like, well, like a fraggin' stone. And when it hit the ground, it broke, man.)<<<<<
—Shark (20:15:58/3-10-51)

>>>>>(Want to know how to catch bats? Remember roasting marshmallows when you were a kid? O.K., burn one, then peel off the crispy outer shell, leaving just the sticky part. Throw it as high as you can. To a bat, the sticky little marshmallow has the same echo signature as a nice, juicy moth. When the bat hits it, wrapping its wings around it, the wings stick to the marshmallow. Down he plummets, the little bugger. No drek. It works.)<<<<<
—Douglas (20:18:10/3-10-51)

>>>>>(And if it's a stonebinder, it spits on you and you die. Fun game, chummer.)<<<<<
—Salient (20:21:22/3-10-51)

GAME INFORMATION

	B	Q	S	C	I	W	E	R	Attacks
Stonebinder	2	4 x 4	1	—	1/4	2	(6)	4	3L1

Powers: Enhanced Senses (Sonar), Immunity to Poisons, Petrification, Venom

Weaknesses: Allergy (Sunlight, Severe)

Note: The effect of the stonebinder's saliva is similar to the Petrify spell, except that it is limited to one extremity or body area. The gamemaster must determine the area hit, taking into account tactical considerations, angle of attack, and so on. Note that a hit to the head is immediately fatal, but a hit to the torso is probably not. Normal armor cannot protect the body from this enzyme. Only a full chemsuit will prevent its effects.

Unless the calcified area is excised, the effect spreads every six hours to the next adjacent body area. To prevent the spread, the victim makes an Unopposed Willpower or Body Test (whichever rating is higher), with a Target Number of 8.

Cyberware limbs and prostheses are not affected by a stonebinder hit and will stop the spread of the calcification to other areas of the body.

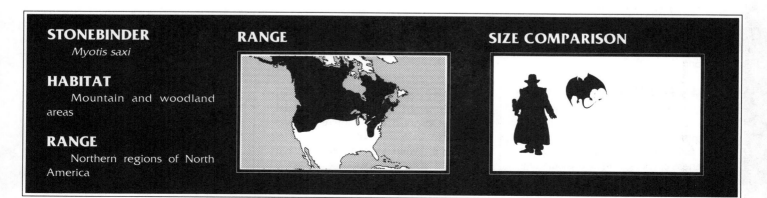

STONEBINDER
Myotis saxi

HABITAT
Mountain and woodland areas

RANGE
Northern regions of North America

RANGE

SIZE COMPARISON

STORMCROW
Corvus procellae

IDENTIFICATION

The stormcrow is a large raven that achieves a wingspan of 1.5 meters. Its plumage is glossy black, its beak sharp and powerful, and its talons long and curved. The bird's hoarse croak is even more raucous than the call of the non-Awakened raven.

MAGIC CAPABILITY

Parabiological.

HABITS

Stormcrows are omnivores, though they especially relish moles and other small burrowing animals. Able to hear its prey burrowing below the surface, the stormcrow pecks hard at the ground above, hoping to kill the burrowing animal with the impact. It can then dig up and devour the creature. Stormcrows also eat fruits, berries, and insects. If really desperate, they will even scavenge for carrion or garbage.

Stormcrows usually congregate in huge flocks of more than 100 individuals. It is not uncommon, however, to see them hunting or scavenging alone. Individual stormcrows are cautious, fleeing immediately from anything even remotely threatening. A flock of stormcrows, on the other hand, seems to generate a "mob mentality." If the flock is threatened, individuals will attack the intruder, pecking and gouging with their beaks and buffeting with their wings to drive the menace away.

Stormcrow flocks are always ringed by individuals acting as "sentries" who alert the flock to the approach of a threatening creature or other danger to the group. These sentries make it almost impossible to surprise a flock of stormcrows.

Like crows, magpies, and other similar birds, stormcrows seem fascinated by shiny objects. Whenever possible, they will steal such items and take them back to their nests. A stormcrow is, of course, as likely to steal a glass button as a diamond ring.

COMMENTARY

The stormcrow's progenitor species is the common raven (*C. corax*). Strong evidence indicates that the bird has a finely tuned weather sense that gives it awareness of changes in air pressure and humidity.

Much debate still continues as to whether or not this creature has a dual nature. Observation of captive subjects seems to indicate that the animal is mundane, while field observers have proven its astral aspect.

POWERS

Enhanced Senses (Improved Hearing), Weather Control (Flock Only).

WEAKNESSES

None.

>>>>>(Frag that "weather sense" drek. Stormcrows control weather. Why the frag do you think they call them stormcrows?)<<<<<
—Brat (11:34:08/4-1-51)

>>>>>(It's never been proven.)<<<<<
—Doc (11:36:01/4-1-51)

>>>>>(Watch them sometime, Doc. That's what I did. They like real drekky weather, and if they don't get it, they make it. If you're looking for a campsite and see stormcrows around, move on.)<<<<<
—Brat (11:36:42/4-1-51)

>>>>>(Oh, drek.)<<<<<
—Casper (11:39:19/4-1-51)

>>>>>(One thing that isn't drek is the bit about sentries. That's dead serious. And here's something even more interesting. When the sentry calls out, the flock's response is appropriate to what the sentry's seen. How do you read that?<<<<<
—Trent (12:55:38/4-1-51)

>>>>>(Are you proposing that they use language?)<<<<<
—Doc (12:57:57/4-1-51)

>>>>>(I'm not proposing anything, Doc. What's your take on it?)<<<<<
—Trent (12:59:15/4-1-51)

>>>>>(Not having seen the behavior you're describing, I can't say. But it might be worth more study.)<<<<<
—Doc (13:02:55/4-1-51)

GAME INFORMATION

	B	Q	S	C	I	W	E	R	Attacks
Stormcrow	2	6 x 2	1	—	3/4	3	(6)/6	4	3L1

Powers: Enhanced Senses (Improved Hearing), Weather Control (Flock Only)

Note: Stormcrows are dual beings only when in a flock of six or more birds.

STORMCROW

Corvus procellae

HABITAT

Any

RANGE

Throughout the world

RANGE

SIZE COMPARISON

TACHYPUS
Antilocapra celeriter

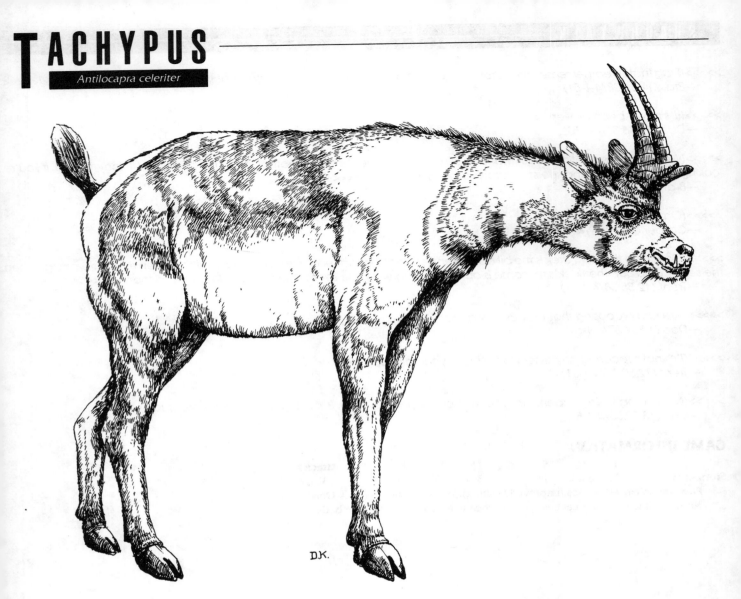

D.K.

IDENTIFICATION

The tachypus resembles a small pronghorn, reaching a height of about 0.7 meter at the shoulder. Its horns are short, sharp, and angled backward (thus the animal cannot use them as weapons). Its short coat is light brown, shading to white on the belly. Some individuals show a broad brown stripe down the back, running from the brow to the short tail. The creature has a narrow muzzle, and its jaws are filled with sharp, carnivorous teeth. Its eyes are lustrous, and its movements graceful.

MAGIC CAPABILITY

Innate.

HABITS

Unlike other members of genus *Antilocapra*, the tachypus is a carnivore. It hunts jackrabbits and other small mammals, using its almost incredible speed to run them down. The tachypus can maintain speeds faster than those of other deer-like animals, and is capable of short sprints approaching 120 kph. While running down its prey, it makes a hissing cry. This sound has the expected effect on its prey, often producing terror so great as to be paralyzing.

Both sexes hunt, though the tachypus tends to be solitary. During the breeding season in early spring, however, dozens of them congregate to mate at the same site year after year. When mating is accomplished, the animals separate again.

No reports exist of either provoked or unprovoked attacks against humans or metahumans. Because of the tachypus's phenomenal speed, the animal rarely encounters a situation where flight is not an option. Also, the creature is normally timid in the presence of larger animals, and usually keeps a respectable distance from such intruders to its home ground.

COMMENTARY

Gene typing has confirmed that the tachypus arose from *Antilocapra americana*, or the pronghorn. It is smaller than its progenitor, a rarity among Awakened creatures. Like its progenitor, tachypus also live in small bands on the open plains.

As an endangered species in the mid-20th century, the pronghorn was confined to protected reservations. In contrast to most other endangered species, the pronghorn made a full recovery and great numbers now roam the plains once more, often becoming the prey of their Awakened brethren.

POWERS

Enhanced Movement, Enhanced Physical Attributes (Quickness, four times per day, for (Essence)D6 turns.

WEAKNESSES

None.

>>>>>(These animals are all over Cal Free State. And they're a beautiful sight.)<<<<<
 —Davey (17:20:23/1-30-51)

>>>>>(What does tachypus mean?)<<<<<
 —Glory (10:34:49/2-12-51)

>>>>>(It's Greek. "Tachy" means fast, and "pus" means foot. "Fast foot" or "fleet of foot." Good name.)<<<<<
 —Bower (10:35:29/2-12-51)

>>>>>(Hey, Davey, did you know a guy down in Cal sells tachypus as pets? If you like 'em so much, why not buy one? Only a couple thousand nuyen.)<<<<<
 —Raster (06:23:42/2-15-51)

>>>>>(Well, for one thing, it can jump like a chipped acrobat. I'd have to put a dome over my back yard. If I had a back yard.)<<<<<
 —Davey (12:25:46/2-15-51)

GAME INFORMATION

	B	Q	S	C	I	W	E	R	Attacks
Tachypus	2	4 x 6	2	—	2/4	3	(6)	6	3M3

Powers: Enhanced Movement, Enhanced Physical Attributes (Quickness, four times per day, for (Essence)D6 turns),

TACHYPUS
 Antilocapra celeriter

HABITAT
 Prairies and deserts

RANGE
 Southwestern and central plains regions of North America

RANGE

SIZE COMPARISON

TALIS CAT
Felis mutabilis

D.K.

IDENTIFICATION

The talis cat is a creature with two forms, and it can shift from one to the other at will. In one form, it is identical to a small tabby housecat. In its other, it is a fast, powerful plains cat like a cheetah (but with the coat of a tabby rather than a cheetah's spotted markings). The housecat form is typically less than 0.6 meter long; the plains cat form achieves a length of 1.8 meters and is almost 1.0 meter tall at the shoulder.

MAGIC CAPABILITY

Innate.

HABITS

In housecat form, the talis cat usually hunts small rodents or birds; the plains cat form hunts larger prey, including humans and metahumans. Some talis cats remain in the wilderness, switching forms to meet the requirements of the moment or their temperaments. Most seem to prefer the city, becoming efficient urban predators. These cats typically spend the day in housecat form, sunning themselves and engaging in other typical behavior. At night, however, they take on their larger form, prowling the streets and alleyways in search of prey. In the urban setting, this usually consists of old, sick, or infirm squatters in the vast slums of most cities.

In plains cat form, these animals are skillful climbers and can leap considerable

distances. Very few unarmed victims are able to escape a talis cat in pursuit.

Talis cats always mate in plains cat form, though the impregnated female soon shifts to her smaller form, remaining so until after the birth. Talis kittens are unable to shift form until at least six weeks old, though this may be longer in individual cases.

COMMENTARY

Talis cats are rare, and were formerly believed to be shapeshifters. In 2049, however, a student of paranaturalism was able to vid-tape a talis cat as it stalked and then killed a new boar. The student watched as the talis cat, in housecat form, moved slowly through the tall grass until only a few meters from the new boar. Changing instantly into plains cat form, the cat then sprang at the boar, ripping out its throat in a blink of an eye.

What is remarkable about this field study is that the vid-tape revealed a different sequence of events than what the observer saw with his eyes. On tape, the talis cat in housecat form moved slowly through the grass, using its small size to remain hidden from the new boar. When the talis cat went in for the kill, however, the tape did not show a cheetah taking down the beast, but rather that exact same tabby! This photographic record revealed that the talis cat used a type of area Illusion or Masking spell that persuaded the student, and presumably,

the new boar that the cat had a form to match its enhanced physical prowess.

After much further study, it has been proven that the talis cat's physical enhancements are active only while the cat is projecting its illusion. Why the illusion is necessary remains the subject of considerable debate. Some paranaturalists argue that the illusion increases the cat's efficiency as a hunter because frightened prey are easier to dispatch. Most scientists reject this thesis, arguing that the cat more likely developed the illusion as a defense mechanism, with the enhanced physical powers following still later.

Perhaps even more interesting is the talis cat's adaptation to hunting humans in their natural environment of urban complexes. From an evolutionary standpoint, this combination of habitat and prey has only existed for an instant in time. For a species to adapt to new conditions in so short a span of time is remarkable.

POWERS

Desire Reflection (Self, Cheetah Only), Enhanced Movement, Enhanced Physical Attributes (Quickness, Body, and Strength), Enhanced Reactions, Enhanced Senses (Low-Light Vision).

WEAKNESSES

None.

>>>>>(So the moral of the story is: don't kick a stray cat or it might tear your leg off. And when those alley cats start howling outside your window, better not throw a bucket of water on them.)<<<<<
—Mad Dog (14:02:56/2-1-51)

>>>>>(I hear that if you treat them well, talis cats might "adopt" you and protect you—as long as you keep feeding them. How about that? A pet cat that can change into a cheetah.)<<<<<
—Bung (16:36:04/2-1-51)

>>>>>(A few days back, I was down on Route 66 (you know, the main sewer tunnel leading south). Up ahead, I saw an Ork chasing a cat, probably just trying to take out its frustration on the little thing. Then they turned a corner and went out of sight. A few moments later, I heard a scream, an Ork's scream. The jerk came pounding back around the corner, hollering, and damn if something that looked like a cheetah wasn't close on his heels. I didn't stick around to see the end of the race, but my money was on the cheetah.)<<<<<
—Mad Dog (14:02:56/2-1-51)

GAME INFORMATION

	B	Q	S	C	I	W	E	R	Attacks
Talis Cat									
As Housecat	1	4 x 4	1	—	2/4	4	(6)	5	2L2, −1 Reach
As "Cheetah"	7	9 x 4	7	—	2/4	4	(6)	5	8L2

Powers: Desire Reflection (Self, Cheetah Form Only), Enhanced Movement, Enhanced Physical Attributes (Quickness, Body, and Strength), Enhanced Reactions, Enhanced Senses (Low-Light Vision)

Note: Treat the Illusion power as a Mask spell with a Rating of 12. It takes one action to activate the Illusion power. Once the Illusion is activated, the talis cat may use the "cheetah" stats above. Remember that in cheetah form, the talis cat gets 3 additional dice to roll for its reaction, due to its Enhanced Reactions power.

TALIS CAT

Felis mutabilis

HABITAT
Any non-mountainous area (preferably urban)

RANGE
Throughout the world

RANGE

SIZE COMPARISON

TORPEDO SHARK

Portheus velocis

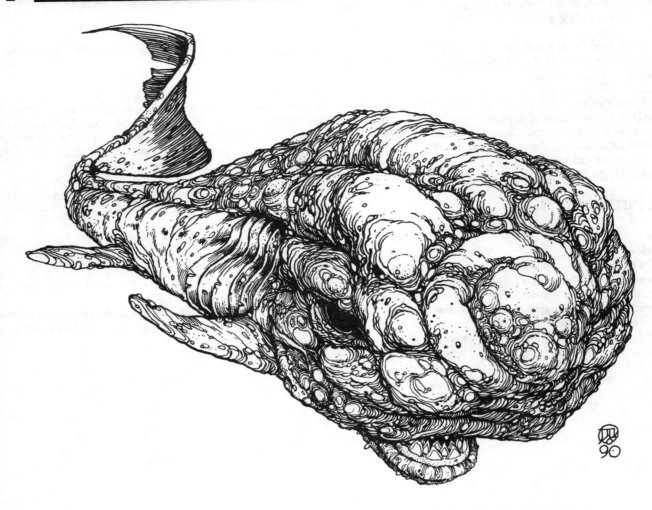

IDENTIFICATION

The torpedo shark has a powerful whale-like body. Surprisingly, its progenitor species is the blue shark. It grows to a length of 5.0 meters and its domed head resembles a torpedo warhead. Its eyes are small and shielded by heavy brow ridges, and its mouth is set back deeply into the underside of its head. Its tail flukes are enlarged, but it lacks a dorsal fin.

The torpedo shark is usually a dark bluish-gray, though some specimens are black or light gray.

MAGIC CAPABILITY

Parabiological.

HABITS

The torpedo shark is a fast-moving predator whose diet is similar to that of the blue shark (i.e., anything from fish, seals, and other sharks to garbage and carrion). There are also authenticated reports of attacks on humans and metahumans. The torpedo shark uses its high speed and bony, domed head in a devastating ramming attack, then tears its stunned prey apart. (Note that the torpedo shark has a mass approaching 1,000 kilograms. The momentum it can build up is very high, giving it the potential to do significant damage with a ram.) Records exist of torpedo sharks ramming small boats with enough force to stave in the hulls or even overturn them.

Torpedo sharks are usually solitary hunters, but they can scent blood over distances of several kilometers, which often draws various other shark species to an attack site. Torpedo sharks will co-operate in killing or driving away any other sharks that try to share their prey. Though torpedo sharks feed voraciously, they do not display true feeding frenzy behavior, and never attack one another over prey. (There are reports of male head-butting challenges during mating season, however.)

COMMENTARY

The torpedo shark is a shark species able to pump water over its gills even when stationary. This ability allows the creature to hang motionless, waiting for prey to come within range.

The ramming charge of the torpedo shark displays incredible speed, but the creature can maintain such velocity for only brief periods. The maximum recorded speed for a ramming torpedo shark was 63 kph (approximately 35 knots). The specimen was able to maintain this speed for less than 10 seconds, however.

POWERS

Enhanced Physical Attributes (Quickness, three times per day, for (Essence – 2) D6 turns), Enhanced Senses (Improved Smell).

WEAKNESSES

None.

>>>>>(They don't call these fish torpedo sharks because of the shape of their heads. If you saw one charge, you'd think it was some kind of World War II torpedo. They swim just below the surface and raise a real big wake. It's scary to watch, especially when you know that rammer is coming straight for your boat.)<<<<<
    —Sid (10:11:13/3-14-51)

>>>>>(It's so easy to confuse one, though. Just drop a barrel or something overboard. They're as likely to hit the barrel as your boat. Torpedo sharks are fast and powerful, but they seem to be equally stupid.)<<<<<
    —Ares (10:16:52/3-14-51)

>>>>>(Probably caused by a concussion.)<<<<<
    —Shamus (10:18:12/3-14-51)

GAME INFORMATION

	B	Q	S	C	I	W	E	R	Attacks
Torpedo Shark	7/2	5 x 4	6	—	1/3	3	6	5	8S3

Powers: Enhanced Physical Attributes (Quickness, three times per day, for (Essence – 2)D6 turns), Enhanced Senses (Improved Smell)

TORPEDO SHARK
    Portheus velocis

HABITAT
    Temperate and subtropical oceans

RANGE
    Pacific Ocean

RANGE

SIZE COMPARISON

TOXIC EARTH SPIRIT

Anima naturalis quisquiliae

IDENTIFICATION

Toxic earth spirits are as mutable in form as other nature spirits. They often appear as small, bubbling puddles of foul-smelling mud, often with shimmering patches of oil on the surface. They can take on a more solid shape, however, which usually resembles a large mass of rotting, oil-soaked garbage.

MAGIC CAPABILITY

Innate.

HABITS

Toxic earth spirits can only manifest in their own territory, which is usually a toxic waste dump, landfill, or other waste-management site. They are malign of intent toward humans and metahumans. Some rare sightings report that toxic earth spirits sometimes leave their waste-dump area, but no knowledge of how or why is yet available.

COMMENTARY

The origin of toxic earth spirits is unknown. Some researchers posit that it is a normal land spirit that has been perverted by the pollution dumped in its territory. Though this writer has seen extensive anecdotal evidence to strongly support this theory, no formal, systematic study has yet been undertaken to prove or refute this theory.

The touch of a toxic earth spirit is highly corrosive and also frequently transmits infection.

POWERS

Alienation, Concealment, Corrosive Secretions, Fear, Manifestation, Noxious Breath.

WEAKNESSES

None.

>>>>>(I know how they're able to leave their territory. If someone challenges a toxic earth spirit to either physical or magical combat on the spirit's own turf, and then leaves without totally destroying the spirit, the latter can leave its dump to exact its vengeance.)<<<<<
—Blacknight (13:36:48/1-15-51)

>>>>>(The toxic nature spirits are a great concern to me. They show how man (and metahumanity) has harmed and perverted the land. Before man's blight fell upon their habitats, toxic spirits were normal nature spirits. As the earth's body was poisoned, so was its spirit ("As above, so below."). We are responsible for creating the toxic spirits, and thus we are responsible for healing them.)<<<<<
—Man-of-Many-Names (10:27:42/1-16-51)

>>>>>(How the drek can we do that?)<<<<<
—Ares (10:33:09/1-16-51)

>>>>>(First, by curing the land, by leaching away its poisons. And then there are certain...rites. So I have learned from Those Who Speak.)<<<<<
—Man-of-Many-Names (10:33:51/1-16-51)

>>>>>(You mean your totem?)<<<<<
—Ares (10:36:02/1-16-51)

>>>>>(I mean Those Who Speak.)<<<<<
—Man-of-Many-Names (10:36:39/1-16-51

>>>>>(If you mean cleaning up all the waste damps, have you got any idea what that would cost?)<<<<<
—Wallace (10:39:55/1-16-51)

>>>>>(Have you seen a toxic waste spirit? Seen its innate purity twisted into something perverted, something evil? When you have, let's see if you still speak of cost.)<<<<<
—Man-of-Many-Names (10:42:34/1-16-51)

GAME INFORMATION

	B	Q	S	C	I	W	E	R*	Attacks
Toxic Earth Spirit	8	2 x 2	8	1	4	4	4A	7/12	4S3, +1 Reach, Special

Powers: Alienation, Concealment, Corrosive Secretions, Fear, Manifestation, Noxious Breath
***Note:** Manifest/Astral Reactions

TOXIC EARTH SPIRIT
Anima naturalis quisquiliae

HABITAT
Toxic waste dumps

RANGE
Throughout the world

RANGE

SIZE COMPARISON

TOXIC WATER SPIRIT
Anima naturalis stagnensis

IDENTIFICATION

Though able to take many forms, toxic water spirits often manifest as patches of muddy-brown foam on the surface of water, or as a foul-smelling oil slick. They can also show more solid forms, sometimes appearing as large gobs of caustic, sticky substance, either floating near the surface or moving slowly along the bottom of a body of water.

MAGIC CAPABILITY

Innate.

HABITS

Toxic water spirits are usually seen only in bodies of water that cannot support normal aquatic life, either because of high concentrations of metal or toxins, or because of low pH. Toxic water spirits can only manifest in their own territory. They are malign of intent toward humans and metahumans. They sometimes prowl the shorelines of their home territory, but rarely move far from water. The few reports of toxic water spirits sighted at great distances from their territory are undocumented.

COMMENTARY

The origin of toxic water spirits is unknown. As in the case of the toxic earth spirit, many believe that the toxic water spirit is a benign water spirit whose essence has been corrupted by man-made pollutants.

The touch of a toxic water spirit is highly corrosive and frequently transmits infection.

POWERS

Accident, Alienation, Corrosive Secretions, Engulf, Fear, Manifestation, Movement, Search.

WEAKNESSES

None.

>>>>>(So, what do you say, Many-Names? The same deal? Cure the water and cure the spirit?)<<<<<
   —Trish (11:13:13/1-16-51)

>>>>>(So it is.)<<<<<
   —Man-of-Many-Names (11:14:57/1-16-51)

>>>>>(I've heard about shamans who can control toxic spirits.)<<<<<
   —Hard Rim (11:24:47/1-16-51)

>>>>>(It is best never to speak of such tings. And if you have heard such tales, you know the reasons why.)<<<<<
   —Man-of-Many-Names (11:25:54/1-16-51)

GAME INFORMATION

	B	Q	S	C	I	W	E	R*	Attacks
Toxic Water Spirit	6	4 x 2	4	1	4	4	4A	10/15	4D4 Stun

Powers: Accident, Alienation, Corrosive Secretions, Engulf, Fear, Manifestation, Movement, Search.
*Note: Manifest/Astral Reactions

TOXIC WATER SPIRIT
   Anima naturalis stagnensis

HABITAT
   Severely polluted bodies of water

RANGE
   Throughout the world

RANGE

SIZE COMPARISON

TROGLODYTE
Pan speluncae

IDENTIFICATION

Troglodytes are slender, bipedal creatures that rarely exceed a height of 1.6 meters. Their heads are large compared to their bodies, and their arms are long. They are totally hairless, have no external genitalia, and their skin is a pallid white. Like an owl's, their eyes are huge in proportion to their heads.

MAGIC CAPABILITY

Parabiological.

HABITS

Troglodytes are omnivores. Though they eat bats, rats, blindworms, and other subterranean creatures, they can also subsist on the lichen and moss growing on the walls of the caves where they live. On rare occasions, troglodytes may form scavenging parties to collect food beyond the entrance to their cave homes. Such parties rarely range more than a few hundred meters from the cave opening. Troglodytes are cannibals who eat their own dead.

A troglodyte's eyes are highly adapted to the dark, with at least limited thermographic vision. Thus do they operate so well in the darkness of deep caves. They cannot abide daylight, however, and any bright light is painful to them.

Troglodytes live in loosely knit bands of up to 50 individuals, organized along the lines of human hunter-gatherer tribes. A single individual is dominant and may be either male or female. This individual is usually the oldest member of the tribe.

Troglodytes occasionally use rudimentary tools, and when necessity demands, weapons. Their tool use is rudimentary, at best, and consists of little more than stripping leaves off branches to create digging implements and clubs. Troglodytes are timid, going to extreme lengths to avoid detection or confrontation.

COMMENTARY

The troglodyte is an Awakened species derived from the chimpanzee (*Pan troglodytes*). Its sapience, or lack of it, continues to be hotly debated. Its cannibalism of the dead is said to be a quasi-religious ritual. The dominant leader of a tribe is reportedly selected by the other adult members of the band. As of this writing, however, no governmental regulatory agency has found the troglodyte to be sapient.

The word "trog" (a derogatory term often applied to Orks and Trolls) is presumably a reference to this creature.

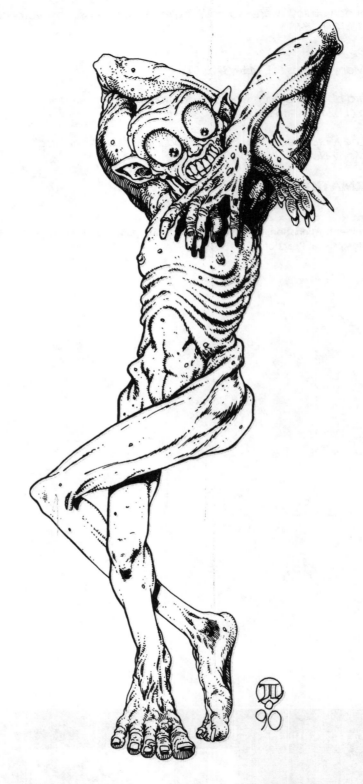

POWERS

Concealment, Enhanced Senses (Thermographic Vision).

WEAKNESSES

Allergy (Sunlight, Mild).

>>>>>(I have spent time studying a troglodyte band near Lake Louise. (I had to get permission from good old Dunkelzahn, and that was a job and a half.) Anyways, I spent some time living with them, and found they'll come to trust you eventually. They have a language and I can almost speak it. All they want from life is to be left alone to do their wall paintings and to tend their lichens.)<<<<<
    —Cahill (13:42:21/2-4-51)

>>>>>(We should help them, give them the assistance they need to take their place in our society. How can we just ignore those less fortunate than we?)<<<<<
    —Deborah Bailey (14:03:23/2-4-51)

>>>>>(You don't get it, do you, lady? They don't need our civilization, and they sure as drek don't want any of it. They have a civilization of their own, even though it's a short one. Like I said, I can almost speak their language, but I understand some of it better. When they're sitting around getting wasted on fermented lichen, you know what they talk about? The concept of a divine creator and his relationship with them. And you know what else? They've discarded the concept as irrelevant to their happiness. Don't mess with these guys. They're getting it right all by themselves.)<<<<<
    —Cahill (14:05:32/2-4-51)

>>>>>(The contention that the troglodyte's progenitor is the chimpanzee is false. Though the pre-Awakening captive populations of lower primates was high, there were not enough breeding bands of chimpanzees, or great apes, to explain present-day populations of troglodytes, dours, or embracers. These Awakened races could have sprung from only one North American primate, and you probably know him better as man.)<<<<<
    —Byron Wordsworth (02:06:03/2-8-51)

>>>>>(That's drek and you know it! Mankind could never sink so low.)<<<<<
    —Ernst (16:23:28/2-8-51)

GAME INFORMATION

	B	Q	S	C	I	W	E	R	Attacks
Troglodyte	3	3 x 4	2	2	3/4	3	6	3	Humanoid

Powers: Concealment, Enhanced Senses (Thermographic Vision)
Weaknesses: Allergy (Sunlight, Mild)

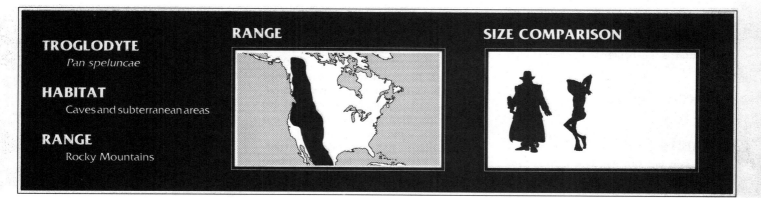

TROGLODYTE
  Pan speluncae

HABITAT
  Caves and subterranean areas

RANGE
  Rocky Mountains

RANGE

SIZE COMPARISON

UNICORN FISH

Monodon novalis

IDENTIFICATION

This animal is misnamed, for it is not a fish at all. It is actually an Awakened mammalian species derived from the narwhal (*M. monoceros*). It grows to lengths of 3.7 to 4.6 meters, with its single, spiral horn adding an additional 1.9 to 2.0 meters. It is dark gray dorsally, shading to white ventrally. The spiral horn is white, sometimes with a slight golden tinge. As with all cetacean species, the tail flukes are horizontal. This powerful, streamlined creature is as capable of high speeds as its appearance suggests.

MAGIC CAPABILITY

Innate.

HABITS

The unicorn fish is a carnivorous whale, feeding on fish and smaller cetaceans. When hunting, its initial approach is a high-speed lunge, attempting to impale—or at least mortally wound—its prey with its horn. If the attack is successful, the unicorn fish scrapes the impaled prey from the horn by rubbing against the ocean floor or against an icecap or iceberg. The creature then feeds. A unicorn fish can remain underwater for as much as an hour without needing to come up for air, and so is well-equipped to hunt beneath the arctic icecap.

Unicorn fish are highly aggressive, ferociously attacking almost anything smaller. Though normally solitary, they sometimes hunt in small pods that sometimes attack and kill creatures considerably larger than the unicorn fish. The creature's ferocity is sometimes its downfall.

Unicorn fish occasionally attack surface vessels, often breaking off their horns in the effort. Because a hornless creature is unable to hunt effectively, it will soon starve to death.

Unicorn fish have well-developed sonar.

COMMENTARY

The horn of the unicorn fish is highly valued as material for a spell focus, though no magical properties are attributed to the horn itself. This is the motive for those who hunt the unicorn fish, in direct violation of the laws of most countries and the international protocols protecting such water-borne mammals from human predation.

POWERS

Immunity to Pathogens, Magical Resistance.

WEAKNESSES

None.

>>>>>(Why protect these things? They're nasty fraggers.)<<<<<
    —Hollis (13:04:44/2-28-51)

>>>>>(I think most of the laws are carry-overs from times when all cetaceans were protected. Laws change only slowly. Did you know there's still a law on the books in England that makes it a capital crime to spit on the London Bridge? Even though London Bridge is in slotting Atzlan?)<<<<<
    —Wilson (13:05:23/2-28-51)

>>>>>(I used to crew on a boat out of the Aleutians. It was made of wood to keep from setting off magnetic mines. And believe me, there are still lots of those around from the last gasp of the Cold War. Well, by the by, a pod of narwhals decides to attack, and before we could drive them off, one rammed the boat. Drove its horn a good meter right through the hull. After we limped back to port, I pulled the nasty fragger's horn out of the hull. I've still got it as a souvenir. A meter and a half long and sharp as a spear.)<<<<<
    —Farsight (09:25:15/3-10-51)

>>>>>(How did you drive them off?)<<<<<
    —Lila (09:29:13/3-10-51)

>>>>>(We used things called squealers that one of the crew made. I guess they screw up their sonar, but I don't know for sure. And serious fire-power. We killed at least two. Guess that makes me a criminal, huh, Wilson? Maybe I should go spit on London Bridge just to complete my life of crime.)<<<<<
    —Farsight (09:30:26/3-10-51)

GAME INFORMATION

	B	Q	S	C	I	W	E	R	Attacks
Unicorn Fish	7	5 x 4	9	—	2/4	3	(6)	4	6S3, +1 Reach

Powers: Immunity to Pathogens, Magical Resistance

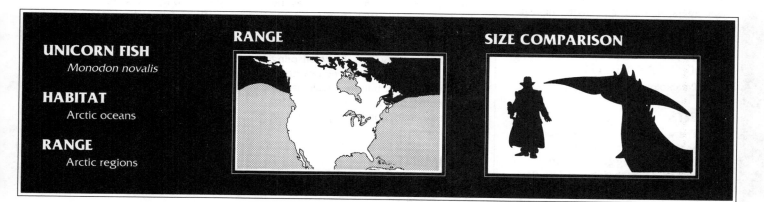

UNICORN FISH
   Monodon novalis

HABITAT
   Arctic oceans

RANGE
   Arctic regions

RANGE

SIZE COMPARISON

WHITE BUFFALO

Bison bison blanc

IDENTIFICATION

As its taxonomic classification implies, the white buffalo is derived from the plains bison (*B. bison*). It is considerably larger, however, with a height of 3.0 meters at the shoulder and an overall length of 5.3 meters. It is, like its progenitor, a stocky and powerful creature, with muscular chest and shoulders. Its coat is brilliant white; its short horns are gray shading to dark brown or black at the tips.

MAGIC CAPABILITY

Parabiological.

HABITS

The white buffalo is a herbivore that grazes the plains and prairies. It is more territorial and aggressive than its progenitor, often charging at intruders. These charges are more threat displays than actual attacks, but if the intruder does not leave, the white buffalo will butt and trample creatures as large as a Troll.

Thanks to a NAN-funded attempt to repopulate the plains with bison, a large population of common buffalo again roams the plains of North America. The white buffalo is much less common.

White buffalo are often seen among herds of common buffalo, usually as the dominant member. White buffalo are able to interbreed with their progenitors, but their offspring may or may not express their parent's coloration. These offspring inherit none of the Awakened powers of the white buffalo, but are usually larger than common buffalo. They, too, frequently hold dominant positions in buffalo herds.

COMMENTARY

Myths of the white buffalo are significant among many Amerindian plains tribes. These tribal nations believe that the reappearance of the white buffalo symbolizes their return to significant power in North America. It is unknown whether these myths are related to an appearance of the white buffalo, or whether they are based on the tendency to mythologize an ordinary animal into a bigger, stronger version.

The creatures have a low tolerance to airborne or waterborne pollutants. This might explain their relatively small numbers.

POWERS

Animal Control (Buffalo), Enhanced Senses (Improved Hearing and Smell), Immunity to Pathogens, Search.

WEAKNESSES

Allergy (Pollutants, Severe).

>>>>>(I believe that the myths of my people spring from accurate observation and not from imagination. The white buffalo probably appeared thousands of years ago. My people have a long memory. I have seen the white buffalo, and it matches the ancient paintings and tales too well to be coincidence.)<<<<<
   —Big Sky (14:36:22/3-21-51)

>>>>>(Mystical drek. If they'd existed previously, we'd have evidence in the fossil record.)<<<<<
   —Barre Sinister (14:38:18/3-21-51)

>>>>>(The fossil records do include the bones of giant bison whose size matches quite closely that of the modern white buffalo.)<<<<<
   —Big Sky (14:40:18/3-21-51)

>>>>>(Old or new, white buffalo are potentially dangerous. Once, out near Edmonton, I saw a wrecked car that had been overturned and smashed damn near to bits by something butting it. Some buffalo, a few of them white, were still nearby, so I couldn't get near enough to see whether the driver's body was still inside. Poor bleeder.)<<<<<
   —Mac (18:36:51/3-21-51)

GAME INFORMATION

	B	Q	S	C	I	W	E	R	Attacks
White Buffalo	9	4 x 4	7	5	2/4	5	6	3	5D3, +1 Reach

Powers: Animal Control (Buffalo), Enhanced Senses (Improved Hearing and Smell), Immunity to Pathogens, Search
Weaknesses: Allergy (Pollutants, Severe)

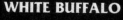

WHITE BUFFALO
   Bison bison blanc

HABITAT
   Prairies and plains

RANGE
   Central and northern regions of North America

RANGE

SIZE COMPARISON

WODEWOSE
Cebus wodewosnis

IDENTIFICATION

The wodewose is a small but exceptionally well-muscled primate that stands perhaps 1.0 meter tall, but weighs as much as 50 kilograms. It is covered with short black fur. Hands and feet are clawed, and its teeth are oversized compared to its mouth. Its tail is short and definitely not prehensile. It is a well-adapted and fast-moving carnivore.

MAGIC CAPABILITY

Parabiological.

HABITS

The wodewose is an arboreal carnivore that feeds on smaller animals and birds. A major part of its diet is made up of eggs that it steals from nests. It is ferocious if threatened, but is not actively territorial.

Wodewose live in tightly knit tribal bands, reminiscent of baboon tribes. The dominant member can be either male or female, but is always the most physically formidable. Younger creatures often challenge for dominance. Though these challenges are rarely to the death, serious wounding is common.

Despite their hominoid appearance, wodewose are neither intelligent nor sentient.

COMMENTARY

Gene typing has established that the wodewose arose from the capuchin monkey (*Cebus capucinus*). The wodewose has changed significantly, however, most notably in the loss of the capuchin's prehensile tail. As capuchin monkeys commonly served as experimental subjects in many labs before the Year of Chaos, it is likely that the wodewose arose from a base population of capuchins released from these labs by animal rights groups.

Wodewose are often carriers of a virus similar to VITAS-3, though they show no symptoms. Considering the creature's probable derivation, the progenitor capuchins had probably been infected as part of immunological studies at the time of their liberation or escape from captivity.

The lifespan of the wodewose is unknown, but enzymological studies indicate that it may be long-lived.

The species was named by its discoverer, Candace Harrigan.

POWERS

Enhanced Senses (Improved Smell), Immunity to Age, Immunity to Pathogens, Immunity to Poisons, Pestilence.

WEAKNESSES

None.

>>>>>(Hey, Peachy. You think these bleeders got out of the same labs that were messing around with the agropelter?)<<<<<
—Mr. A (10:47:52/2-8-51)

>>>>>(Don't know. Neddy didn't say anything about wodewose.)<<<<<
—Peachy (14:21:47/2-8-51)

>>>>>(If wodewose live for a long time, is it likely that they'll become intelligent?)<<<<<
—Gavin (11:37:39/2-10-51)

>>>>>(I kinda doubt it. Longevity often goes with low reproductive rate, which isn't conducive to fast evolution. At least, that's what my old biology prof used to say.)<<<<<
—Bilbo (16:49:30/2-11-51)

>>>>>(Wodewose might not come from the same place as agropelters, but they've got some of the same nasty habits. These bleeders drop drek on you, too.)<<<<<
—Manta (09:36:02/2-19-51)

>>>>>(Let's get back to intelligence for a minute. Anybody ever seen them use tools or weapons?)<<<<<
—Nighthawk (11:38:48/2-20-51)

>>>>>(Sometimes they use little sticks to dig out insects, but nothing more sophisticated than that. Baboons do the same thing. That doesn't count as real tool use, does it?)<<<<<
—Mac (19:26:53/2-20-51)

GAME INFORMATION

	B	Q	S	C	I	W	E	R	Attacks
Wodewose	2	4 x 4	6	—	2/4	3	6	4	3M2, +1 Reach

Powers: Enhanced Senses (Improved Smell), Immunity to Age, Immunity to Pathogens, Immunity to Poisons, Pestilence

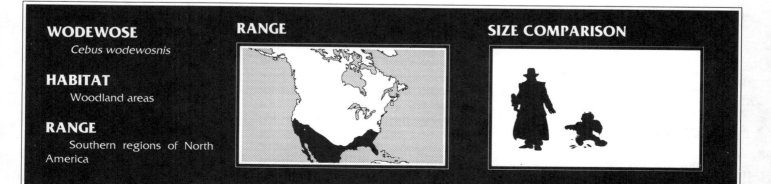

WODEWOSE
Cebus wodewosnis

HABITAT
Woodland areas

RANGE
Southern regions of North America

RANGE

SIZE COMPARISON

WYVERN
Alatuserpens pili americanus

IDENTIFICATION

The North American wyvern resembles a small, denuded, feathered serpent. Alternatively, it might be described as similar to a pterodactyl or pteranodon. Its head is smaller, proportionately, and its skull more sharply sloped than a dragon's, indicating considerably less brain mass. Its long, sinuous tail ends in a wicked-looking stinger. Its hind feet have sharp, curved claws. The wyvern is dark brown. It can achieve a total length of 11.0 meters, with a wingspan of 20.0 meters.

MAGIC CAPABILITY

Innate.

HABITS

The wyvern inhabits desolate places, preferably far from human habitation. It is a carnivore and scavenger, feeding on birds, large fish, animals up to the size of a cow, and even carrion. It hunts like an eagle, spotting its prey from altitude and swooping to snatch it up in its powerful talons. Having grasped its prey, the wyvern uses its venomous tail to kill it. (The wyvern is completely immune to its own venom, of course.) It usually returns to its nest, or at least the vicinity, to actually eat its prey. Wyverns are highly territorial.

Wyverns have a reptilian appearance and share some physiological features with reptiles. It is assumed that they are oviparous. Wyverns are solitary creatures.

One might suppose that overgrown forests would pose problems for creatures as large as wyverns, but the creatures can easily fly through the branches of all but the largest trees. They do this by attaining some airspeed, then tucking their wings back and crashing through the branches like a projectile. Wherever adequate space is available, they beat their wings to maintain velocity. For this reason, one can often hear hunting wyverns from great distances.

Nothing is known about the wyvern's reproductive behavior. Because they have no overt genitalia, it is impossible to determine the sex of a wyvern without dissection.

The wyvern is nocturnal.

COMMENTARY

Although many wish to assign it to genus *Draco*, it seems unlikely to this cataloguer that the wyvern is actually related to the western dragon. A strong indicator of this is that the western dragon has three sets of limbs—forelimbs, hind limbs and wings—while wyverns have only two. Unfortunately, no progenitor species has been identified through gene mapping. There are similarities in the gene map between wyverns and the various species of drake—and, it must be admitted, with dragons—but these similarities are only partial.

POWERS

Enhanced Senses (Low-Light Vision), Immunity to Poisons, Influence (Fear), Venom.

WEAKNESSES

None.

>>>>>(Paterson calls it the North American wyvern. Does that mean there're wyverns in other places?)<<<<<
—Harry the Horse (14:19:50/2-18-51)

>>>>>(Yeah, Harry. The European wyvern looks like those heraldic beasts, you know, the ones you see on old coats-of-arms.)<<<<<
—Corbeau (18:31:48/2-18-51)

>>>>>(But you don't really know.)<<<<<
—Harry the Horse (19:11:54/2-18-51)

>>>>>(No. I don't know.)<<<<<
—Corbeau (22:38:14/2-18-51)

>>>>>(I've seen wyverns in the bayous. They're fast, chummer, and old Paterson's right. They just go straight through stuff, like a big missile. I think they nest in trees, but I'm not sure. And believe me, they're not built for life on the ground. They're almost graceful in the air, but on land, they're ungainly bleeders, moving kind of in hops, real clumsy. They'd be funny if they weren't so fragging big.)<<<<<
—Easy (14:24:42/3-22-51)

>>>>>(I must say, I have found your constant chatter highly entertaining... and not unenlightening. So many significant insights, mixed in with so much dross. You ephemerals continue to amaze me. My congratulations.)<<<<<
—Dunkelzahn (**:**:**/**-**-**)

>>>>>(FRAG!! Dunkelzahn, the fragging dragon? How the frag did he get in? Check his entry. No time-date stamp. What type of deck is he using?)<<<<<
—Blacknight(04:31:48)/6-4-51)

>>>>>(A dragon running the Matrix? Boys and girls, I think everything just got a little more interesting.)<<<<<
—Fastjack (04:33:51/6-4-51)

GAME INFORMATION

	B	Q	S	C	I	W	E	R	Attacks
Wyvern	9	3 x 2	8	—	2/4	4	(6)	4	8S3, +1 Reach

Powers: Enhanced Senses (Low-Light Vision), Immunity to Poisons, Influence (Fear), Venom
Note: Flying multiple is 6.

WYVERN
Alatuserpens pili americanus

HABITAT
Forests and mountains

RANGE
Central to southern regions of North America

RANGE

SIZE COMPARISON

The

End